Children's Book Corner

Children's Book Corner

A READ-ALOUD Resource

with Tips, Techniques, and Plans
for Teachers, Librarians, and Parents

Level Grades 5 and 6

Judy Bradbury

Photographs by Gene Bradbury

LIBRARIES
UNLIMITED
A Member of the Greenwood Publishing Group

Westport, Connecticut • London

Library of Congress Cataloging-in-Publication Data

Bradbury, Judy.
  Children's book corner : a read-aloud resource with tips, techniques, and plans for teachers,
 librarians and parents : grades 5 and 6 / by Judy Bradbury ; photographs by Gene Bradbury.
    p. cm.
  Includes bibliographical references and indexes.
  ISBN 1-59158-045-5 (pbk : alk. paper)
  1. Oral reading. 2. Reading (Elementary) 3. Children—Books and reading. 4. Book selection.
 I. Title.
 LB1573.5.B732 2006
 372.45'2—dc22   2006017478

British Library Cataloguing in Publication Data is available.

Library of Congress Catalog Card Number: 2006017478
ISBN: 1-59158-045-5

First published in 2006

Libraries Unlimited, 88 Post Road West, Westport, CT 06881
A Member of the Greenwood Publishing Group, Inc.
www.lu.com

Printed in the United States of America

⊗™

The paper used in this book complies with the
Permanent Paper Standard issued by the National
Information Standards Organization (Z39.48–1984).

10 9 8 7 6 5 4 3 2 1

Dedication

For those children, now adults, who were members of my fifth- and sixth-grade class at the College Learning Laboratory on the SUNY College of Buffalo campus my first two years of teaching, with thanks for what they taught me in our time together. Angela, Verdell, Robert, Sandra, Mary Beth, Victor, all of you . . . *I remember.*

Contents

Acknowledgments

We read to know we are not alone.—C. S. Lewis

My first two years of teaching, my most precious years of teaching, were filled with wonder, memorable moments, and a lot of hard work. Those inner-city fifth and sixth graders were tough, but at 20 years old, I was up for the challenge, and together we reached for the stars.

I sat in the middle on the couch—the one I hauled into my classroom on a dreary Saturday morning when the school building was deserted—and read to my kids every day. By the third or fourth week, they fought (we're talking fists and flying chairs here) over who got to sit next to me on that couch when it was time for our daily read aloud.

And so we set up a system. It was sort of like the system parents set up before a long car trip. You get the window the first 100 miles; your sister gets it after the pit stop. For the most part it worked, except that Angela seemed to wangle her way to my side most days to lay her head on my shoulder as I read. She was taller than I and fearsome to most of her peers, but she was putty in my hands when I sat on that couch with a book.

So like a family on a car trip, we traveled together short and long distances. We trekked mountains, solved mysteries, felt joy and pain, relived history, and made our own. We did it together, through books. When I moved on to first one and then another high school to teach the remedial readers the system had failed, I found another couch and continued to read aloud every day.

Years later, when my daughter was born, I read to her every day. We read books you'll find in the previous volumes of Children's Book Corner and books you'll find in this one. We read every Chronicles of Narnia tale, countless poetry books, *American Girl* magazines, and more. She eventually went on to read and re-read countless times every Anastasia and Sam book written by the powerful, wonderful author Lois Lowry. At 16, she still finds time to have a reading fest with her mom. We are readers together, she with her book and I with mine.

Although I write alone, the making of this book was a group effort. There are many people to whom I owe gratitude. First and foremost, there are the authors who wrote such fabulous books and the illustrators who created such memorable art, and who graciously contributed new material for the Up Close and Personal reflections that accompany the read-aloud plans. Their generosity of spirit and the stories they shared are treasures.

Right behind them in line are those kind and patient souls at the publishing houses who generously and enthusiastically gave of their time, participating in this project by sending books, putting me in contact with the right person, and arranging for cover art to appear in this resource: Kimberly Lauber, Marketing Coordinator, Education & Library, Simon & Schuster Children's Publishing; Anne Irza-Leggat, Educational Marketing Supervisor, and

Kristin Seim, Contracts & Rights Assistant, Candlewick Press; RasShahn Johnson-Baker, School and Library Marketing Coordinator, and Angus Killick, School and Library Marketing Director, Hyperion Books for Children; Nancy Hogan, Associate Publisher and Director of Marketing, Front Street Books and Director of Institutional Marketing and Subsidiary Rights, Boyds Mills Press; Karolina Nilsson, Marketing, School and Library Department, HarperCollins Children's Publishing; Jason M. Wells, Publicity and Marketing Director, Abrams Books for Young Readers and Amulet Books; Lucille Rettino, Director Advertising and Promotion, Adult & Books for Young Readers, and Kathryn Sibiski, Marketing Assistant, Henry Holt and Company; Jeanne McDermott, Director of Marketing, Farrar Straus Giroux Books for Young Readers; Andrea Cruise, Associate Director, School & Library Marketing, Penguin Young Readers Group; Erin L. Falligant, Editor, Pleasant Company Publications; Molly O'Neill, Marketing Assistant, Clarion Books; Kim Biggs, Publicity Associate, and Ron Hussey, Manager, Permission & Serial Rights, Houghton Mifflin; Kathleen Morandini, Publicist, and John Briggs, President, Holiday House; Tracy Mack, Executive Editor, and Jennifer Rees, Associate Editor, Scholastic; Kathy Tucker, Editor-in-Chief, and Heather Boyd, Promotion Coordinator, Albert Whitman & Company; Jen Bechard, Marketing Assistant, Kids Can Press; Kia Neri, Author Promotions Manager, and Barbara Fisch and Sarah Shealy, Associate Directors of Publicity, Harcourt Children's Books Division; Megan McGinnis, Editor, Meadowbrook Press; Susan Raab, Raab Associates; and Cecile Goyette, Executive Editor, Alfred A. Knopf & Crown Books for Young Readers.

For taking time out of their busy schedules to be a part of this book and for their good humor while Gene photographed readers reading, sincere thanks go to Kathy and Laura Back, Doug and Andy Cassidy, Jeffrey, Rachel, and Benjamin Lackner, Dianna and Piava Rioli, Chris Bagneschi, Kelsey Bradbury, and Julie Terry, Guidance Counselor at Amherst Middle School, Amherst, New York. Smile, and look down at the book!

This project, from the first book through the fourth, was a dream realized and a joy to work on due to the support and hard work of the people with whom I interact at Libraries Unlimited/Greenwood Publishing. There are many, but special thanks go to Sharon Coatney, Editor; Mike Florman, Senior Project Manager; Melissa Mazzarella, Exhibits Coordinator; and Debbie LaBoon, Author Support and Workshops Manager. Without their attentiveness, efficiency, professionalism, and dedication, this series would not be what it is.

Closer to home, here's a belly rub for you, Sadie, for nuzzling me insistently every so often to get up from the computer and find you a bone, and a bit of milk for you, Tasha, for curling up in front of the computer screen. I really didn't mind when you stretched out a paw and added a string of letters to my read-aloud plan. Thank you, Rozanne, for double-checking those quotations in *Bartlett's Familiar Quotations* in the eleventh hour; and Annette, fine neighbor that you are, for coming through with your marvelous camera when ours went on strike, hours before the deadline.

Finally, it is with a full and grateful heart that I thank the two people who are closest to me, Kelsey and Gene. You have watched this project evolve (and overtake the dining room and every closet and bookcase in the house), helped with simple as well as loathsome tasks, kept me laughing, and offered suggestions as well as your unstinting support. You remind me that I am not alone. Without you this book, this project, this life, simply would not be.

Introduction

"Let me hear you read it" is a test. "Let me read it to you" is a gift.—Katherine Paterson

This resource book contains 25 **Read-Aloud Plans** for outstanding books to read with children in the fifth and sixth grades. Hundreds of related titles are suggested following the read-aloud plans and in the **Tips and Techniques for Teachers and Librarians** and **Book Notes** sections. Fiction as well as nonfiction titles are represented. Look for books reflecting a spectrum of genres on popular themes and content area subjects, holidays and special events, biographies, memoirs, poetry, and more. Thought-provoking books, funny stories, illuminating studies, history, mystery, and math, as well as issues such as death, divorce, prejudice, and civil rights are addressed. School and family matters, learning about oneself, and friendship are prevalent themes in books written for this age group.

The books chosen to be included in this volume celebrate reading by the very excellence they bring to the advanced picture book, nonfiction book, and novel. As examples of the best there is to offer in literature for children in the upper elementary grades, they nourish and sustain the independent reader while encouraging the reluctant reader to embrace the wonderful world of books. A variety of interests and a range of levels of reading difficulty are represented here. The plans offer suggestions that weave in the four strands of language arts: reading, listening, writing, and speaking.

In addition to read-aloud plans, look for **Tips and Techniques for Teachers and Librarians.** In this section are more titles for reading aloud, reading together, or reading alone, and an extensive list of poetry anthologies, collections, and professional resources for teaching poetry. Other useful and accessible resources and references found in this section will augment a read-aloud program and keep it thriving. **Parent Pull-Out Pages** are intended to be reproduced and sent home on a regular basis throughout the year to inform and motivate parents about reading aloud to their children. An extensive **Book Notes** section lists hundreds of curriculum-related children's books, cross-referenced by subjects and briefly summarized. Finally, consult the **subject, title, author**, and **illustrator indexes** to find just the right book for a special group or a particular child.

How Do You Define Upper Elementary Grades?

Although reading levels and interests vary among individuals, for the purposes of this volume in the Children's Book Corner series, upper elementary grades refers to youngsters in the 10- to 12-year-old age range. These children are also referred to here as preteens. Books written for children in the upper elementary grades intend to guide them in understanding themselves as they grow and mature and find their place in the world, including peer groups, school situations, and their family. Current social problems and growing so-phistication are mirrored in plot lines of fiction and discussed in nonfiction written for this age group. At times tough, contemporary issues are grappled with honestly. Both nonfiction and fiction offer hope to readers. Through quality literature, children are ultimately encouraged to meet problems head-on and feel empowered to make a difference in their own lives and the larger world.

Because this is a resource for teachers, librarians, and parents, its aim is to offer suggestions and recommend books and other media suitable for fifth and sixth grade children. It is the responsibility of the adult using this resource to choose accordingly those materials they deem appropriate for the children with whom they interact.

How Were the Choices Made About Which Books to Include?

In deciding which children's books to include in this resource, several criteria were used to determine whether a book would be highlighted with a **read-aloud plan**, listed in the **Book Notes**, mentioned on a **Parent Pull-Out Page**, or not included in the resource at all. The determination was based on several factors, the most important of which was whether the book told an original story in an appealing way or approached a nonfiction topic in a memorable and fresh fashion *for a child in the upper elementary grades*. In the case of a picture book, how the subject was handled and whether the text and art created a package suitable for preteens were essential considerations for inclusion. Books chosen for read-aloud plans are worthy titles, both new and older, that teachers, librarians, and parents might not be familiar with, rather than well-known classics or popular children's titles. How-ever, time-honored, timeless classics ought to be the foundation of every classroom and school library, as well as fully represented in the children's collections of public libraries. The fiction books listed in the **Tips and Techniques for Teachers and Librarians** section of this resource will encourage and stimulate young readers and are ideal for reading aloud, reading together, or for youngsters to read independently.

What Do I Need to Know in Order to Find the Recommended Books?

Publication information is provided for each book recommended in this resource. This reflects the most up-to-date information available on the book at the time of the printing of *Children's Book Corner.* As there are a number of editions available for most ti-tles, from hardcover to softcover to library binding, I have listed information on the hardcover edition unless the book is not available in hardcover. By referring to the title information and looking up its listing in library catalogs, online bookstores, publishers' catalogs, or publish-ers' Web sites, you can access information on the edition that best suits your needs.

Which Edition Should I Get?

There are typically several editions available for each of the titles presented here. The edition you choose to select will depend on your needs, budget, and purposes. If you are a classroom teacher trying out a book, planning to use it just once, or if you have a limited budget, consider borrowing the title from the public library. If the school library owns it, all the better! Should you decide to purchase the book, consider which edition will work best for you.

Hardcover editions are the most common and most durable for use in the classroom library. Although they cost more initially than softcover copies, they will last longer and will not need to be replaced as often.

Library binding editions are especially designed for the longer shelf life of library settings, but these sturdy editions can be perfect for the classroom library as well. As they tend to be a bit more expensive, you may want to choose this edition for those books in the classroom library that you think will see the most use over an extended period of time.

Softcover editions are ideal when funds are limited and for multiple copy purchases for classrooms where a library-lending program for students and their families will be instituted. Special printings of books are arranged by school book clubs and appear in softcover or specially priced hardbound editions. These are available for purchase at very reasonable prices only through that club and are usually available for a limited time only.

Each edition bears its own ISBN, so be sure to note the correct one when ordering books for purchase.

How Do I Know What the Books Featured in Read-aloud Plans Are About?

In addition to publication information, subject categories are listed for each read-aloud book. Use this handy reference when you are trying to find just the right title to augment a unit of study, a particular season, or an issue you want to explore. The subject index provided at the back of this book will help with this search as well.

Books included in the **Book Notes** section of this resource are also cross-referenced by subject as well. Books are listed in all subject categories to which the book relates.

How Does the Read-Aloud Plan Work?

Each plan follows the same approach. At the top of the read-aloud plan is the publication information and an estimate of the time and number of sessions it ought to take to read the book aloud (*not* including questions and follow-up activities, as these are used at the reader's discretion, and the time spent on them will vary). Next is a brief summary of the book. The teaching plan itself consists of four parts.

The read-aloud session begins with a **Pre-Reading Focus,** which includes suggestions for introducing the book or chapter. This is an important step in the read-aloud plan because it focuses the group on the book, its format, and its subject. Discussion before reading aids in building prediction skills and draws upon experiential background, enabling children to use their personal experiences to bring meaning to the story. As children discuss and answer questions, they verbalize thoughts and feelings and relate their experiences. Each read-aloud plan launches the reading of the book or chapter with a **Let's read to find out** focus for listening to the story.

The **While Reading** portion in many of the read-aloud plans suggests questions to pose as you read the book or chapter aloud. Answers are given in parentheses for even the simplest and most obvious questions for ease in following the plan while preparing in advance for the read-aloud session. Specific suggestions for reading the book aloud are also in this section.

Write Away! suggestions offer writing activities related to the theme, plot, characters, student responses to events in the story, or personal reflections.

The **Follow-Up Discussion** offers ideas for bringing the read-aloud session to a meaningful close. Questions that relate to the outcome of the story or chapter are posed. Discussion is encouraged.

Some of the suggested **follow-up activities** extend beyond a simple, short follow-up. Fiction elements, such as setting, characterization, or conflict, or terms important to the story or subject, are often explored. Introduce these words in context rather than as isolated vocabulary. At the end of the plans you will find additional information and related titles.

The **Up Close and Personal** segments contain comments submitted by the books' authors or illustrators, or both, about the making of the book, where the idea came from, challenges they faced in creating the book, and so on. Share these reflections with children as an extension activity.

It is advisable to become familiar with the read-aloud plan as well as the *entire* book prior to presenting it to children. This will ensure that the book's theme, plot, and vocabulary are appropriate for your students.

Note: Plan to have an easel with chart paper or a chalk or dry-erase board available in the read-aloud area. Have dictionaries available as well. Many of the read-aloud plans suggest activities that make use of these tools.

How Do You Recommend I Use the Questions Provided in the Plans?

Use questions at your discretion as time and student needs permit.

When asking the suggested questions, rephrase children's answers into complete sentences. Reinforce responses by beginning with an affirmative. If a response is incorrect or not what you are after, accept the answer and rephrase the question. Avoid negative responses. ("No, that's not right.") Encourage and reinforce appropriate group discussion dynamics.

When asking children to relate personal experiences, be flexible within reason and allow for variance. Encourage complete-sentence answers rather than single-word responses whenever possible. When you are looking for a specific response, allow children to throw out answers and consider prompting with, "Yes, anything else?" or "I hadn't thought about that! Any other ideas?" To bring a discussion to a close, consider saying something such as, "I'll take one more answer and then we will go on with the story."

Several questions are suggested in each part of the read-aloud plan. You are encouraged to use some or all of these questions according to your schedule, the attention span of your listeners, and their needs as you perceive them.

How Should I Use the Tips and Techniques for Teachers and Librarians Section of the Book?

This portion of the book is designed to provide practical suggestions for professionals who work with independent and developing readers. Resources, tips, and techniques are outlined and explained, with the hope that teachers and librarians will utilize this section of the book as needed and find it to be a handy reference tool.

What Is the Purpose of the Parent Pull-Out Pages?

Provided in this section of the book is material developed especially for parents or caregivers responsible for the children with whom you work. Permission is granted to reproduce the **Parent Pull-Out Pages** for distribution. It is recommended that these pages be sent home on a regular basis throughout the year. Their purpose is to reinforce the importance of reading aloud to children and to provide useful techniques and information about books and reading to parents and caregivers. It is essential to reinforce the key role adults play in fostering a lifelong love of reading in children.

What Will I Find in the Book Notes?

This section of the book offers hundreds of additional titles, cross-referenced according to the subject(s) the book addresses, with a brief summary of each title. Publisher information and a general reading level are also included.

Why So Many Indexes?

Subject, title, author, and illustrator indexes are provided at the back of the book for your convenience in quickly and easily locating the information you need on just the right book. Use these indexes when you need to locate information on any book included in this resource.

What If I Have Questions, Comments, or Feedback?

I'd love to hear from you! If you have information you'd like to share with me or would like to arrange a school visit, parent program, or teacher in-service training, send an e-mail to my attention at judyreads@bluefrog.com. Place "Children's Book Corner" in the subject line so it's sure to reach me. For information on other books in the Children's Book Corner series or this author, visit www.lu.com.

Read-Aloud Plans

No reading lesson is complete unless it leaves children with the sound of sentences ringing in their ears and the sharp taste of words lingering on their tongues. —Bill Martin Jr.

Hyperion Books for Children.

Title	SAHARA SPECIAL
Author	Esmé Raji Codell
Publisher	Hyperion
Copyright Date	2003
Ages	9 and up
Read-Aloud Time	10–12 minutes per chapter
Read-Aloud Sessions	13
Themes	School, friendship, self-esteem, divorce, family, writing

Note: This story is an excellent read-aloud choice for the beginning of the year, to set the stage for read-alouds, storytelling, and writing in journals.

Sahara is not going to give the school any more of herself, now that they've taken her letters to her absent father. They know *a* history, but not "the history" of her. They know she doesn't do school work; they do not know that she is a writer. They do not know that she reads books with her mom as well as when she is alone while her mom works. How the new teacher, Miss Poitier—or Miss Pointy, as the children lovingly call her —changes all that, makes for a touching and affirming story set in a fifth-grade classroom in inner-city Chicago, just a heartbeat away from the waters of Lake Michigan, and hope.

> **PRE-READING FOCUS:** Introduce the book by showing the cover and reading the title. Ask: What do we know about this story from the cover? (A girl who lives in a high-rise in the city is the main character; she might like to read since she's holding a book.) Discuss the stars on the cover and what they might represent. Ask: What do you think the title means? **Let's read to find out** whom we meet in the first chapter and if we learn more about what the title means.

Chapter One: "Me and Darrell Sikes"

> *While reading:* After reading the first section of Chapter One, list the characters we have met so far. (Fifth grader Sahara, who is the narrator and main character; her mom; and her school counselor, Mr. Stinger.) Discuss what we know from this first scene. (Setting: school; plot: Sahara misses her dad, who is divorced from her mom; Sahara writes her dad letters but never sends them; Mr. Stinger is concerned about Sahara and has called in her mom for a conference; Sahara loves to read and be read to by her mom; Sahara is angry that her letters have been taken by Mr. Stinger; Mom is furious with Sahara for causing herself to be labeled "special ed.") Sahara feels that her school file is "*a* history" but not "*the* history" of her. **Let's read to find out** more about that. Read through the end of the chapter.

Follow-up:

- We meet Sahara Jones, the **narrator** of the story, in this first chapter. What words could be used to describe this character? (Angry, stubborn, sad, smart, misunderstood, funny.)

- Discuss Sahara's feelings at having to meet with the Special Needs teacher in the hall.

- Explore how the author uses words that appeal to our senses to make us feel what Sahara is feeling when she is in the hall.

- We also meet Darrell Sikes. Review what Sahara tells us about him. (Darrell has been designated "Special Needs" for a very long time; he has, according to rumor, been violent toward teachers; he is abusive toward "Peaches.")

- At the second conference with Mr. Stinger, Sahara asks for her letters back. Why? Sahara's mother wants the school to fail her daughter if she doesn't complete her school work instead of labeling her "Special Needs." Discuss Mom's motives.

- At the end of the chapter we are offered added insight into Sahara. Discuss. (Sahara loves to write more than just letters; she would rather not try than fail; Sahara knows she is not stupid; she has a solid relationship with her mom.)

- The last sentence of the chapter is a great example of *foreshadowing.* Bring it to students' attention.

- Discuss what the title means.

Write Away! Think about how Sahara felt when she was in the hallway with Peaches. Write about a time when you were really embarrassed by something you had to do. Use as many senses as you can to describe how you felt.

Write Away! Sahara's mom once told her not to judge a book by its cover. Sahara remembers this when she relates the rumors about Darrell. Tell about a time when you learned the importance of not judging a book by its cover.

Note: In preparation for the next chapter, collect a few Beezus and Ramona books by Beverly Cleary to show to the class.

Chapter Two: "My True Ambition"

Pre-reading: Read the chapter title. Ask for predictions about what Sahara's true ambition might be. **Let's read to find out.**

Follow-up:

- We've met three new characters in this chapter. What do we know so far about Rachel Wells? (She is Sahara's cousin and her best friend; she is one year younger than Sahara; she has a baby brother named Freddie; Rachel's mom is a single mom; Rachel is shy.)

- How do we know that Rachel is shy? (She talks in a "whispery" voice, her cheeks get pink and she looks at her feet when she speaks; she won't join in jump rope games at school.)

- Discuss Sahara's view of shy people.

- Why is Rachel Sahara's best friend? (Rachel came back; Sahara always has to look out for her; and Rachel is the only one who knows Sahara's true ambition.)

- What is Sahara's true ambition? (To be a writer.)

- What do we know about Mrs. Rosen? (She watches out for Sahara; she is old, short, and "shrunken.")

- What do we know about Cordelia Carbuncle? (She is friends with Rachel but excludes Sahara; she talks to boys and wears makeup.)

- Discuss the conversation Sahara has with her mom about wearing makeup.

- Sahara says that Rachel is shy. Do you think Sahara is shy? Discuss.

- Introduce Beezus Quimby to listeners. Read the dedication of *Sahara Special.*

Write Away! Write a paragraph about your best friend. Describe the way your friend does things that show what he or she is like, just as Sahara has described Rachel's voice, her pink cheeks, and her actions to help us see Rachel and feel as if we know her.

Write Away! Write about your true ambition.

Chapter Three: "At the Library"

Pre-reading: Read the chapter title. Ask: What do we know about Sahara and the library? (She loves to read and check out books; she hides her writing there.) **Let's read to find out** what happens at the library.

Follow-up:

- We met a new character in this chapter. What do we know so far about Paris? (She goes to the library every Saturday with her older brothers; she loves to read; she is friendly.)

- At the end of the chapter, Sahara doesn't feel like reading. Why?

Chapter Four: "New Things All the Time"

Pre-reading: Read the title. **Let's read to find out** what the title means.

Follow-up:

- Review why Sahara is failing fifth grade. (She does not do her work.)

- We learned a bit more about the **setting** of this story. Where does the story take place? (Inner-city Chicago.)

- Discuss the meaning of the title of the chapter. (New teacher, new school year, new resolve to do better.)

- What are "first impressions"?

> **Write Away!** At the beginning of this chapter, Mom gives Sahara a "poison eyeball." What does that mean? (A dirty look.) Earlier in the story, the author wrote that Rachel looked at Sahara like she "was homework." When an author uses phrases like these, it helps us see the characters or places the author is describing. Think of ways to describe a few of these feelings or actions: tired, angry, ashamed, silly, a frown, a giggle, excitement, fear, sadness, joy, a handshake, a hug, a smile, a voice.

Note: In preparation for the next chapter, consider getting composition books for each member of the class. After reading the chapter aloud, distribute the composition books. Begin journal writing in your class using Miss Pointy's simple rules. See the Write Away! suggestion below. If children already have journals, allow them to personalize their journals to make them feel new and fresh, and then institute Miss Pointy's rules.

Chapter Five: "We Got Her"

Pre-reading: Read the title. **Let's read to find out** what the new teacher is like.

While Reading: Show the journal entries Sahara imagines so that listeners can see the different fonts used to indicate different entries. Read the entries in different voices to differentiate between them.

Follow-up:

- What is Miss Pointy like? (Funny; unconventional; different from any teacher the kids have ever had.)

- What did you like best about Miss Pointy or what she did in this chapter?

- Show the last page of the chapter. Discuss Sahara's entry. Who do you think wrote the last part? (Miss Pointy.)

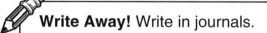

Write Away! Pass out journals. Assignment: Tell me everything I need to know about you!

Note: In preparation for the next chapter, have available a copy (or several different versions) of Aesop's fables. One wonderful edition is the Caldecott winner FABLES by Arnold Lobel (HarperCollins).

Chapter Six: "The Lion's Lesson"

Pre-reading: Read the title. **Let's read to find out** what the lion's lesson is.

Follow-up:

- Discuss how Miss Pointy tries to reach Darrell.

- Talk about the troubles basket.

- Discuss the desk-kicking incident.

- Why do you think Miss Pointy reads Aesop's fables to her class?

- Look at fables. If time allows, ask children to tell a fable they remember and/or read the lion's lesson.

- Ask: What do you think will happen next in the story?

Write Away! Write in journals.

Note: In preparation for the next chapter, find a lamp. Plan to read aloud by its light.

Chapter Seven: "George Gets Busted"

Pre-reading: Read the title. **Let's read to find out** what the title means.

Follow-up:

- Why does Miss Pointy smile when Sahara raises her hand? (She likes that Sahara is participating; she likes her comment.)

- Why do you think Sahara did not want Miss Pointy to read what she wrote in her journal?

- What does the title of this chapter mean? (George refers to George Washington; Darrell "gets busted" by the class for his dishonesty.)

- When Darrell's mother arrives, what does the class's behavior tell you about how the students feel about Miss Pointy? (They stick up for Miss Pointy because they like and respect her.)

Write Away! Write in journals.

Note: In preparation for the next chapter, write Miss Pointy's writing pointers on a chart and post them in a prominent place in the classroom.

Chapter Eight: "The Way Things Are Built"

Pre-reading: Read the title. **Let's read to find out** what happens at recess.

Follow-up:

- What does "Trying your best is a success in itself" mean?

- Review the writing advice Miss Pointy gives to Sahara.

- How does Sahara feel about what she has done? (Regretful.)

- Sahara calls Paris a hero. Why? (Paris took the blame for someone else rather than tell on that person; she did what's hard, and she lost her friend over it.)

- Refer to the star on the cover of the book that resembles the one Sahara lifted from Luz's journal.

Write Away! Write about an everyday hero you know or about a time when you did something similar to what Paris did. How did you feel?

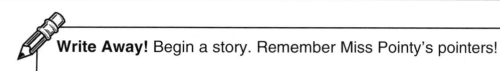

Write Away! Begin a story. Remember Miss Pointy's pointers!

Note: In preparation for the next chapter, have a copy of JULIE OF THE WOLVES
by Jean Craighead George (HarperCollins) on hand.

Chapter Nine: "Miss Pointy Gets Me Where I Live"

Pre-reading: Read the title. What does it mean? (Miss Pointy knows how to get to someone.) **Let's read to find out** how this happens.

Follow-up:

- What does the chapter title mean? (Miss Pointy comes to Sahara's home; Sahara overhears Miss Pointy telling her mother something that makes a difference to Sahara—she is failing herself.)

- What does it mean to "fail yourself"?

- Why do you think Sahara feels so strongly about not failing herself?

- Something big happens in this chapter. What is it? (Sahara writes.)

Write Away! Sahara says, "Time moves more quickly with my book friends than my real friends." Have you ever felt that way about books you've read, pets, TV characters, radio show hosts? Write about it.

Write Away! Continue working on stories. Remember Miss Pointy's pointers!

Chapter Ten: "Orphans"

Pre-reading: Read the chapter title. What is an orphan? (A child without parents; one deprived of protection or advantage.) **Let's read to find out** how this plays into the story.

Follow-up:

- What does the chapter title mean? (Miss Pointy's poem, in Darrell's hands, is misunderstood.)

- Sahara finally gets a sticker of her own. Why does she give it to Paris? (So Paris can give it to Luz, to make up for the one Sahara took off Luz's journal.)

- How does Sahara feel? (Relieved.)

Write Away! Write about a time when you set something right as Sahara has done in this chapter.

Write Away! Continue working on stories. Remember Miss Pointy's pointers!

Chapter Eleven: "Why Teachers Get Apples"

Pre-reading: Read the chapter title. **Let's read to find out** why.

Follow-up:

- What does the chapter title mean? (Miss Pointy made up a story to help Darrell see the error of his ways.)

- What do you notice about the journal entries at the end of the chapter? (We are seeing another side of Darrell; Darrell is warming up!)

Write Away! Write what you would wish for.

Write Away! Continue working on stories. Remember Miss Pointy's pointers!

Chapter Twelve: "Name-calling"

Pre-reading: Read the chapter title. **Let's read to find out** about Sahara's name, how she got it, and what it means to her.

Follow-up:

- What does Sahara tell us through her writing about her name? (We learn that her dad named her, what she thinks about a desert; how she felt about changing her name; how she felt when other kids called her "Sahara Special" last year; why she likes her name. We learn Sahara is one terrific writer!)

Write Away! Write about how you got your name and how you feel about your name.

Write Away! Continue working on stories. Remember Miss Pointy's pointers!

Chapter Thirteen: "Autobiographia Literaria"

Pre-reading: Read the chapter title. Where did we hear those words before? (It is the name of the poem Sahara loved and copied for Darrell.) **Let's read to find out** why this chapter is named after the poem.

Follow-up:

- Recall the discussion in the classroom in Chapter 10 (page 113) about spending poems and the discussion about extra credit in Chapter 11 (page 131) as you consider the ending of the story.

- How has Sahara changed by the end of the story?

- Review Miss Pointy's writing pointers. Has the author followed these pointers in writing this book?

Write Away! Continue working on stories. Remember Miss Pointy's pointers!

Look for the sequel to this book, VIVE LA PARIS (Hyperion). For other books by Esmé Raji Codell suitable for fifth and sixth graders, refer to the author index of this resource. For information on her resource book for teachers and parents, turn to the Tips and Techniques for Teachers and Librarians section of this resource.

Up Close and Personal · · · · · · · · · · · ·

A Note from the Author, Esmé Raji Codell

About names . . .

My parents named me after a girl in a short story, "For Esmé with Love and Squalor" by a man named J.D. Salinger. Since then I have learned it is a common name in England for both boys and girls, and that it is also an English version of the French *Aimée*, or Amy, which means "beloved." My middle name is from India, I think it means something like "goddess of the moon." I am from America, and I consider that to be my ethnicity. My great-grandparents came a long way and had a very hard time just so someday I could call myself American.

Names are very important in the stories I write. In Scott O'Dell's ISLAND OF THE BLUE DOLPHINS, Karana is very careful about whom she tells her true name to, because she feels there is power attached to her name. I agree with that. When I was in fifth grade myself, kids used to call me "Pippi Longstocking." I didn't mind, because I liked that story. Sometimes I asked my friends to call me "Maggie," because that seemed like a name that was a lot more simple and cheerful than my own name, but they would usually forget (and so would I). When I was a fifth grade teacher, I let the children call me "Madame Esmé because I thought it was funny, and every time I heard that name, it would make me smile. In SAHARA SPECIAL, the main character doesn't get to choose what name she gets called, but she does choose to own it and make it a source of pride. Names are important in SAHARA SPECIAL, and in its sequel, VIVE LA PARIS, because I want readers to remember that we are more than the names that other people give us.

I always like going to school assemblies, because they give out programs full of the names of children. When I am looking for a character's name for one of my books, I often take out my collection of programs so I can pick from names of real people. Having a very unusual name myself that is never on any pre-printed stickers or mugs, I imagine some child will be very excited to see his or her unique name in print!

About writing . . .

I use the skill of writing every day in my work as an author, but I also used it as a children's bookseller, an elementary school teacher, a librarian, a website designer, to help my friends, and for pleasure. You don't have to be an author to use that skill. Think about that!

To learn more about Esmé Raji Codell and her books for children, teachers, and parents, visit her Www.onderful World of Children's Literature at www.planetesme.com.

Hyperion Books for Children.

Title	MATH POTATOES
Author	Greg Tang
Illustrator	Harry Briggs
Publisher	Scholastic Press
Copyright Date	2005
Ages	9–12
Read-Aloud Time	5–7 minutes per poem
Read-Aloud Sessions	16
Themes	Math can be easy and fun, problem-solving strategies, poetry

In this seventh book in a best-selling series by Greg Tang, older readers are treated to 16 poems that offer "common sense strategies" meant to make math fun and easy. Each problem is presented in light and humorous rhyme facing a full-page, full-color illustration. The reader is offered one of three tactics: make "smart sums"; find patterns and symmetries; or look for groups of equal size, which makes it possible to multiply instead of add. "Answers" are offered at the back of the book.

Note: For each poem in the collection, consider having props that students can use to try out problem-solving strategies.

PRE-READING FOCUS: Consider setting aside a regular time in which you treat students to one of Tang's math strategies offered in light and appealing poems. Use props to introduce each poem. For example, in the first poem in the book, "Math-ter Cards," show a hand of five numbered playing cards. Ask: How would you add up these cards? Take answers and discuss which method is easiest, quickest, and most efficient. **Let's read to find out** what the author suggests.

WHILE READING: After reading the poem in its entirety, ask listeners what the key words in the poem mean. In "Math-ter Cards," for example, Texas Hold 'em, 5-Card Draw, 7-Card Stud, and Omaha are card games; a straight (five cards numbered consecutively) and a flush (five cards of the same suit) are card game terms. Ask: In a card game, what does it mean to hold? (Not throw in any cards.) To fold? (Throw in the hand.)

FOLLOW-UP DISCUSSION: "Math-ter Cards": Look at the playing cards in the illustration. Ask: How would you add up these cards? Go to the Answers page in the back of the book and compare student answers with the author's suggestion. Ask: Do you agree with his method? (You may not always! But in every instance, children will be thinking about numbers, patterns, and connections.) Pass out five numbered playing cards to each team of two or three children. Ask groups to come up with the quickest, easiest way to add up the sum of the cards. Allow each team to explain their strategy to the class. Discuss.

Write Away! After reading a number of Tang's math poems, let children try their hand at writing math poems of their own. For helpful suggestions, refer to Tang's article for teachers on creating math poems with children, on his Web site (www.gregtang.com). Have children illustrate poems and provide "answers" to their poem problems as Tang has done in his books.

Other books in Tang's series include THE BEST OF TIMES, MATH APPEAL, MATH-TERPIECES, and THE GRAPES OF MATH, all published by Scholastic Press.

For additional math-related books, turn to the Book Notes section of this resource.

<u>Notes:</u>

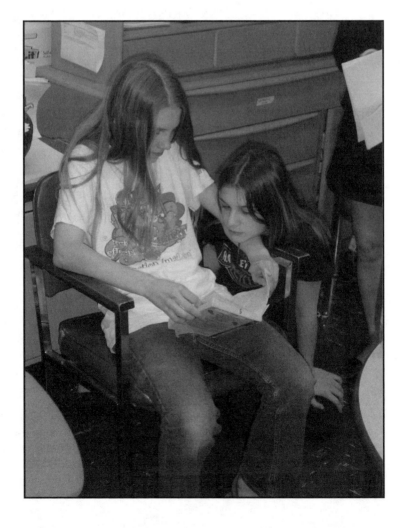

 Up Close and Personal

A Note from the Author, Greg Tang

Writing poems . . .

Here's a little "inside" knowledge about how I go about writing my poems. Have you ever had a great idea for a poem but then you get stuck trying to find the right rhymes?

To avoid this problem, I work backwards. I don't start with the idea, I start with the rhyme. I just play with words, and the rhymes give me ideas that I never would have thought of otherwise. I never get stuck trying to find a rhyme, because I start with it!

Here's an example. I knew my book would be called MATH POTATOES as a play on "mashed potatoes." So I started to think about rhymes: mash and hash, which led to different ways we eat potatoes. For six months I thought this would be a promising idea: potatoes au gratin, the kind that are best forgotten! Finally, I ran it by some kids and they told me it was really dumb. They were right. But then all this thinking about different ways to cook a potato started me thinking about the life of a potato, which isn't really very good, and I ended up with one of my favorite poems:

Math Potatoes
Boiled and baked and often mashed,
Peeled and fried and sometimes hashed.
No wonder spuds hide underground,
Life is painful when they're found!
Can you add up these pour souls,
For whom the bell already tolls?
In groups of 10 you'll hear their cries,
"Please don't turn us into fries!"

For Tang's bio, recommended reading lists, and an article about writing math poems written by Tang for Instructor *magazine, visit Tang's Web site at www.gregtang.com.*

See also the "At Home Activities" related to Tang's books on the Scholastic Web site at http://www.scholastic.com/schoolage/activities/k_2/mathriddles.htm.

Cover of WHEN I HEARD THE LEARN'D ASTRONOMER by Walt Whitman, illustrated by Loren Long. Copyright © 2004. Used with permission of Simon & Schuster Books for Young Readers, an imprint of Simon & Schuster Children's Publishing.

Title	WHEN I HEARD THE LEARN'D ASTRONOMER
Author	Walt Whitman
Illustrator	Loren Long
Publisher	Simon & Schuster
Copyright Date	2004
Ages	8 and up
Read-Aloud Time	5–7 minutes
Read-Aloud Sessions	1
Themes	Astronomy, imagination, Walt Whitman, poetry

In lush acrylics, Loren Long creates a dreamy paean to the stars and the imaginings they inspire in his interpretation of this simple, spare poem from LEAVES OF GRASS, written by one of America's most celebrated poets. Above, beside, and below the words of the poem, readers are treated to the fanciful artwork of Long's two young sons, Griffith and Graham. This book has won numerous awards, including the Parents' Choice Gold Award and the Society of Children's Book Writers and Illustrators Golden Kite Honor Award for picture book illustration.

Note: Have a copy of LEAVES OF GRASS on hand for the pre-reading focus.

PRE-READING FOCUS: Read the words of Walt Whitman's short poem to children before showing them Long's picture book. Ask: What is this poem about? (An astronomer's heady lecture; the beauty of a starry night.) Who do you think is speaking? Where does the poem take place? (A lecture hall; outdoors beneath the stars.) What do you think this poem is about? What is the mood of this poem? How does it make you feel? What is the message? **Let's read to find out** what the illustrator suggests through his pictures.

WHILE READING: Read the book in its entirety, taking time to appreciate the illustrations.

FOLLOW-UP DISCUSSION: Ask listeners what they think the poem means. Discuss how the poet was able to condense that message into just a few lines. Discuss how the illustrations help readers understand Whitman's message. How do the illustrations create a mood? Compare what they know and feel about the poem now with what they knew and felt about the poem when you read it to them without the benefit of illustrations. Ask which of Whitman's words or phrases they most liked. Why? Discuss the choice of words in the last line of the poem. (Perfect; silence.) Tell listeners that the simple drawings around the words of the poem were created by the illustrator's sons. Ask why they think Long chose to do that. Share the illustrator's comments found on the Up Close and Personal page with listeners.

Write Away! At the back of the book, readers will find Albert Einstein's famous quotation: "Imagination is more important than knowledge. Knowledge is limited. Imagination encircles the world." Ask students to respond to the message of Einstein's words.

Write Away! Have children read and select (or create) a poem to illustrate. Share poems. Read them aloud and then display the accompanying illustrations.

Other picture books that offer interpretations of classic poems through inspiring illustrations include LEWIS CARROLL'S JABBERWOCKY, illustrated by Jane Breskin Zalben, with Annotations by Humpty Dumpty (Boyds Mills Press); HIST WHIST, written by e. e. cummings and illustrated by Deborah Kogan Ray (Crown); and LITTLE TREE, written by e. e. cummings and illustrated by Deborah Kogan Ray (Crown).

For an extensive listing of poetry books suitable for students in grades 5 and 6 and resources for teaching poetry, turn to the Tips and Techniques for Teachers and Librarians section of this resource.

For an illuminating picture book biography of Walt Whitman, see the Robert F. Sibert Honor Award–winning, WALT WHITMAN: WORDS FOR AMERICA, written by Barbara Kerley and illustrated by Brian Selznick (Scholastic).

Notes:

Up Close and Personal ....

A Note from the Illustrator, Loren Long

How this book came about . . .

Many times ideas simply come from a daydream or something you see or hear or a conversation you have with another person. My editor, Kevin Lewis, and I were having one of those fun conversations about things we like. We stumbled across poetry, and in no time we learned that we both admire the famous American poet, Walt Whitman. Kevin had long loved Whitman's simple, but profound poem, "When I Heard The Learn'd Astronomer." I remembered it from school myself, but it was Kevin who suggested the idea of making it into a picture book for children. I gave it some thought and soon agreed that it would be a worthwhile project. Walt Whitman wrote these words almost 150 years ago, but to me, the message from this poem is even more powerful and meaningful today than it was when he first wrote it all those years ago.

Creating the art . . .

I must admit that taking on the challenge of creating art to accompany this eight line poem was somewhat difficult. Visually, Whitman's text does not offer much detail. For example, he tells us nothing about our main character, the narrator. Is the character male or female? Young or old? In what time period does the story take place, and where? In fact, when I studied Whitman's words, I realized the only detail he offers is that our narrator goes somewhere to listen to a noted astronomer.

I was given the task of coming up with my own little storyline based on Whitman's words. This was the fun part! I decided the narrator was a young boy who had a room decorated with space elements. He dresses up for this important occasion and is taken to an important building where he ponders an astronomy exhibit. He is the only child in our story, and we focus on his evening. From here, Whitman's words guided my visual interpretation as we follow our character outside in nature to exhale and soak in the beauty and wonder of the stars.

I felt the boy needed to carry a toy from home (the rocket) that is sort of a symbol of his youth and imagination. I also felt that my formal paintings should be offset by playful, more childlike drawings—almost as if my art is what we see the character going through, but the simple drawings throughout might be what our character is thinking or feeling.

Notice how there is nothing at all on the page opposite the lines, "How soon, unaccountable, I became tired and sick"! At this point, I imagine the little guy has had enough of the lecture and his mind is total mush. We've lost him.

It was great fun to involve my sons in one of my books. I supplied them with lots of paper and pens and pencils. In just a few sittings, they came up with over fifty drawings which I shipped to the art director at Simon & Schuster Children's Books, who then went about picking and choosing what he felt would work on the pages opposite my pictures.

We felt Einstein's quote was a fitting way to end the book, and I had the boy bring Mom and Dad out to share what he found—that science and technology are amazing and necessary, but we must never forget to go out in the "mystical moist night air and from time to time look up in perfect silence at the stars."

A message for all of us, young and old.

Shoot for those stars!

For more information on Loren Long and his other books, visit his Web site at http://www.lorenlong.com/.

Drawings by Griff and Graham Long. Used with permission.

Title	CHASING VERMEER
Author	Blue Balliett
Illustrator	Brett Helquist
Publisher	Scholastic Press
Copyright Date	2004
Ages	10 and up
Read-Aloud Time	8–10 minutes per chapter
Read-Aloud Sessions	21
Themes	Mystery, art, Vermeer, pentominoes

Note: This mystery story, set in Chicago, revolves around a Vermeer painting. It begins in October. As an introduction to the story, develop an appreciation of Vermeer's art by showing examples of his work. If possible, have a set of pentominoes to show children. To further enhance the read-aloud experience, check information on Scholastic's Web site (www.scholastic.com/chasingvermeer) about the hidden message the illustrator, Brett Helquist, has placed in the chapter illustrations.

Three letters, countless unexplainable coincidences, and the theft of a Vermeer painting add up to one absorbing mystery. This first novel, written by a teacher, was the result of her class wanting to read something as good as FROM THE MIXED-UP FILES OF MRS. BASIL E. FRANKWEILER by E. L. Konigsburg. When Balliett couldn't find anything that measured up, she decided to write a story herself for her University of Chicago Laboratory School students. Although she no longer teaches, she still writes in her laundry room, where it all began several summers ago.

> **PRE-READING FOCUS:** Introducing the book: Show the cover and read the title. Ask: What kind of story do you think this is? (Mystery.) When you look at the cover, what are the clues that this is a mystery story? (Color of the jacket; expressions on the characters' faces; door has appearance of puzzle pieces.) Ask if anyone is familiar with the artist Jan Vermeer. Give background on Vermeer to the extent that you deem appropriate for the group. Show examples of his artwork. Study the map of the setting of the novel found on the beginning pages of the book. Read "About Pentominoes and About This Story" and "About the Artwork: A Challenge to the Reader." Write the hint on the board or an easel, where it can be referred to throughout the read-aloud of this mystery story.

Chapter One: "Three Deliveries"

Pre-reading: **Let's read to find out** what the three deliveries are.

Follow-up:

- Discuss the letter that three people received at the beginning of the chapter. Note the salient points on the board or easel paper. (A painter was wronged. The crime is centuries old. Each will be rewarded for helping. They may not show the letter to anyone. The three will work together, but they may never meet.)

- Ask listeners which person seems most interesting. Why? Plan to write down the names of those who received a letter as it is revealed in the story.

Chapter Two: "The Letter Is Dead"

Pre-reading: Review what we know so far about this story. **Let's read to find out** what the title of this chapter means.

Follow-up:

- Discuss what we have learned about Ms. Hussey (She teaches sixth grade at the University School; she believes in learning by doing; she does not follow a set curriculum.)

- Discuss what we have learned about Calder Pillay (He is one of the narrators of the story; he likes the adventure of Ms. Hussey's classroom; he enjoys puzzles; he plans to solve a great mystery; he is 11 years old; he helps out once a week at Powell's Used Books; according to Petra, he is disheveled, he mutters to himself, and he is kind of "weird".)

- Discuss what we have learned about Petra Andalee (She is one of the narrators of the story; she loves to write; Powell's Used Books is one of her favorite places; according to Calder, she is "exceptionally" weird, a loner, quiet, and she has a triangle of hair on her forehead.)

  – Petra believes that humans need questions more than answers. What do you think this means?

> **Write Away!** Do the assignment Ms. Hussey asked her class to do: Ask an adult to tell you about a letter he or she will never forget. This should be a piece of mail that changed his or her life. How old was the person when he or she got it? Where was the person when he or she opened it? Does the person still have it? Write about what you find out.

Note: In preparation for the next chapter, have several art books available for children to peruse for the Write Away! assignment. If possible, find a book of paintings by Degas, Monet, Picasso, and Auguste Bernard.

Chapter Three: "Lost in the Art"

Pre-reading: Briefly discuss the Write Away! assignment. Did anyone find a really unusual letter? **Let's read to find out** more about our narrators and what letters the class members came up with.

Follow-up:

- Review what we have learned about Petra Andalee's family in this chapter. (Petra is the oldest of five siblings; her household is like a "tornado"; every first girl in her mother's family has been named Petra after an ancient city in Jordan; she likes that she was named after a "mysterious place of buried secrets.")

- Discuss the argument Petra overhears between her parents.

- What have we learned about Calder's family? (His father plans gardens for cities; he speaks calmly; Mom teaches math at the university; Calder is an only child.)

Write Away! Look through an art book to find a painting with a letter in it. Describe what is happening in the painting.

Note: In preparation for the next chapter, find a picture of Caillebotte's painting Rainy Day.

Chapter Four: "Picasso's Lie"

Pre-reading: **Let's read to find out** what Picasso's lie is.

Follow-up:

- What do you think Picasso meant when he said that art is a lie, but a lie that tells the truth?

- Show listeners Caillebotte's painting *Rainy Day* and discuss Petra's reaction to it. Ask: What do you think the book by Charles Fort has to do with the story?

Write Away! Do the assignment Ms. Hussey asked her class to do: Choose an item at home that feels like a work of art to you. It can be anything. Describe the object without saying what it is.

Chapter Five: "Worms, Snakes, and Periwinkles"

Pre-reading: Look up the words *credulity* (readiness or willingness to believe, especially on slight or uncertain evidence) and *premise* (assumed or taken for granted). **Let's read to find out** what Petra's new book is about.

Follow-up:

- What do you think Petra's dream means?

- What does it mean to be "educated by surprises"?

- Discuss the sentence that intrigues Petra: "We shall pick up an existence by its frogs."

Note: In preparation for the reading of the next chapter, copy the code onto chart paper or make a copy for each listener. You may also want to copy the letters the boys wrote to each other for ease in decoding them as a group.

Chapter Six: "The Geographer's Box"

Pre-reading: Ask: What do you think Calder will find as his piece of art? **Let's read to find out**.

While Reading: Decode the letters.

(From Tommy: Calder—name—of—kid—next—door—is—frog—vanished—last—week—I—think—kidnapped—have—to—stay—inside—mom—afraid—new—york—stinks—Tommy; From Calder: Tommy—so—sorry—about—frog—maybe—you—can—solve—mystery—and—be—hero—be—careful—Calder.)

Follow-up:

- What do you notice about what is happening in Petra's part of the story and what is happening in Calder's? (Both have to do with frogs!)

 **Write Away!** Write a letter in code to the person on your left. Exchange.

Note: In preparation for the reading of the next chapter, find a copy of Vermeer's painting The Geographer to show to listeners.

Chapter Seven: "The Man on the Wall"

Pre-reading: Ask: What is a geographer? (One who studies the physical features of the earth's surface.) **Let's read to find out** what Calder gets himself into.

Follow-up:

- Explain roman numerals and how MDCLXVIII translates into 1668.

- Look at Vermeer's paintings. Find the geometry, symmetry, and objects that appear again and again in his work, as Calder did.

- Why do you think Vermeer is interesting to Calder and will be to Petra? (He left behind more questions than answers.)

Write Away! Find more information about Vermeer. Write down a few interesting facts to share with the class.

Note: In preparation for the reading of the next chapter, have available a copy of a collection of Vermeer's paintings that includes A Lady Writing, 1665 to share with listeners.

Chapter Eight: "A Halloween Surprise"; Chapter Nine: "The Blue Ones"

Pre-reading: **Let's read to find out** how Petra and Calder dress for Halloween. (Petra—the writer in her dream; Calder—a *pentomino*.)

Follow-up to Chapter 8: Look at the painting *A Lady Writing, 1665.*

Pre-reading for Chapter 9: **Let's read to find out** what happens next.

Follow-up:

- Look at the other paintings of the woman in the yellow jacket.
- Compare the facts on Vermeer's life listed in the story with those the students have collected.
- Begin to look for clues in the novel's illustrations.

Chapter Ten: "Inside the Puzzle"

Pre-reading: **Let's read to find out** what strange thing occurs in this chapter.

Follow-up:

- How would you feel if you were Calder?

Chapter Eleven: "Nightmare"

Pre-reading: Ask: What is a nightmare? (A bad dream; a terrible occurrence.) **Let's read to find out** what kind of nightmare happens in this chapter, and to whom.

Follow-up:

- Discuss the letter.
- Look at the paintings again.

Note: In preparation for the reading of the next chapter, make a copy of the letter for each listener so all can decode it.

Chapter Twelve: "Tea at Four"

Pre-reading: Ask: Who do you think will be having tea at 4:00? (Petra, Calder, and Mrs. Sharpe.) What do you think the kids will learn from Mrs. Sharpe? **Let's read to find out!**

While Reading: Decode Tommy's letter.

(Calder—fred—caught—me—looking—for—clues—on—frog—got—mean—took—my—bike—mom—and—fred—fighting—Tommy)

Follow-up:

- Do you think Mrs. Sharpe is involved in the theft? Ms. Hussey? Mr. Andalee? Mr. Watch?

> **Write Away!** Choose a character you feel might be involved in the theft. Explain why you think it might be him or her.

Note: In preparation for the reading of the next chapter, make a copy of the letter for each listener so all can decode it.

Chapter Thirteen: "The Experts"; Chapter Fourteen: "Flashing Lights"

Pre-reading: Ask: What might "Flashing Lights" refer to? **Let's read to find out!**

While Reading: Decode Tommy's letter.

(Calder—fred—moved—out—we—want—to—come—home—but—no—money—Tommy)

Follow-up:

- What does it mean to "frame" someone for a crime? Do you think Mrs. Sharpe framed herself?

Chapter Fifteen: "Murder and Hot Chocolate"

Pre-reading: **Let's read to find out** who gets arrested. (Ms. Hussey.)

Follow-up:

- Look for clues in the chapter illustration.

Chapter Sixteen: "A Morning in the Dark"; Chapter Seventeen: "What Happens Now?"

Pre-reading: **Let's read to find out** what Calder gets himself into.

Follow-up:

- Do you agree with what the author of the art book said in his message to the thief? Discuss.
- Do you think the thief's mission has been successful?
- Look for clues in the chapter illustrations.

Chapter Eighteen: "A Bad Fall"

Pre-reading: **Let's read to find out** who takes a bad fall.

Follow-up:

- What clues do you think the author has placed in this chapter?
- Check the illustration for additional clues!

Chapter Nineteen: "The Shock on the Stairs"

Pre-reading: **Let's read to find out** what the shock is!

Follow-up:

- What do you think Petra has figured out? Study the illustration for clues.

Chapter Twenty: "A Maniac"

Pre-reading: Ask: To whom do you think the chapter title is referring? **Let's read to find out**.

Follow-up:

- Where do you think Petra is going?

Chapter Twenty-one: "Looking and Seeing"

Pre-reading: Ask: What is the difference between looking and seeing? **Let's read to find out** what happens in this chapter.

Follow-up:

- What do you think Petra's father is doing on campus?
- What do you think happened to the package he was carrying?
- Do you think Petra's father is involved in the theft?

Chapter Twenty-two: "Twelves"

Pre-reading: **Let's read to find out** what the chapter title means.

Follow-up:

- Where do you think Petra and Calder are heading?

Chapter Twenty-three: "Help!"

Pre-reading: **Let's read to find out** where Petra and Calder are headed.

Follow-up:

- How do you think Calder ended up with the painting?

Chapter Twenty-four: "Pieces"

Pre-reading: **Let's read to find out** the pieces to the puzzle of this mystery story.

Follow-up:

- Discuss which pieces of the story are believable and which seem to be a stretch of the imagination.

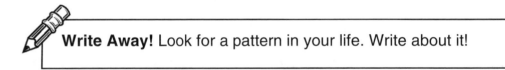

Write Away! Look for a pattern in your life. Write about it!

For activities related to CHASING VERMEER, visit the publisher's Web site at www.scholastic.com/titles/chasingvermeer/index.htm.

Be sure to look for the sequel to this book, WRIGHT 3, in which Calder and Petra are joined by Tommy, the off-stage character in CHASING VERMEER, as they work to solve another art mystery, this time revolving around Frank Lloyd Wright's Robie House in Chicago.

For a list of other mysteries suitable for grades 5–6, refer to the Tips and Techniques for Teachers and Librarians section of this resource.

Up Close and Personal

A Note from the Author, Blue Balliett

About the process of writing . . .

The most surprising part of writing CHASING VERMEER was discovering how much I really had to say, and that I really could write a book, a page at a time, even though my life was so busy.

Part of the secret of getting it done was writing down what felt right to me and not worrying about what was going to happen to it. Because I was sure this book was probably too wild to go anywhere outside of my classroom, I did exactly what I wanted with it. When it actually got published, I was shocked. I think I'm still a bit surprised to see it out in the world, and not in a huge pile on the laundry room floor where I do my writing!

When I was working on this book, I reached lots of dead ends and sometimes went too far in one direction or another. Writing is a messy process, and you don't always manage to say things instantly in a way that feels "just right". I spend lots of time crossing out and erasing and rewriting. And sometimes, when I sit down to figure something out, it keeps slipping out of my grip, and I don't feel like I'm getting anywhere. But what I've discovered is that often the answer to that same problem will pop into my mind later, when I'm not even really thinking about it. Weird but true.

Sometimes I figure out an idea just as I'm falling asleep. When I was trying to decide on the ending of CHASING VERMEER, it was winter and very cold outside. Suddenly, out of nowhere, the solution simply appeared in my head. I usually keep something to write on next to the bed, but I didn't have any paper that night. I had a pen, and I saw a piece of cardboard in the waste basket. It was too cold to get up, so I grabbed the cardboard and wrote the end of the book in the streetlight coming in the window. The next morning, I realized I'd written on the liner from a package of boxer shorts I'd bought for my son. He didn't think I should tell anyone about this, but I kind of like the idea that writing can happen in unpredictable places and at all times of day . . . I still have that piece of cardboard.

Cover of THE FLAG WITH FIFTY-SIX STARS by Susan Goldman Rubin, illustrated by Bill Farnsworth. Published by Holiday House. Reprinted by permission.

Title	THE FLAG WITH FIFTY-SIX STARS: A GIFT FROM THE SURVIVORS OF MAUTHAUSEN
Author	Susan Goldman Rubin
Illustrator	Bill Farnsworth
Publisher	Holiday House
Copyright Date . .	2005
Ages	10 and up
Read-Aloud Time .	12–15 minutes
Read-Aloud Sessions .	1
Themes	World War II, concentration camps, strength of spirit, hope, freedom, American flag

This account is at once both heart-wrenching and heartwarming. It is an unforgettable story of human resolve and hope in the face of one of history's most reprehensible crimes. As the author takes readers back in history, facts are presented in mesmerizing, storytelling fashion. Rubin enables us to experience the depth and strength of the human spirit inspired by the hope of liberty and explains beautifully how the American symbol of freedom added to the triumph of the prisoners of Mauthausen.

Note: Have an American flag on hand for the read-aloud of this book.
Find an illustration of the American flag with 48 stars, as it existed during WW II.

PRE-READING FOCUS: Review the history this book explores. Ask children what they know about World War II, the Nazi regime, concentration camps, and the Holocaust. Discuss racism and religious persecution. Read the title. Explain that Mauthausen was the last concentration camp built by the Nazis. Ask what is puzzling about the title. (The illustration on the cover shows the American flag, yet the title mentions 56 stars. The American flag has 50 stars.) Discuss what the American flag *symbolizes*, or stands for. **Let's read to find out** about the title and why Mauthausen is the subject of this book.

WHILE READING: Read the book in its entirety, with minimal interruptions. As you come upon difficult words, such as *subterranean, sabotaged, espionage, foraged,* and *evacuated,* help listeners use context to determine the meaning of the words.

FOLLOW-UP DISCUSSION: Ask listeners why they think the author chose to write this book. What was her purpose? What message did she hope to bring to readers? Review what the American flag means to Americans and others around the world. What did it mean to the prisoners at Mauthausen and to the soldiers who rescued them? Read Simon Wiesenthal's words regarding the American flag in paragraphs two and three of the Afterword. Ask: What words would you use to describe the prisoners? The soldiers who freed them?

Write Away! In this book we learn about hope in the face of terrible, tragic experiences. A teen prisoner is quoted in the book as saying, "I never gave up my belief. Dreaming of freedom is really what kept me going. In my mind I was still a free person." Write about a time when hope made a difference in your life or the life of someone you know.

Write Away! Research Simon Wiesenthal. You may want to begin with the Afterword at the back of the book. See also the references listed on pages 37–39. Report to the class about Wiesenthal's life beyond the concentration camp.

Other outstanding picture books that offer perspectives on World War II and other historical events can be found in the Book Notes section of this resource. See also the read-aloud plan for THE JOURNEY THAT SAVED CURIOUS GEORGE: THE TRUE WARTIME ESCAPE OF MARGRET AND H. A. REY, written by Louise Borden and illustrated by Allan Drummond (Houghton Mifflin).

For other books by Susan Goldman Rubin suitable for grades 5–6, refer to the author index of this resource.

For more information on Susan Goldman Rubin and her books, visit her Web site at http://www.susangoldmanrubin.com/index2.html.

Notes:

Up Close and Personal

A Note from the Author, Susan Goldman Rubin

From idea to published book . . .

THE FLAG WITH 56 STARS started with my friend, Adaire Klein. Adaire is the Director of the Library and Archives at the Simon Wiesenthal Center/Museum of Tolerance in Los Angeles. She showed me the flag with fifty-six stars that is displayed in the museum and told me the story behind it. I immediately felt tingly all over and knew this should be a book for young people. The problem was: how to write it?

Colleagues thought that it should be fictionalized. But I felt that the story had to be told accurately as nonfiction. In researching I used primary sources—interviews with those who had been at Mauthausen Concentration Camp, both prisoners and liberators. I hoped that someone somewhere in the world would remember who had made the flag. I never did find out for sure but along the way I uncovered new information. I called people in Paris, London, and Dallas, Texas. One contact led to another. Finally I spoke to a G.I. in Pennsylvania. He is the historian of the 11th Armored Division, the American soldiers who liberated Mauthausen. Not only had he been there but he had taken movies with cameras left behind by the fleeing Nazis. And he had edited these into a video. I bought the video and also became an honorary member of the 11th Armored Division.

While I was working on the manuscript I wrote to Simon Wiesenthal in Vienna. He had been imprisoned at Mauthausen and was there, in the hospital in the Death Block when the Americans arrived. Although Mr. Wiesenthal did not remember the flag, he sent me his thoughts about what the American flag meant to him, and I treasure his letters.

The most moving moment for me came at the launch of the book on May 15, 2005. Our program at the Museum of Tolerance included Mike Jacobs and Shirley Sweetbaum, survivors of Mauthausen; and Duane Mahlen, a member of the 11th Armored Division, and Susan Seibel McKnight, daughter of Colonel Richard Seibel, the commanding officer. Both Duane and Mike were exactly the same age—19 years old—in May 1945. They both had saved their hats and wore them at the program. Mike's was a striped prisoner's cap, and Duane's was a khaki soldier's cap. When they sat at a table side by side, reminiscing, tears came to my eyes. I felt gratified for doing this book and bringing these people together to celebrate courage and hope.

Title	GRANNY TORRELLI MAKES SOUP
Author	Sharon Creech
Illustrator	Chris Raschka
Publisher	HarperCollins
Copyright Date	2003
Ages	10 and up
Read-Aloud Time	8–10 minutes per session
Read-Aloud Sessions	12
Themes	Family, friendship, jealousy, cooking, grandparents

Twelve-year-old Rosie is stubborn, smart, impatient, and loved by Granny Torrelli. Lucky for her, and lucky for readers, who eavesdrop on Rosie and Granny as they make soup and salad and pasta while working out the wrinkles and snags—and doing the mending—necessary to keep the fabric of life fitting comfortably.

Note: Consider making the meals that are described in the book to serve to listeners at key points in the read-aloud of the book. Mangia! Mangia!

PRE-READING FOCUS: Introducing the book: Show the cover and read the title. Ask: What do the title and the cover of the book tell us about the story? (This is a contemporary story; a grandmother, a boy, a girl, and a dog are central to the story; soup plays a part in the story.)

Part I: Soup: "That Bailey"; "I'm Mad"; "Granny Torrelli Says"; "Why I Liked Bailey"; "Granny Torrelli Makes Soup"

Pre-reading: **Let's read to find out** who the characters on the cover are and what the problem is.

Follow-up:

- Review the characters we have met in the first 10 pages. (Rosie—narrator; Bailey—Rosie's neighbor and best friend since they were babies; Granny Torrelli.)

- What do we know about these characters? (Rosie is mad at Bailey; Granny is trying to find out what's going on; Granny makes soup; Rosie describes Granny as patient, reasonable, and calm; Granny doesn't like being called an old lady; Granny is feisty, which we glean from the story Rosie tells about how Granny handled the meter reader imposter. According to Rosie, Bailey smiles all the time; he is better than a brother to Rosie; he's quiet, and not pushy, selfish, or mean; and he has hair that sticks up.)

- What is the *conflict*, or problem in the story? (Rosie is mad at her friend, Bailey, for something he has said.)

- Which character seems most interesting? Why?

- Why do you think Granny Torrelli makes soup for Rosie? (To make her feel better.)

- Consider the title. Why do you think Creech has put Granny and not Rosie in the title?

- Why does Rosie love Granny Torrelli? (She is always making good things, she is calm and patient, and she tells Rosie she is smart.) Discuss.

- Begin a list of Granny Torrelli's Italian words and what they mean in English. (*Zuppa* = soup.)

Write the ingredients for zuppa on the board or chart paper. (Celery, carrots, onions, mushrooms, chicken, salt, pepper, soy sauce. Also, from the next chapter, "pasta dots," or acini de pepe.) If you plan to make the soup, ask for volunteers to bring in one of the ingredients. You will also need a small bowl and spoon for each member of the group. Napkins wouldn't be a bad idea, either!

Write Away! Granny says that when you are angry with someone, you should think of the good things about that person, the nice things he or she has said, and why you liked that person in the first place. Think about someone you are mad at, or have been mad at, and write down what you would say about him or her, following Granny Torrelli's advice.

Write Away! Rosie says that Bailey is better than a brother because she chose him and he chose her. In what ways are friends better than brothers and sisters? In what ways are brothers and sisters better than friends?

Write Away! Write about your granny (or another member of your family). What is she like? What does she do that makes her special to you? Tell a story, as Rosie did, about something your relative has done that will help us know his or her personality.

Note: Have a tissue available for each student for the reading of the next section.

Part I: Soup: "You Going to Tell Me?"; "Pardo"; "Bambini"; "Just Like Bailey"

Pre-reading: Yesterday we learned that Rosie is mad at her best buddy, Bailey. What do you think will happen next? **Let's read to find out.**

Follow-up:

- Discuss what we have learned about the characters in this section. (Rosie and Bailey are 12 years old; Granny used to have a good friend named Pardo; Bailey is visually impaired.)

- If you plan to make the salad, write the ingredients on the board. (Oranges, parsley, olive oil.) Ask for volunteers to bring in the ingredients. You will also need small plates, forks, and napkins.

- Add *bambini* (babies) to Granny's word list.

- Give tissues to the students so they can see like Bailey.

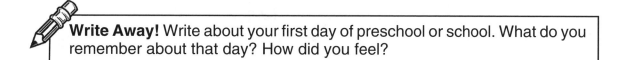

Write Away! Write about your first day of preschool or school. What do you remember about that day? How did you feel?

Note: In preparation for the next section, find a Braille book to show to listeners. Make two copies of the play on pages 28–29. Find a stuffed tiger or other animal to use as a prop for the play. Begin soup in a crock pot to be ready for tomorrow's read-aloud session. Enjoy the smells throughout the day!

Part I: Soup: "Put Your Feet Up"; "Plays"; "The Blind Woman"

Pre-reading: Read the chapter titles. Ask listeners to predict what we will learn about Bailey and Rosie in these chapters. **Let's read to find out**.

While Reading: Ask for two volunteers to read the Mother and Father parts of the play.

Follow-up:

- Discuss what Rosie did to Bailey's book.

- Why does Granny say that Rosie is stubborn sometimes?

- Add *si* (yes) to the list of Granny's words.

Part I: Soup: "Stubborn Streak"; "Tutto Va Bene"; "Pasta Party"

Pre-reading: Read the chapter titles. **Let's read to find out** what *tutto va bene* means and what other words Granny uses are new to us.

Follow-up:

- Add Granny's words to the list: *completamente* (completely), *piccolino* (little), *nero* (black), *bene* (good), *stupido* (stupid), *tutto va bene* (all is well), *disastro* (disaster), *tutto non va bene* (all is not well).

- Enjoy the *zuppa*!

Write Away! Find out more about guide dogs. Write down a few interesting facts to share with the group.

Part I: Soup: "Tangled Head"; "Lost"; "The Prince"

Pre-reading: Share guide dog facts. Read the chapter titles. In one of these chapters, Bailey takes "a short walk that got very long." What do you think that means? (He got lost.) **Let's read to find out**.

Follow-up:

- Add Granny's word to the list: *molto* (very).

- What makes someone a good friend?

Write Away! Write about a time when you were looking for someone or something that was lost. How did you feel when you found the person or thing? Or, tell about a time when you were lost. Be sure to give lots of details so the reader knows what it was like and how you felt, just as Rosie did in the story.

Write Away! Write about a time when you were bullied or you bullied someone else.

Note: Have the salad ready to serve after the next read-aloud session.

Part I: Soup: "The Rescuer"; "Why, Why, Why?"; "In My Head"

Pre-reading: Read the chapter titles. **Let's read to find out** why Rosie is mad at Bailey.

While Reading: Stop reading after "Why, Why, Why?"

- Why do you think Bailey is mad at Rosie?

- Continue reading to find out.

Follow-up:

- What do you think will happen next?

- Enjoy the salad!

Part I: Soup: "The Door Opens"; "Tutto"; Part II: Pasta: "She's Back"

Pre-reading: Read the chapter titles. Ask if anyone knows what *tutto* means (all). **Let's read to find out** what happens when the door opens.

While Reading: Read through "Tutto." Note that the next section of the book is Part II: Pasta.

- Why do you think the author has divided her book into two parts?

- What do you think will happen next?

- Read the chapter title. ("She's Back.") To whom might this be referring? **Let's read to find out**.

Follow-up:

- What is bothering Rosie? (The hug.)

- Ask for volunteers to bring in cavatelli pasta, spaghetti sauce, tiny meatballs, plates, forks, and lotsa napkins! Or, if time permits and you are very brave, plan to make the pasta, meatballs, and sauce from scratch as Granny, Rosie, and Bailey do!

Part II: Pasta: "Ciao"; "My Warm and Cold Heart"; "What's New?"

Pre-reading: Read the chapter titles. Ask if anyone knows what *ciao* means. (Hello or good-bye.) Add it to Granny's list of words. **Let's read to find out** whether *ciao* means hello or good-bye in this chapter.

Follow-up:

- What is bothering Rosie? (She is unsure of her new neighbor, Janine, and her feelings for Bailey are confusing.)

- What does it mean to have a warm heart? A cold heart?

- Is it possible to have an instant best friend? Discuss.

- Is it strange to have a boy for a best friend if you are a girl, or a girl for a best friend if you are a boy? Discuss.

- What do you think of Janine?

- Rosie calls herself odd. Do you think Rosie is odd?

- Add Granny's word to the list: *niente* (nothing)

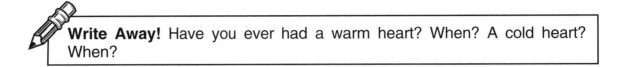

Write Away! Have you ever had a warm heart? When? A cold heart? When?

Part II: Pasta: "Violetta"; "Janine"; "Haircut"

Pre-reading: Read the chapter titles. What do you think "Violetta" is about? **Let's read to find out.**

While Reading: Stop after reading "Violetta."

- Who is at the door?
- What do you think Rosie will do?
- Continue reading.

Follow-up:

- What is bothering Rosie? (She is jealous of Janine.)
- Why does Granny whisper "Violetta"?

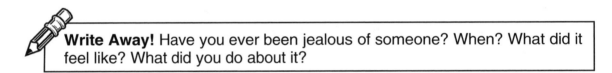

Write Away! Have you ever been jealous of someone? When? What did it feel like? What did you do about it?

Part II: Pasta: "A Long Pause"; "Snakes"; "Sauce"

Pre-reading: Read the chapter titles. Ask for predictions about what will happen in these chapters. **Let's read to find out.**

Follow-up:

- What do you like best about each of the characters in this story?

Write Away! Imagine you are Janine. How do you feel? What are you thinking?

Part II: Pasta: "The Yellow House"; "Meatballs"; "Not So Fast"

Pre-reading: Read the first sentence of "The Yellow House." Ask for predictions about what will happen next. **Let's read to find out.**

Follow-up:

• Tomorrow we will finish this book. How do you think it will end?

> **Write Away!** Write an ending to the story from one character's point of view. Choose Rosie, Granny, Bailey, Janine, or one of the new boys.

Note: Prepare to have your own pasta party following the read-aloud of the conclusion of the book. Allow sauce and meatballs to simmer in a crock pot prior to the read-aloud, if possible, to fill the air with the wonderful aroma. Mangia! Mangia!

Part II: Pasta: "The Baby"; "The Pasta Party"

Pre-reading: **Let's read to find out** how the story ends.

Follow-up:

• Rosie says she feels that her world is a little bigger. Discuss.

• Enjoy a pasta party!

> **Write Away!** Describe a big dinner you have been a part of. What was it like? Tell about its sounds, smells, tastes, how the table looked, and what the settings felt like. How did you feel at that party? Try to use all five senses to help the reader feel as if he or she is there, too.

Sharon Creech is the author of several books for children, including the Newbery Award–winning WALK TWO MOONS. Teacher's guides for her books can be found on her Web site at http://www.sharoncreech.com/teach/teach.asp.

The following Web sites have additional information about Sharon Creech:
http://www.harperchildrens.com/hch/author/author/creech
http://www.ala.org/alsc/creech.html
http://falcon.jmu.edu/~ramseyil/creech.htm
http://www.achuka.co.uk/scsg.htm
http://www.indiana.edu/~eric_rec/ieo/bibs/creech.html
http://www.sdcoe.k12.ca.us/score/walk/walktg.htm

Note: Although Web sites can be valuable resources that provide a wealth of information, the author cannot guarantee the accuracy of their information or their safety for children. Use the Internet wisely.

Cover from SKETCHES FROM A SPY TREE by Tracie Vaughn Zimmer, illustrated by Andrew Glass. Jacket illustrations © 2005 by Andrew Glass. Reprinted by permission of Clarion Books, an imprint of Houghton Mifflin Company. All rights reserved.

Title	SKETCHES FROM A SPY TREE
Author	Tracie Vaughn Zimmer
Illustrator	Andrew Glass
Publisher	Clarion
Copyright Date	2005
Ages	9 and up
Read-Aloud Time	8–10 minutes per session
Read-Aloud Sessions	6
Themes	Family, divorce, twins, new baby, neighbors, sketching, hope

Nestled in a neighborhood tree with her sketchbook, Anne Marie, the narrator, and twin of Mary Anne, watches the neighbors and works out her problems. Over the course of a year, there is much to ponder about life, family, love, disappointment, and, ultimately, hope. Told in well-crafted poems and illustrated in a variety of media that mirror Anne Marie's moods, this deep yet simple story is certain to launch many discussions and strike a chord with many a child.

Note: Consider making or purchasing individual sketchbooks or journals for listeners to use throughout the read-aloud of this book. On each double-page spread there should be one side for writing and one side for illustrations.

To aid in the discussion of the poetic devices found in the poems that make up this story, see the author's simple and useful definitions and the "Poetic Devices Scavenger Hunt" found on the author's Web site at www.tracievaughnzimmer.com. See also the resources for teaching poetry listed in the Tips and Techniques for Teachers and Librarians section of this resource.

PRE-READING FOCUS: Introducing the book: Show the cover and read the title. Ask: What do the title and the cover of the book tell us about the story? (This seems to be a contemporary story; setting: a tree; from the looks of the tree, it is either spring, summer, or early autumn; the two girls look alike, but they dress differently; one of the girls has a sketch book; from the title we can conclude that the girls "spy" from the tree.) Ask: What might they spy on from the tree? What might they see? Which girl do you think is the main character? (The one with the sketch book.) This story is written in verse. Explain that this means the story is a series of poems. Encourage listeners to think about that as you read the story aloud.

"Early Spring"; "Family Portrait"; "Across the Back Fence"; "The Twins"

Pre-reading: **Let's read to find out** about the characters on the cover and what they are doing in the tree.

Follow-up:

- Discuss what we have found out in these first few poems. (Narrator, Anne Marie, is a twin; there are three children in the family; Dad left two years ago; Anne Marie and her twin, Mary Anne, have similarities as well as differences.)

- Discuss how Anne Marie and Mary Anne are the same and how they are different. Ask: Do you know any twins? Do they look alike? Do you think of them as the same? How are they different? Show the photos on the back flap of the book jacket and read about the author and illustrator, who are both twins. To learn more about the author's experience as a twin, visit her Web site.

- What have we learned about Anne Marie? (She has wild red hair that is tangled; she loves to wear cutoff jeans and coveralls; she has scraped knees, grimy bare feet, and a scar from injuring herself while running in the house; she likes to draw, paint, and play street hockey)

- What do we know about Mary Anne? (She has wild red hair that she wears in French braids with satin bows; she loves ballet; she plays piano) How do we know this? (We are told by Anne Marie.) Note that we have not yet met Mary Anne.

- What are some of Anne Marie's *characteristics*? (One characteristic is that Anne Marie is angry.) Ask: How do we know that Anne Marie is angry? (She cuts Dad out of the photograph and "crumples his face"; she blows seeds across the back fence into Mr. O'Brien's yard; she describes herself as the twin "with hate painting my heart black.")

- Why is Anne Marie angry? (Dad left the family.)

- What is the *conflict*, or problem, in the story? (Anne Marie is angry at her dad.)

- What words or phrases in the poems we read today help you see the characters and feel what Anne Marie is feeling? (Personification: "First light of morning winks . . ."; "hate painting my heart black"; Imagery: the description of the smells of the pizza box.)

- Review the sensory images in "Family Portrait" in preparation for the **Write Away!** assignment below.

- What physical characteristic does Dad share with the twins? (Wild red hair.)

- Begin a log about Anne Marie's neighbors, with brief descriptions of each. Start with Mr. O'Brien.

- Pass out individual sketchbooks or journals.

Write Away! Write a poem that describes you or one of your family members, or a comparison of you and one of your family members, as Anne Marie has done. Try to use words and phrases that will create strong images in your reader's mind. Illustrate your poem.

> **Write Away!** Describe a special place in your house where you play, like Anne Marie and Mary Anne's closet. Use words and phrases that will appeal to the reader's senses.

"Maple Street"; "And She Does"; "Best Friend"; "The Cat Lady"; "Streetlights"

Pre-reading: Share sketches and descriptions from the **Write Away!** assignment listed above. **Let's read to find out** more about the spy tree.

Follow-up:

- Discuss the variety of art media used to illustrate the poems. Discuss why the artist may have chosen to illustrate this story in this way. (To complement the mood of the poem.) Which illustrations do you like best? Why?

- In "And She Does" we learn a little about Anne Marie's mom through Anne Marie's description of her. What is she like? What are her *characteristics*?

- Add the neighbors we have met today to the log (Jamie Hamilton, Paul and Carrie O'Brien, Miss Emory).

- What did we learn about Dad in these poems? (He loved to paint landscapes.)

- What is troubling Anne Marie in the poems we read today? (Her dad's friend, Mike, has moved in.) Discuss.

- Identify the poetic devices found in these poems. (Alliteration: "faithful fans of college football . . . favorite teams"; "quilt of cats"; Simile: "hair like two flags in the wind"; "smile like we've got the winning lottery ticket"; "sauerkraut that smelled like dead rats"; Imagery: "a quilt of cats folded around her legs"; "lace curtains drip from tall windows".)

> **Write Away!** Write a poem that describes one of your neighbors. Try to include a simile, personification, and lots of sensory images. Illustrate your poem using a variety of media, as the illustrator of this book, Andrew Glass, does.

"Chores"; "Bubblegum in Braces"; "Not to Brag, but . . .";
"Dad's Roses"; "New Neighbor"; "Sheets"; "A Dare";
"Hey, Bullfrog"

Pre-reading: **Let's read to find out** how the author helps us see Anne Marie's world. Listen for alliteration, similes, and vivid images.

Follow-up:

- Review the characters we meet in this section. (Younger sister Emily, Mr. and Mrs. Kramer, May Ching, Mrs. Green, bullfrog.) What are their characteristics? Discuss what we learn about each of them from Anne Marie. Add the neighbors we met in this section to the log.

- Look closely at "Bubblegum in Braces" for an abundance of poetic devices.

- What did we learn about Dad in the poem "Dad's Roses"? (He loved to nurture roses; he left three days before the narrator's ninth birthday.) What do we learn about Anne Marie in this poem? (We see her anger toward her father for leaving the family three nights before she and Mary Anne turned nine played out in her destruction of the rose bushes.)

- Discuss the benefits of being a twin according to Anne Marie. What might be the disadvantages?

> **Write Away!** Write a poem that describes your relationship with one of your siblings or a member of your extended family. Use poetic devices to make your descriptions come alive. Illustrate your poem.

In preparation for the next read-aloud session, make a copy of "It Must Be September"
for each listener.

"The Kiss"; "Get Rich Quick"; "It Must Be September";
"Stepdad"; "The Book Lady"; "Mr. Grouch"; "Tasting"; "Regret"

Pre-reading: Review what we know about Anne Marie's family. **Let's read to find out** about more of Anne Marie's neighbors.

Follow-up:

- How does Anne Marie feel in "The Kiss"? Discuss the fact that Anne Marie carries a single rosebud as a "silent protest" and gives Emily rose petals to scatter at the wedding. Contrast Anne Marie's actions here with what she did in "Dad's Roses."

- Anne Marie says, "the air feels like a wool coat." Discuss why this simile is powerful. Note that the setting of the poem is an outdoor wedding. Find other examples of great similes and metaphors in these poems. (My favorite is "Splitting Mom's attention like an extra-small pepperoni pizza.")

- "It Must Be September" is full of sensory images. Explore these. Give a copy of the poem to each listener. Ask children to highlight or underline sensory images with different colored markers according to which sense they appeal to; for example, blue = sight, yellow = taste, pink = sound.

- Note the example of personification in this poem. (Yellow school bus stealing freedom.)

- Discuss why Anne Marie might aspire to be "The Book Lady" when she grows up.

- Add Mr. Grouch to the neighbor log.

- Why is Anne Marie staring out the front window watching other kids play in "Regret"? (She is grounded.)

Write Away! The author has written about Popsicles in "Tasting." Write a poem about a food that is the "taste" of your favorite season. Use poetic devices. Illustrate your poem.

Write Away! Write a poem about a regret of yours.

"The Turtles"; "What She Sees"; "Names"; "Nightmare"; "Overnight"; "March Winds"; "That Dog"

Pre-reading: **Let's read to find out** about more neighbors.

Follow-up:

- How does Anne Marie help Mee Song? (She helps her improve at reading by reading with her, making flashcards, taking her to the Kramers' house for tutoring.) What do Anne Marie's actions in this poem tell us about her? (She is kind, helpful, and charitable.)

- Find a metaphor in this poem. ("Her tongue a twisted jump rope.")

- Discuss Anne Marie's concern as revealed in "What She Sees." (She is worried that she reminds her mother of her father.)

- Anne Marie wishes for another name. Have you ever wished for another name? What name would you choose? Why?

- List the vivid verbs the author chooses in "Nightmare." (Roar, howls, scratching, bound, chases, nestle, swallow, matching.)

- Note how "Nightmare" starts with long lines and ends with very short ones. Why do you think the author wrote it this way? How do the line lengths help you feel what Anne Marie is feeling?

- How does Anne Marie feel in "March Winds"? Why is Anne Marie so angry? What do you think she is referring to when she says, "But it DID happen! It DID!"? (She is thinking about her dad and his leaving.)

- Add the neighbors we met to the log. Don't forget the mean dog!

Write Away! Write a poem about the parent you look or act like. Write a verse for each characteristic you share, as Anne Marie does in "What She Sees."

Write Away! In "That Dog" Anne Marie writes about a mean dog down the street that scares her "so bad." Write about an animal or person you might feel sorry for if he or she didn't scare you "so bad." Illustrate!

Write Away! Revise one of your poems, concentrating on replacing plain verbs with vivid verbs.

"Perspectives"; "Free First Lesson"; "Never Mind"; "Potential"; "Baby Sister Sarah"; "Mom Calls Her Loquacious"; "Self Portrait"

Pre-reading: **Let's read to find out** how Anne Marie is feeling at the end of the book.

Note: Ask the first follow-up question following the reading of "Perspectives" and then read on to the end of the book.

Follow-up:

- What advice does Mary Anne give her sister? (Give Mike a chance.) Do you think it's good advice? Discuss. Do you think Anne Marie will take her sister's advice?

- Call attention to the alliteration in "First Free Lesson."

- What is "potential"? (Capable of development; promise.) Discuss Anne Marie's comment in "Potential": "I think I'll paint a picture to fill the black spot he wiped clean in my heart." Compare how she feels here with how she felt in "The Twins," where she referred to her "black" heart.

- In "Baby Sister Sarah" Anne Marie imagines all the things she will do with her new sister. How would you describe Anne Marie here? (Hopeful; happy.)

- After hearing the poem "Mom Calls Her Loquacious," what do you think *loquacious* means? (Talkative.)

- How would you describe Anne Marie at the end of the book? (Happy; she has accepted her new stepdad.)

- What events helped Anne Marie get over her anger? (See "Perspectives" and "Potential".)

- Add the neighbor we met to the log.

- Which neighbor(s) did you like best? Why? Which neighbor(s) do you think Anne Marie liked best? Why?

Write Away! Write a poem about your private "dreaming spot." Illustrate it.

Write Away! Write about a time when you had to get over something that was very upsetting to you. How did you do it? How long did it take? Who and what helped you get over it?

Notes:

Up Close and Personal

A Note from the Author, Tracie Vaughn Zimmer

From fact to fiction . . .

So much of SKETCHES FROM A SPY TREE had its start in this seed of the truth—all the details about what it feels like to be a twin are completely based on my real life. My twin sister and I really did lose the same teeth on the same day, and we scored identically on our IQ tests. We even answered the same way on the questions we missed.

But the story part of SPY TREE is just a wild ride into my imagination. That's how writing works for me. I take this feeling (anger or hope or loneliness, for example) and then I think, *what if*? What if my character's dad just dropped out of her life? What if her mom remarries and has a new baby? What if she still misses her old life and wants things to be like they were? Then I just run with it. I never know where the story will go until I'm writing it. I can't plot it out ahead of time like I used to think real writers do. To me, that would be like reading the last chapter of a book first. *Boring!* So I snag some true details or real feelings from my life and then give them to a character. I build a story around her and sometimes my characters surprise me. For example, I didn't know Anne Marie would pull down her dad's rose bushes until she did it. Writing, to me, is just the flip side of reading—staying with a story until I see what happens. I get to live inside the life of someone else for a while, and when I come home I'm changed from the journey.

Visit Tracie Vaughn Zimmer at her Web site at www.tracievaughnzimmer.com, where you will find information about the author of interest to students, teachers, and parents; suggested poetry activities related to SKETCHES FROM A SPY TREE; activities for a number of other poetry books and picture books the author recommends; links related to the theme of SKETCHES FROM A SPY TREE; and more.

Up Close and Personal

A Note from the Illustrator, Andrew Glass

Through Anne Marie's Eyes . . .

I did lots of drawings (I always do a lot of drawings!) as I tried to imagine how Anne Marie felt making sketches for each poem in SPY TREE. I thought about what kind of stuff she might have around to make collages with too. Finally, I chose drawings that looked as if they really might be found in a sketchbook. My way of drawing just naturally got mixed up with the way I imagined hers might be. I like to try seeing through a character's eyes and drawing what the character sees "from his or her point of view" like a fly on the wall, maybe. How would a fly draw?

Drawing ideas . . .

My favorite part of illustrating a book is making the sketches, so in working on SPY TREE I got to do a lot of what I enjoy most. Often, my sketches are loose lines and overlapping pictures held together with tape. I do whatever it takes to help me find the picture, using a pencil or a brush, paper, and glue. Drawing, for me, is like thinking out loud. Since I enjoy drawing so much and like the way sketches look, I try to leave some of the sketchiness in the illustrations. The difficult and in-teresting part is allowing my thoughts to have life of their own. In that way, drawing is much like writing a story: you have to be very persis-tent and try not to think about being finished before your drawing draws you there or you will go a little or a lot crazy.

A lot of work is like that . . . I remember homework being like that!

Look for Tracie Vaughn Zimmer's interview with Andrew Glass, on her Web site at http://www.tracievaughnzimmer.com/Andrew%20Glass%20Interview.htm.

Notes:

Cover of THE LETTER HOME, by Timothy Decker Copyright © 2005. Published by Front Street, an imprint of Boyds Mills Press. Reprinted by permission.

Title	THE LETTER HOME
Author/Illustrator	Timothy Decker
Publisher	Front Street
Copyright Date	2005
Ages	10 and up
Read-Aloud Time	8–10 minutes
Read-Aloud Sessions	1
Themes	World War I, letter-writing, fable

This first book by a photographer and artist who currently teaches writing to young adults is haunting and thought-provoking. The illustrations extend and deepen the spare text about the emotional trials of war. The narrator, a medic, tries to explain his war experiences to his young son in a letter home. His struggle to do so is palpable; the words and images, though simple, speak volumes.

PRE-READING FOCUS: Show the cover of the book. Look at the title page illustration, in which the setting and date are given. (Europe, 1918.) Note the look of the airplanes. Review with children what they know about World War I. Identify the objects in the illustration on the page facing the copyright page. (Helmet, satchel, barbed wire, pieces of wood.) Return to the cover illustration. Ask: Who do you think is standing with his back to the reader? (Father; a soldier.) Where do you think he was when he wrote the letter? (Somewhere at war in Europe.) **Let's read to find out** about the letter this soldier writes to his son.

WHILE READING: Note the illustration details: the dress and the circumstances of World War I. Discuss how they extend and deepen the meaning of the spare text. Consider where the boat was going. (Europe.) What type of a voyage does it seem to have been? (Rough, rocky.) Note the flags. What country do you think the soldiers are walking through? (France.) Note the narrator's armband, denoting his responsibility as a medic. What is he carrying? (A rolled-up cot.) Discuss what a medic is. (Corpsman engaged in medical work.) As you read on, note how the father describes the war in a way that will not scare his son. ("Nights alive with fireworks," "hide and seek," "school," "schoolboys playing in the mud.") What lines help us know about this man's fear? ("We didn't really play much," "Slept when we could for as long as we could with our heads down and our ears open," "[time] passed slowly.") Discuss how the details in the illustrations tell us what this man is feeling. (Downcast heads, sad expressions on faces, body stance, the starkness of the sketches.)

FOLLOW-UP DISCUSSION: Ask: What is compassion? (Sympathy for the pain or distress of others.) Discuss the quotation at the end of the book: "Compassion as action to ease the pain of the world." What do you think the author's purpose was in writing this book? What message did he hope to bring to readers?

Write Away! In this book we learn about tragic wartime experiences through a father's letter to his son. Write about how war has affected humankind throughout history.

Write Away! Thinking about the quotation that ends this book, write about a time when you used "compassion as action" to ease someone's pain.

Write Away! Write about how you might show compassion to someone.

For other books that reflect on the experience of war or teach about wars in history, refer to the Book Notes section of this resource.

Notes:

Up Close and Personal

A Note from the Author/Illustrator, Timothy Decker

On creating the art for his first picture book . . .

I love to draw. I have been drawing for years and find it incredibly rewarding. However, focusing my mind and energy on drawing THE LETTER HOME was the hardest work that I had ever done. It was hard because it required my attention for a very long time, and that meant that I risked getting bored or quitting before I was finished.

I didn't want that to happen, so I started to think like a professional athlete. Practice makes perfect in creating art, just as it does when throwing a baseball or riding a surf board. The only way to get good at something is to do it over and over, to make mistakes and to learn from them.

In the Tour de France, which is a very long bicycle race that lasts for weeks, cyclists have two days when they don't have to race. They can do whatever they want, yet all of them spend those days riding their bicycles and practicing. Much like that, I drew hundreds of drawings while working on THE LETTER HOME. Some of them were good and became the pictures in the book, but most of them were just practice—something from which I could learn.

I learned that I had to draw everyday, even when I when I didn't quite feel like it, because that was the only way that I would be happy with THE LETTER HOME when I was done with the project.

Courtesy Harcourt, Inc.

Title	HARVESTING HOPE: THE STORY OF CESAR CHAVEZ
Author	Kathleen Krull
Illustrator	Yuyi Morales
Publisher	Harcourt
Copyright Date	2003
Ages	9 and up
Read-Aloud Time	15 minutes
Read-Aloud Sessions	1
Themes	Migrant workers, immigrant experience, biography

This biography of Cesar Chavez, a leader of migrant workers, demonstrates how passion can cause a shy, soft-spoken boy to rise to lead his people in the fight for civil rights. Written by a skilled biographer for children and lushly illustrated, this book has won numerous awards.

Note: Have a map of the state of California available for the read-aloud of this book.

PRE-READING FOCUS: Show the cover of the book. Read the title. Who is this man? (Cesar Chavez.) What do you think that is behind him? Look at the title page illustration. Does this give more clues? (Sunrise.) Make connections between the illustration and the title. Explain that this is a biography of Chavez's life. **Let's read to find out** about Cesar Chavez and what the title means.

WHILE READING: Read the first page. List what we know about Chavez from this page. (Until he was 10 years old, Chavez lived on an 80-acre ranch in Arizona; he was part of a large extended family that enjoyed spending time together in the summer.) Ask: What clue does the author give that things changed for Chavez? ("Until he was ten.") Read the next two spreads. Discuss what we have learned about Chavez as a young boy. (He was shy and stubborn, but he did not fight.) Read the next two spreads. Ask: What is a migrant? Use the context to define. (A person who moves regularly to find work, especially in harvesting crops.) Contrast Chavez's life now with his life on the ranch. Read the next spread. Discuss how the author has helped you feel what Chavez felt as he worked the fields. (Sensory images: swallowed bitter homesickness, eyes sting, lungs wheeze, hot spasms shoot through his back, years blurred together.) Read the next three spreads. Discuss the discrimination Chavez encountered and the choice he made, at age 20, to fight for change. Discuss what other choices he could have made. Read the next spread. Discuss Chavez's personality traits—those that helped him in his cause (patience, compassion, stubbornness, being demanding, single-mindedness, being a problem-solver) and those that didn't (shyness). Ask for examples of behavior that demonstrate each of these qualities. Read the next spread. Discuss: "Truth is a better weapon than violence" and "Nonviolence takes more guts [than violence]." Ask listeners to name other leaders in history who would have agreed with these words. (Martin Luther King Jr., Jesus Christ, and Mahatma Gandhi.) Before reading the next spread, ask if anyone knows what *huelga* means. (Strike.) **Let's read to find out.** Read the next spread. Trace the path from Delano to Sacramento. Ask: What do you think happened when they reached the capitol? Read the next five spreads. Locate Ducor, Fresno, Modesto, Stockton, Beverly Hills, and Sacramento on the map as you read about Chavez's progress. Show 15 miles on the map. Keep track of the growing numbers of supporters who joined the march. Read the next spread. Ask: How many began on the journey with Chavez? (67.) How many made the entire journey? (57.) What does the celebration in Sacramento remind you of? (The fiesta we read about on the first page.) Read the next spread.

FOLLOW-UP DISCUSSION: Discuss Chavez's powerful words: "[T]here must be courage but also . . . in victory there must be humility." Choose excerpts from or read aloud all of the Author's Note found at the back of the book and discuss.

Write Away! In this book we learned about Cesar Chavez's personality characteristics. Some of these qualities helped him reach his goals, while others were obstacles he had to overcome. List up to five of your personal characteristics, both positive and those that need work. Tell briefly something about yourself that serves as an example of each characteristic you list.

For a poem about Chavez, perfect for a poetry pause, see "The Organizer" in HEROES AND SHE-ROES: POEMS OF AMAZING AND EVERYDAY HEROES, by J. Patrick Lewis (Dial). For a novel set in this era about a girl who emigrates to the United States from Mexico after her family loses their wealth, see ESPERANZA RISING, by Pam Muñoz Ryan (Scholastic).

Refer to the Tips and Techniques for Teachers and Librarians and the Book Notes sections of this resource for other books written by Kathleen Krull that are suitable for this age group.

Notes:

Up Close and Personal

A Note from the Author, Kathleen Krull

On what inspired her to write the book . . .

Most people my age remember Cesar Chavez's struggles during the 1960s, and the spotlight he put on the grim lives of grape-pickers. A few years ago when I discovered most kids hadn't heard of him, I was shocked.

In my earliest computer searches for what was written about Chavez, I kept running into the boxer, Julio Cesar Chavez, whom I'm sure is very nice, but not a great American civil rights leader. When I found out how little was published for younger readers about Cesar Chavez, the hero of the 1960s, I was motivated to try to write about him in ways children could understand.

Injustice, nonviolence, and hope . . .

All kids can relate to injustice. And the people who pick our fruits and vegetables have the longest hours, lowest wages, harshest conditions, shortest life spans, and the least power of any group of workers in America. How can one person try to change such a system? The key to Chavez, I believe, was his opposition to violence.

"Nonviolence takes more guts," Chavez once said—and this was a sentence I felt would grab kids' attention. It means using truth and imagination in the fight against powerlessness. The peaceful march Chavez organized from Delano to Sacramento was a brilliant example of his nonviolent techniques. Actually, my original title for the manuscript was "Fighting Without Violence," and it is thanks to an editor at Harcourt that this awkward title segued into HARVESTING HOPE.

Many, many drafts later, this became a story about hope.

For more information on Kathleen Krull, her long list of insightful biographies for young readers, as well as a listing of her other children's books, visit her Web site at www.kathleenkrull.com.

Up Close and Personal

Title	PROJECT MULBERRY
Author	Linda Sue Park
Publisher	Clarion
Copyright Date	2005
Ages	9 and up
Read-Aloud Time	15 minutes per session
Read-Aloud Sessions	16
Themes	Friendship, writing process, silk worms, prejudice, research

The Newbery author known for her historical fiction offers a contemporary story about two friends who raise silkworms for a club project. This novel won the 2005 Chicago Tribune Prize for Young Adult Fiction, an award that honors an author whose work concerns young people's role and importance in society and has "special resonance" with readers from 12 to 18 years of age. Intriguing in the novel is the material found *between* chapters, in which the main character, Julia, and the author discuss the story. It's an effective tool for young, inquisitive minds and for avid readers who may wonder how authors develop their plots. Throughout the book there is detailed information about raising silkworms. Visit the author's Web site for photos of the actual project her father commandeered to add authenticity to Park's story. See also the author's note at the back of the book.

Note: This is a great book to read before introducing or while working on class research projects.

Consult the list of reference books on silkworms found at the back of PROJECT MULBERRY. Try to have one or more on hand for the read-aloud of Chapter 9 and subsequent chapters.

If kimchee is available in your area, consider offering samples to listeners following the read-aloud of the first chapter. Or, use a recipe to make kimchee from cabbage yourself or with the group.

PRE-READING FOCUS: Introducing the book: Show the cover and read the title. Ask: What do we know about this book from its cover? (The cover looks like a notebook. The book could be about a school project. There are doodles on the cover of the notebook. These give us a few clues. The book is a novel, which means it is fiction.) There is something unusual about this novel that will be revealed as we read the first chapter. Be on the lookout for it!

Chapter 1

Pre-reading: **Let's read to find out** who the main character is and to meet some of the other characters in this story. Look for clues to what kind of story this is, the setting, and the problem, or conflict.

While Reading: After reading Chapter 1, move into the dialogue between character and author. Consider having one of the listeners read the character's lines (Me) and you read Ms. Park's lines to get the feel of a dialogue. After reading it, show listeners the change in print font. Discuss the novel's format. Do listeners like the idea of the character and author chatting about the story? As you progress through the read-aloud of the book, encourage listeners to think of questions they might ask Ms. Park if they were Julia.

Follow-up:

- In this chapter we meet Julia and Patrick. Through Julia we learn much about Patrick: his habits, his likes, and his family. Review the details about Patrick that the author has woven into the first chapter. (He comes from a large family. He is the third oldest of six children. He has two older sisters—one is Claire, whom we meet in this chapter—and three younger siblings. The younger children include a set of male twins and a brother who is a year older. They are known as Hugh-Ben-Nicky. He loves kimchee. Patrick spends a lot of time at Julia's house. Patrick loves to read and gets excited about things.

- What do we know about Julia? (She has one brother, Kenny, whom she refers to as a snotbrain. She has moved a few times. She is in seventh grade. She isn't crazy about reading, and she deplores kimchee.)

- What is the Wiggle Club? (It stands for Work-Grow-Give-Live! and its purpose is to teach kids about farming.)

- In this chapter Julia and Patrick are trying to decide on their Wiggle Animal Husbandry project. The best projects will be exhibited at the state fair in August.

- What is the setting of this story? (A town named Plainfield; it is March.)

- Who is the main character? (Julia.) How do you know? (The story is told from her point of view; she gets to talk to Ms. Park.)

- What type of story is this? (Contemporary fiction.)

- In this chapter, Julia and Patrick are having trouble deciding on an animal for their project. What animal do you think they might decide on?

- Sample kimchee!

> **Write Away!** Ms. Park tells Julia, "Fiction is about the truth, even if it's not always factual." Think about a story or book you've read that was about truth even though it wasn't factual. Tell about it, giving details of the story.

> **Write Away!** Begin a list of questions you would ask Ms. Park if you were Julia. Plan to add to it as we progress through the story.

Chapter 2

Pre-reading: **Let's read to find out** what animal Julia and Patrick decide to study for their Wiggle Club project.

While Reading: After reading Chapter 1, stop before reading the dialogue between Julia and Ms. Park and consider the questions below.

Follow-up:

- In this chapter Mrs. Song has an idea for the animal husbandry project. What do you think of the idea of raising silkworms?

- Note Julia's reaction. Why do you think she is not excited about this idea?

- Julia and Patrick collect quarters. Do you collect anything? Do you collect the state quarters? Do you have a favorite?

- Read the dialogue.

- Ask listeners what questions they might ask Ms. Park.

> **Write Away!** Choose a state quarter and research what's on it, as Julia and Patrick have done. Be ready to share what you have learned with the group.

> **Write Away!** Julia and Patrick are very good friends, but they are different in some ways. She likes hands on; he likes research. Tell about a good friend of yours who likes some things you don't and vice versa, and explain whether that makes your friendship stronger and more interesting or not. Give details and use examples.

Chapter 3

Pre-reading: Although this is a fiction story, you will learn many facts as we read it. Review what facts have been learned so far. Record these on chart paper and add to the facts list as you progress through the story. **Let's read to find out** what bothers Julia.

While Reading: After reading the chapter, answer the questions below before moving on to the dialogue between Julia and Ms. Park.

Follow-up:

- In this chapter learn a bit more about Julia. Why doesn't she want to do the silkworm project? (It's too Korean.)
- Julia thinks about the prejudice she has experienced. Discuss.
- Have you ever experienced or witnessed prejudice? Discuss.
- In Julia's eyes, Kenny is a pain. Patrick disagrees. Do you have younger siblings? Are they a pain?
- What word did we learn in this chapter? (Maelstrom.) Review its meaning. (A giant, violent whirlpool.) Have you ever heard that word before? Can you think of a word you didn't know that you learned from a game, TV, an amusement park ride, or a book?
- Add to the facts chart.
- Read the dialogue.
    - What do we learn from this dialogue? (The main character must have a problem or two.)
- List the problems, or conflicts, in this story.

Write Away! Julia calls Kenny the Maelstrom or Snotbrain. Do you have a nickname for a young sibling? Tell me about it! Fill me in on how you decided on it and what your sibling does that makes the nickname fit him or her.

Write Away! Do you have a nickname that an older sibling has given you? How do you feel about this nickname? Do you think it fits?

Note: In preparation for the read-aloud of the next chapter, find a picture of a mulberry tree to show to listeners.

Chapter 4

Pre-reading: **Let's read to find out** what Julia learns from her mother, and why.

While Reading: Read the chapter and the dialogue between Julia and Ms. Park before moving on to the questions.

Follow-up:

- In this chapter Julia learns about embroidery. Has anyone tried embroidery? Do you think it would be fun? Do you think it would make a good project?

- We will be starting class projects soon. Be thinking about a project you'd like to do. Do you prefer a hands-on project, like Julia, or a research project, like Patrick?

- Do you think the silkworm project will be a flop?

- Show a picture of a mulberry tree.

- Add to the facts chart.

 Write Away! Ms. Park says that sometimes the story is the boss. What do you think this means?

Write Away! Start a list of projects you might be interested in doing.

Chapter 5

Pre-reading: **Let's read to find out** what develops in the silkworm project.

While Reading: Read the chapter and the dialogue following it before moving on to the Follow-up questions.

Follow-up:

- In this chapter Julia feels like a spy. Do you think she is being fair to Patrick? Discuss.

- The friends plan to look for the car. Do you think they will be successful?

Write Away! Continue to work on your list of possible projects. Is one topic more special than the others? Is it narrow enough? If it is too general or broad, how could you narrow it down? Begin to think about how you would go about doing the project. Keep notes.

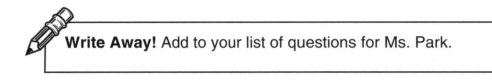

Write Away! Add to your list of questions for Ms. Park.

Chapter 6

Pre-reading: **Let's read to find out** if Julia and Patrick find the Mulberry Man.

While Reading: Be sure to use a slight Southern accent when reading Mr. Dixon's lines. After reading the chapter, answer the questions below before moving on to the dialogue between Julia and Ms. Park.

Follow-up:

- In this chapter Julia gets a call from Mr. Dixon and must make two decisions. What are they? (Whether to go to Mr. Dixon's; whether to tell Patrick.)

- What does she decide? (To go to Mr. Dixon's; to tell Patrick.)

- What does this tell you about her character? (It speaks to her morals and values.)

- We haven't seen Kenny in a while. Why do you think that is? (Ms. Park is keeping her promise to Julia!)

- What did we learn about Mrs. Song in this chapter? (She is prejudiced against black people.) Discuss Julia's feelings about this.

- Read the dialogue.

  – What do we learn from this dialogue? (Sometimes an author learns things about her story as she writes it.)

Write Away! Begin a story of your own. Think of the things Julia has learned from Ms. Park. Use these insights as you develop your story.

Chapter 7

Pre-reading: **Let's read to find out** what happens at Mr. Dixon's house.

While Reading: After reading the chapter, answer the questions below before moving into the dialogue between Julia and Ms. Park.

Follow-up:

- In this chapter we get to know a bit more about Mr. Dixon. What is he like? (Friendly, honest, neat, and particular.)

- Explore how Julia's mom behaves.

- Try memorizing a phone number the way Mr. Dixon does!

- At the end of the chapter, Julia is mad at herself. Why? (She is putting herself before her friend. She has embarrassed and humiliated Patrick.)

- Read the dialogue.

- What do you think Julia will do next?

Write Away! Continue working on your story.

Write Away! Do you agree with Julia that what she told Patrick about the money so they wouldn't be able to order the worms is like telling someone that you like his or her present when you don't? Support your opinion.

Write Away! Search for books and/or Internet sites that may have information about one or more of the project ideas you have, as Patrick does in the beginning of the book. Jot down a few titles or site addresses. How does this search help you determine the subject of your project?

Chapter 8

Pre-reading: Julia is feeling guilty. **Let's read to find out** why and what Julia does about it.

While Reading: After reading the chapter, answer the questions below before moving on to the dialogue between Julia and Ms. Park.

Follow-up:

- In this chapter we learn where the title of the book comes from. Do you think it is a good title? Discuss other possible titles.

- Tell about a favorite title of yours. Why do you like it so much?

- Do you have any ideas about what Julia could do to make the project more American?

- Add questions for Ms. Park to your list.

- Read the dialogue.

  – What do we learn from this dialogue? (The author imagines herself to be Julia when she needs to figure out what her character would do.)

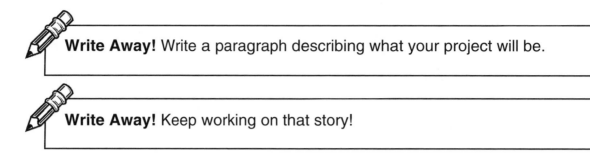

Write Away! Write a paragraph describing what your project will be.

Write Away! Keep working on that story!

Chapter 9

Pre-reading: In this chapter the silkworm eggs arrive. **Let's read to find out** what Julia and Patrick do to begin the hands-on portion of their Wiggle project.

While Reading: Read the chapter and the dialogue that follows before answering the questions below.

Follow-up:

- Review what Patrick and Julia do on their project in this chapter.

- How does Patrick involve Kenny in the project? (Kenny will keep track of the temperature to make sure it doesn't go below 50 degrees F.)

- Do you think involving Kenny is a good idea? Discuss.

- Show the books on silkworms that you have collected. Look at some of the photos. Look at a few of the photos on Linda Sue Park's Web site, too. Consider doing this periodically throughout the remainder of the read-aloud of this book.

- Julia tells Ms. Park to write down a word. What is it? (Cycle.)

- Why do you think she did this?

- Add facts you have learned from the book to the list.

Chapter 10

Pre-reading: In this chapter the silkworm eggs go from periods to commas to hairs! **Let's read to find out** what Julia and Patrick do to help them survive.

While Reading: Read the chapter and answer the questions below. Then read the dialogue between Julia and Ms. Park.

Follow-up:

- Julia is concerned about her mother's attitude toward Mr. Dixon. She uses the word *racist*. What does this word mean? (One who is prejudiced or discriminates against others of a particular race or creed.) Do you think her mother is prejudiced?

- Do you think Julia's mom overreacted to Julia being gone so long? Discuss.

- Review the steps Julia and Patrick take to help the silkworms survive.

- Add to the facts list.

- Read the dialogue.

- Ms. Park reveals that she rewrote this novel early on. What is this process called? (Revision.)

- Ms. Park reveals that she enjoys the revision process. Why do you think it is satisfying to revise? (Your work gets better.)

Write Away! Revise a piece of your writing to make it better.

Chapter 11

Pre-reading: In this chapter Julia and Patrick go on a field trip with the Wiggle Club to a sustainable farm. **Let's read to find out** what that is and what they learn while there.

While Reading: Read the chapter and answer the questions below before moving on to the dialogue between Ms. Park and Julia.

Follow-up:

- Review what Patrick and Julia learn about farming in this chapter.

- Julia gets upset because Mr. Dixon thinks she is Chinese and makes a general statement based on that belief. He is *stereotyping*. Review her thoughts at the end of the chapter (page 141) and discuss.

- Do you think Mr. Dixon is a racist? (No.) How do his comments and behavior differ from Mrs. Song's? Discuss.

- Add to the facts list.

- Read the dialogue.

- Discuss the writing tips Ms. Park gives.

Write Away! Continue working on your research project.

Write Away! Continue working on your story. Use Ms. Park's tips!

Chapter 12

Pre-reading: In this chapter we learn how Ms. Park used the word *cycle*. **Let's read to find out** how it fits into the story.

While Reading: Read the chapter and the dialogue that follows before answering the questions below.

Follow-up:

- How did Ms. Park work *cycle* into the story?

- Patrick has revealed his phobia to Julia. Are you as surprised as Julia is?

- What do we know about Patrick from the fact that he admitted his phobia to Julia? (He trusts her and is sure enough of himself to be able to reveal this about himself to his good friend.)

- What have we learned about Ms. Park? (She has a worm phobia.) What does this piece of information tell you about authors? (They write what they know.)

- Add to the list of questions for Ms. Park.

- Add to the facts list.

Write Away! Do you have a phobia? Tell about it.

Write Away! Continue working on your project.

Chapter 13

Pre-reading: In this chapter the worms move into a new stage, and Kenny helps solve a problem. But problems keep cropping up. **Let's read to find out** what happens next.

While Reading: Read the chapter and the dialogue that follows before answering the questions below.

Follow-up:

- Julia didn't read the book about silkworms, so she didn't know a crucial piece of information. How does she feel when Patrick reveals the information about the silk thread to her? (Upset.)

- At the end of the chapter Julia says something that reminds us of an earlier part in the book. What was it? (When Julia was trying to work out her feelings about prejudice after Mr. Dixon referred to her as Chinese.)

- What have we learned about Ms. Park in her dialogue with Julia? (She needs Julia to finish the story.)

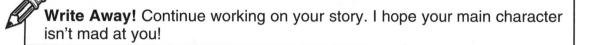

Write Away! Continue working on your story. I hope your main character isn't mad at you!

Write Away! Continue working on your project.

Chapter 14

Pre-reading: In this chapter Patrick and Julia have a fight. **Let's read to find out** how this affects their Wiggle project.

While Reading: Read the chapter and answer the Follow-up questions below before reading the dialogue that follows the chapter.

Follow-up:

- Patrick and Julia are upset with one another. How does Patrick try to make Julia feel better? (By sending her an e-mail with a link to an article about Susan B. Anthony and a silk dress.)

- When Julia is talking with Mr. Maxwell and she realizes something about him that makes her upset, what does she do? (She puts on a perfect face.) Who does this remind you of? (Her mother.)

- What do you think will happen next?

- Read the dialogue.

Write Away! Work toward the ending of your story.

Write Away! Continue working on your project.

Chapter 15

Pre-reading: In this chapter Kenny has another good idea, and Julia does some thinking while she embroiders. **Let's read to find out** about both of these events.

While Reading: Read the chapter and answer the Follow-up questions below before reading the dialogue that follows the chapter.

Follow-up:

- Julia thinks maybe everything in life has messy parts: things others don't see, things they didn't know they didn't know, or things they didn't want to think about. Who and what is she thinking about? (Herself, her mom, Patrick and Mr. Dixon; prejudice, solutions, phobias.)

- Discuss what Kenny does at the end of the chapter.

- There is no dialogue at the end of this chapter. Why do you think Ms. Park chose to leave it out?

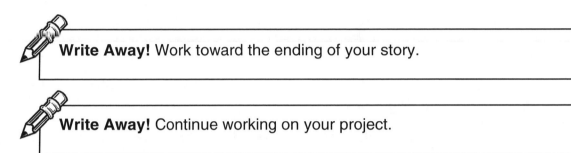

Write Away! Work toward the ending of your story.

Write Away! Continue working on your project.

Chapter 16

Pre-reading: In this chapter Patrick and Julia head for the state fair. **Let's read to find out** what happens there.

While Reading: Read the chapter and the dialogue that follows the chapter.

Follow-up:

- What parts of this story did you like best?

- Which details do you wish Ms. Park had "wrapped up," and which ones are you glad she didn't?

- Are you one of those people who like the inside story, or one of those who don't? Discuss.

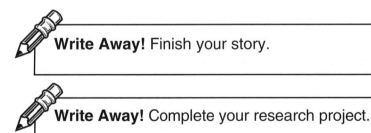

Write Away! Finish your story.

Write Away! Complete your research project.

Notes:

Up Close and Personal

A Note from the Author, Linda Sue Park

On the format of the book . . .

I'm often asked about the sections between the chapters in PROJECT MULBERRY, where Julia and "Ms. Park" discuss the progress of the story. Many authors say that their characters talk to them, but in my first four novels, it happened to me only "once". A character spoke to me late one night when I was almost asleep, then vanished immediately and never "came back". It was a striking experience, and I found myself envious of those writers whose characters talked to them regularly.

Be careful what you wish for! During the writing of PROJECT MULBERRY, Julia talked to me. Oh boy, did she talk! Jabber, prattle, chatter, prate—her voice was in my head almost constantly! Mostly she would ask questions about the story. *Why had I written such-and-such a scene? Why was her little brother so bratty?* She also complained about what was happening when things weren't going well for her. In general, whenever she talked to me, she was not a happy camper.

As usual for me, I often got stuck while I was writing PROJECT MULBERRY. I hated sitting there staring at the blank screen, so I got into the habit of typing out what Julia was saying to me. And whenever she had questions, I typed out the answers as well. It started out as just a writing exercise, but I was delighted to find that it often had the effect of getting me "unstuck". Once I discovered that, I began doing it regularly, and pretty soon, the typed conversations felt like part of the story itself.

So I decided to include them. Originally the conversations were very short—just a few lines—and they were scattered throughout the manuscript. My editor, Dinah Stevenson at Clarion Books, found that these frequent interruptions distracted her from the story. If I wanted to keep them, I had to figure out a way to make them less of a distraction.

I collected the bits and pieces of conversation, condensed and edited them, and put them in between the chapters. And that's how the book was eventually published—with those in-between sections that give the reader an idea of the way Julia's story came to be written.

For more about Linda Sue Park, her award-winning books, and her advice for young writers, visit her Web site at www.lspark.com. For a listing of other books written by Linda Sue Park suitable for fifth and sixth graders, refer to the author index of this resource.

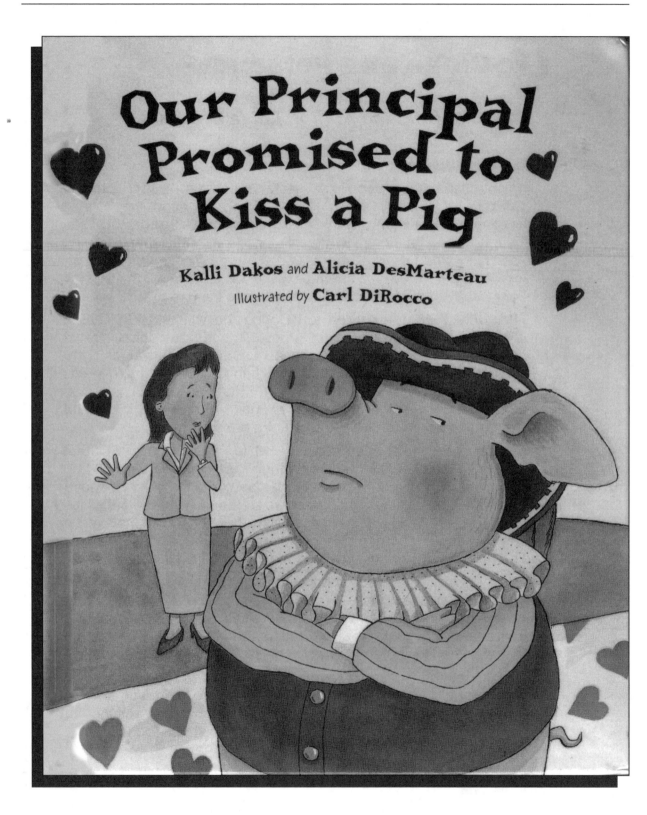

Cover illustration by Carl DiRocco from OUR PRINCIPAL PROMISED TO KISS A PIG by Kalli Dakos and Alicia Des Marteau. Illustrations © 2004 by Carl DiRocco. Reprinted by permission of Albert Whitman & Company.

Title	OUR PRINCIPAL PROMISED TO KISS A PIG
Author	Kalli Dakos and Alicia DesMarteau
Illustrator	Carl DiRocco
Publisher	Whitman
Copyright Date	2004
Ages	10 and up
Read-Aloud Time	15 minutes
Read-Aloud Sessions	1
Themes	Shakespeare, quotations

This picture book offers an excellent introduction to William Shakespeare. It's nonthreatening, lighthearted, and fanciful. Following the reading of this book, you have the option of moving on to more serious study of the bard and his work with one or more of the excellent picture book treatments of Shakespeare's well-known plays and sonnets listed at the end of this plan.

Note: Have available brief information on William Shakespeare to present to children as part of the read-aloud of this book. Pictures of the bard in period dress would be great, too. Copy Hamlet the pig's quotations, listed at the back of the book, onto index cards.

PRE-READING FOCUS: Show the cover of the book. Read the title. What do you notice about this pig? (He is dressed in costume.) What else do you see on the cover? (Hearts.) From these picture clues, what predictions can you make about this story? (It's fiction; a silly story.) **Let's read to find out** if our predictions are correct.

WHILE READING: Read the first page. Note the pig's name. Ask listeners what they know about Hamlet. Briefly introduce William Shakespeare to listeners. Read the next two spreads. Ask: What kind of person do you think the principal is? Read the next spread. Note that now we know how Hamlet the pig got his name. Read the next spread. What is funny on these pages? (Ham sandwich; pig having feelings; Hamlet's dress and facial expressions; Hamlet's words.) Draw attention to Hamlet's words. Tell children that these words are similar to words one of William Shakespeare's characters uses in one of his plays. Read the next spread. Again, note that Hamlet's words are similar to those that one of William Shakespeare's characters uses in one of his plays. Read the next two spreads. Ask: What do you think will happen next? **Let's read to find out.** Read the next spread. Ask: What do you think Hamlet has planned? Show the next spread and then read this and the next spread. Ask: Why do you think the kiss never came? Read to the end of the story.

FOLLOW-UP DISCUSSION: The Shakespearean references are listed at the back of the book. Give one of Hamlet the pig's quotations to each team. Their mission: find the actual words Shakespeare wrote! This makes a super library project in which students can make use of reference books, such as *Bartlett's Familiar Quotations,* and online resources. If the picture books listed below are available, encourage children to use these books for their research as well.

Write Away! Using three different colored inks, copy the actual words Shakespeare wrote beneath Hamlet the pig's words. Beneath that, explain what Shakespeare's words might mean. Illustrate, and present your work to class.

For wonderfully illustrated retellings of works by Shakespeare, look for the following:

WILLIAM SHAKESPEARE'S TWELFTH NIGHT, retold by Bruce Coville and illustrated by Tim Raglin (Dial)

WILLIAM SHAKESPEARE'S MACBETH, retold by Bruce Coville and illustrated by Gary Kelley (Dial)

WILLIAM SHAKESPEARE'S ROMEO AND JULIET, retold by Bruce Coville and illustrated by Dennis Nolan (Dial)

SHAKESPEARE'S ROMEO & JULIET retold by Michael Rosen and illustrated by Jane Ray (Candlewick)

WILLIAM SHAKESPEARE'S A MIDSUMMER NIGHT'S DREAM retold by Bruce Coville and illustrated by Dennis Nolan (Dial)

WILLIAM SHAKESPEARE'S HAMLET, retold by Bruce Coville and illustrated by Leonid Gore (Dial)

WILLIAM SHAKESPEARE'S THE TEMPEST, retold by Bruce Coville and illustrated by Ruth Sanderson (Doubleday)

TALES FROM SHAKESPEARE: SEVEN PLAYS, distilled and illustrated in panel art done in watercolor and ink by Marcia Williams (Candlewick)

See also:

BARD OF AVON: THE STORY OF WILLIAM SHAKESPEARE, written by Diane Stanley and Peter Vennema and illustrated by Diane Stanley (HarperCollins)

UNDER THE GREENWOOD TREE: SHAKESPEARE FOR YOUNG PEOPLE, edited by Barbara Holdridge and illustrated by Robin DeWitt and Pat DeWitt (Stemmer House)

See also the Shakespeare Stealer series, by Gary Blackwood (Dutton) in which Widge, a fictional orphan living in Elizabethan England, solves Shakespeare-related mysteries in stories that also teach about the era and its main drama man. Titles include THE SHAKESPEARE STEALER, SHAKESPEARE'S SCRIBE, and SHAKESPEARE'S SPY.

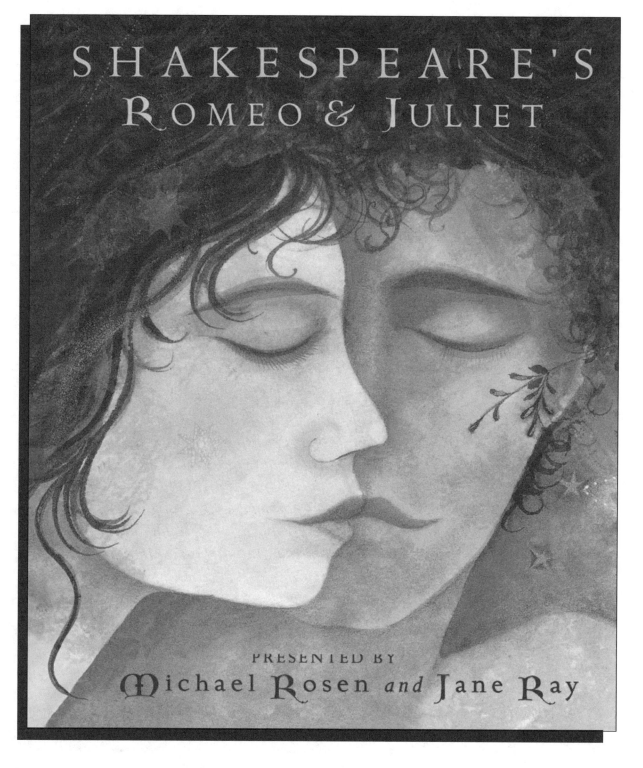

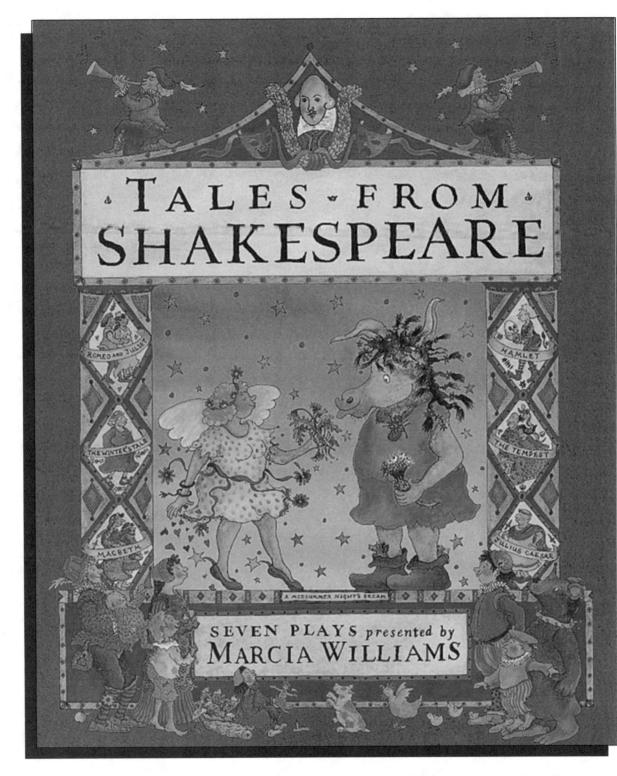

TALES FROM SHAKESPEARE: SEVEN PLAYS. Copyright © 1998 Marcia Williams. Candlewick Press, Inc., on behalf of Walker Books, Ltd.

Notes:

Up Close and Personal

A Note from the Authors, Kalli Dakos and Alicia DesMarteau

On where the idea for the book came from . . .

Kalli Dakos:

OUR PRINCIPAL PROMISED TO KISS A PIG began as a very short poem. I visited a school near my home in Virginia where a principal really did kiss a pig because his students had met his challenge of reading 10,000 books. I love to write poems about school, and I knew this was a perfect topic. That day I began to write:

> Our principal kissed a pig,
> He did,
> He did,
> We saw our principal,
> Kiss a pig.

I decided the story was humorous enough for a picture book, and I imagined how the poor pig must have felt on the day of the kiss. Would you want to be kissed by a strange man or woman you had never met in front of an audience of teachers and children? Of course not; and neither would a pig.

As I'm a poet, I thought it would be fun to have the pig speak in rhyme, but my daughter and co-author, Alicia, took the manuscript one step further. She gave the pig his name, Hamlet, and thought it would be hilarious if he spoke in Shakespearean verse.

On where the idea for Hamlet the pig came from . . .

Alicia DesMarteau:

Shakespeare's Hamlet has always prompted me to picture a porcine poet. I thought my mother's pig should be Hamlet, and that he should speak in Shakespearean verse. I scoured Shakespeare's plays for lines that would be suitable to introduce elementary students to his work. Hamlet emerged as an endearing mishmash of Shakespearean heroes.

Kalli Dakos:

We wove in nineteen references to plays such as ROMEO AND JULIET, HAMLET, MACBETH, THE TAMING OF THE SHREW, AS YOU LIKE IT, A MIDSUMMER NIGHT'S DREAM, JULIUS CAESAR and one of Shakespeare's sonnets. While the original Hamlet says, "To be, or not to be—that is the question" (Hamlet: act 3, scene 1, line 56), Hamlet, the pig, says:

> To kiss or not to kiss,
> The principal in school?
> Why choose a pig
> To be their fool?

Alicia DesMarteau:

I did have some trepidation about placing Shakespeare's most famous lines in the mouth—er, snout of a pig, but my mind was set at ease when I remembered that Shakespeare himself featured a talking donkey (of sorts) in A MIDSUMMER NIGHT'S DREAM.

On the illustrations . . .

Kalli Dakos:

Carl DiRocco was picked to do the illustrations, and we both fell in love with his artistic vision of Hamlet. Look carefully at the artwork because he added lots of funny details.

You can visit teacher, author, and poet Kalli Dakos and learn more about her books, view lesson plans, and sample her writing workshop ideas on her Web site at http://www.kallidakos.com/.

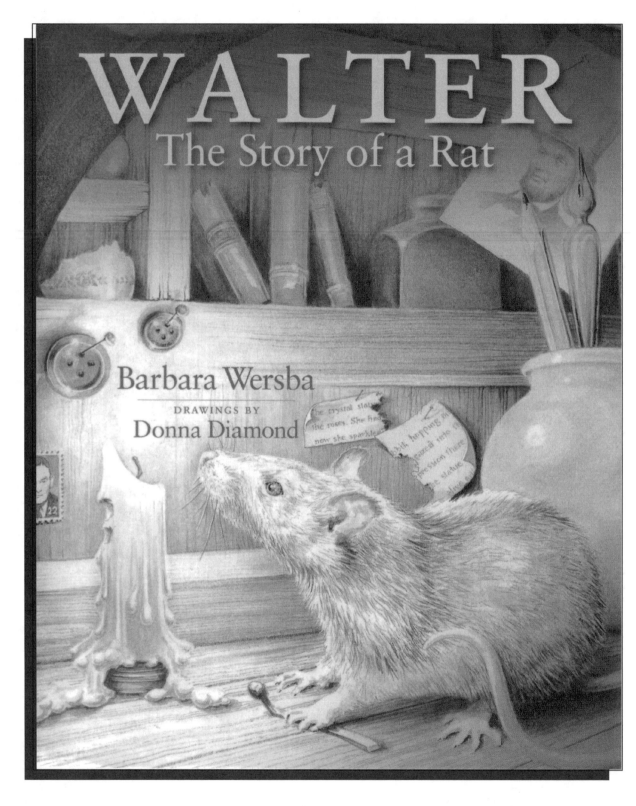

WALTER: THE STORY OF A RAT, by Barbara Wersba, drawings by Donna Diamond. Copyright © 2005. Published by Front Street, an imprint of Boyds Mills Press. Reprinted by permission.

Title . . . . WALTER: THE STORY OF A RAT
Author . . . . Barbara Wersba
Illustrator . . . . Donna Diamond
Publisher . . . . Front Street
Copyright Date 2005
Ages . . . . 8 and up
Read-Aloud Time . . . . 12–15 minutes per session
Read-Aloud Sessions 8
Themes . . . . Fantasy, books, friendship, famous quotations

The author of a number of young adult books, Barbara Wersba has created a sweet story of a reclusive author and the well-read rat who shares her home in this slim volume peppered with illustrations that charmingly convey Walter and his enigmatic roommate. Throughout the book are brief references to great works of literature.

Note: Have dictionaries available throughout the read-aloud of this book so listeners can look up the meanings of words used in the story. Also, if possible, have a copy of Bartlett's Familiar Quotations *or a similar reference on hand (or plan to make use of online resources) to locate the origin of lines from works of literature.*

PRE-READING FOCUS: Introducing the book: Show the cover and read the title. Ask: What do we know about this story from the cover of the book? (Walter is a rat; he is on a desk; books and pens and snippets of paper suggest writing and reading; the burned candle tells us it may be night.) Ask: Who is the main character of this story? (Walter, a rat.) From the cover, what kind of story do you guess this is? (Fantasy.) Discuss what fantasy is. Ask for predictions about what this story of Walter might be about.

Note: In preparation for the reading of these pages, have a copy of A FAREWELL TO ARMS available to study the cover.

Pages 7–Middle of 14

Pre-reading: **Let's read to find out** about Walter and learn why Walter has chosen to live where he does.

While Reading: After reading about Miss Pomeroy on pages 8–9, ask: What do you think *penchant* means? (A strong liking.) Walter learns that *arms* mean armaments, and this relates to war. What do you think *armaments* are? (Weapons.) Walter likes Miss Pomeroy because she is *unconventional,* which he considers himself to be. What does unconventional mean? (Out of the ordinary.) On page 13 we learn that Walter is reading his way through the entire room of books in Miss Pomeroy's house. It says that this is no *mean* feat. What does the word *mean* mean here? (Humble, dull, lowly.) Discuss what this comment means. (It is not easy to read all those books!)

Follow-up:

- In this chapter we have learned much about Walter, his habits, his likes, and his dislikes. What is his favorite activity? (Reading.) Why? (The experience excites him even though he does not always understand what he is reading.) Discuss what else we have learned about Walter. (He is old, he is tidy, he is lonely, and he is curious.)

- In what ways are Walter and Miss Pomeroy different? (He is tidy; she is not. He keeps himself neat; she does not.)

- In what ways are they alike? (They both love books; they are old; they are solitary.)

- We learn about some of the things Walter has gleaned from reading books. As we read this book, let's keep a list of the quotations Walter remembers from the books he has read. From today's reading: "To be or not to be" (William Shakespeare); "I am past my prime."

- A FAREWELL TO ARMS is a novel. Look at the cover. Can you tell this is a story about war? Discuss.

- Investigate the origin of the phrase, "I am past my prime." (Maggie Smith.)

Write Away! Research the *rattus norvegicus,* or common rat. Find out what this rat looks like, what it eats, where it lives, its life span, and so on. Compare to Walter's description on page 8 and the description from *A Field Guide to Small Mammals,* found on page 9.

Write Away! Walter is named after Sir Walter Scott. Learn about this famous person and write a brief report.

Write Away! Would you say your best friends are more like you or unlike you? Explain. What are the advantages of having friends who are like you? Who are unlike? Explain.

Write Away! Find out about the movie Miss Pomeroy loves, *The Maltese Falcon.* Write a brief summary to share with the class.

Pages 14–20

Pre-reading: Show the illustration on page 17. Ask: Who is this? (Miss Pomeroy.) **Let's read to find out** more about her.

Follow-up:

- On pages 16–18 we learn about Miss Pomeroy's behavior. Discuss what she is like and what her behavior tells us about her. (She is shy; she nods curtly at others, but does not chat. She has an awkward gait. She wears old-fashioned clothes. She is expressionless. She likes to feed the gulls.)

- Walter is afraid that Miss Pomeroy would show *revulsion* if she discovered him. What does this word mean? (Strong distaste.)

- Why do you think Walter wonders if Miss Pomeroy has ever been happy? (Because of the way she behaves.)

- Role-play Miss Pomeroy on the pier.

- What do we know Miss Pomeroy likes, and how do we know this? (Books—she keeps her library tidy although the rest of the house is messy; music—she listens to it animatedly; birds—she feeds the gulls on the pier.)

- Find out who wrote "Hope is the thing with feathers that perches in the soul." (Emily Dickinson.)

Write Away! Tell about the things you value. How would someone who observed you know that you value these things?

Write Away! Think about the quotation Walter likes: "Hope is the thing with feathers that perches in the soul." What does this mean? What does the fact that Walter likes this quotation tell you about his character?

Write Away! Thinking about the quotation, "Hope is the thing with feathers that perches in the soul," why do you suppose the author compares hope to something with feathers? Why do you thinks she compares hope with something that flies away?

Pages 20–26

Pre-reading: Walter seems happy living with Miss Pomeroy. **Let's read to find out** what he finds out about her that causes him dismay.

While Reading: Read through the middle of page 23. Ask:

- Why is Walter upset when he comes upon Miss Pomeroy's children's books? (They are about mice.)

- Make a list of books written for children about mice.

- Continue reading through page 26.

Follow-up:

- Why is Walter upset? (He feels betrayed because he feels rats are not treated fairly.)

- Why is he upset specifically with Miss Pomeroy? (Her biography on the back of the book is dishonest.)

- What might be the explanation for why cooking and gardening appear in Miss Pomeroy's biography?

- Find out who wrote, "My candle burns at both ends/It will not last the night." (Edna St. Vincent Millay.)

- What do you think Walter will do?

Write Away! Write a brief biography of yourself that might appear on the back of a book written by you.

Write Away! Interview a friend. Write a brief biography that might appear on the back of a book written by him or her.

Pages 26–32

Pre-reading: Walter is unhappy with what he has learned about Miss Pomeroy. **Let's read to find out** what he does about that.

Follow-up:

- On page 27 the author says Walter's "disappointment in Miss Pomeroy was connected to his admiration for her." Discuss.

- Why does Walter decide to write a letter to Miss Pomeroy? (He is upset about the dishonesty of her biography.)

- What does the word *pompous* mean? (Self-important; arrogant.)

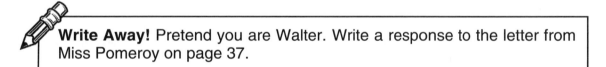

Write Away! When Walter sits down to write a letter to Miss Pomeroy, he discovers it is easier to read words than to write them. Do you think this is true? Explain, using your own experiences.

Pages 33–37

Pre-reading: **Let's read to find out** what Walter does with Miss Pomeroy's response to his letter.

Follow-up:

- Walter and Miss Pomeroy correspond. What do you notice is happening? (They are becoming friends.)

- What do you notice about Miss Pomeroy's letters? (They are getting longer.)

Write Away! Pretend you are Walter. Write a response to the letter from Miss Pomeroy on page 37.

Pages 37–42

Pre-reading: Walter is learning more about his new friend, Miss Pomeroy. **Let's read to find out** what he thinks about her.

Follow-up:

- What troubles Walter about Miss Pomeroy? (She always seems angry.)

- What might be making her angry?

Write Away! Explain what you think the saying, "Be not inhospitable to strangers, lest they be angels in disguise" means?

Note: Prior to reading the next section, collect the following books and stories to have on hand: "The Pied Piper of Hamelin"; THE WIND IN THE WILLOWS; THE DEVOTED FRIEND; THE BOY, THE RAT AND THE BUTTERFLY; and the Harry Potter books.

Pages 42–52

Pre-reading: Thanksgiving and Christmas come. **Let's read to find out** how Miss Pomeroy and Walter make each other happy.

Follow-up:

- Walter reads many children's books about rats. Assign the reading of these to listeners to report back to the class.

- Miss Pomeroy writes to Walter that she feels he has a benevolent view of the world. What does she mean? (He is optimistic.) Discuss.

Write Away! How do you think the friendship between Walter and Miss Pomeroy is helping each of them grow?

Pages 52–60

Pre-reading: Walter wants to give Miss Pomeroy a gift for Christmas. Ask: Do you think she will give him a gift? **Let's read to find out**.

Follow-up:

- What does the word *misanthropic* mean? (Having hatred or contempt for humankind.)

- Walter thinks up a gift for Miss Pomeroy. Do you think she will like it?

- Why is Walter so pleased with his gift? (It is original and especially for him.)

- Why does Walter think the book is so special? (Miss Pomeroy has made him the hero of the book. Walter loves books, and he is the main character in this one.)

- We never see Miss Pomeroy's face in this book. Why do you think the illustrator chose not to show her face?

Write Away! What makes Miss Pomeroy's gift to Walter so special? What makes a gift memorable?

Notes:

Notes:

Up Close and Personal

A Note from the Author, Barbara Wersba

Working from life to create art . . .

I don't have my own anecdote to share about WALTER: THE STORY OF A RAT, because the book came to me in a flash and I barely remember writing it. However, although writing the story was quick, it took three years to go from manuscript to published book. That process included getting an offer for publication from Front Street, a number of revisions, choosing an illustrator, and deciding when the publisher wanted to put WALTER on bookshelves.

Although I don't have a story about writing the book for you, I do have a story to share about the illustrator, Donna Diamond's experience while illustrating WALTER that I'm certain she will not mind my sharing with you.

We worked on a book together several years ago, and I enjoy our friendship as well as our collaborations. Donna Diamond is a wonderful illustrator who also teaches public school. This means she is very busy, so you won't be surprised to hear that she did the art for the book in the middle of the night!

Because she wanted to get the illustrations right for WALTER, Donna bought a rat for $2.00 and placed it near her drawing board in a glass tank when she was working on the book. She hoped the rat would pose for her, but here is an example of when working from life does not work out. The rat refused to pose! He either raced around the tank or slept. Donna's best intentions did not work out. Eventually, Donna used an encyclopedia and other references to get the physical details of Walter just right. I think the illustrations are sweet and lovely. I hope you do, too.

Cover illustration by Julie Collins from MY NIGHTS AT THE IMPROV by Jan Siebold. Illustration © 2005 by Julie Collins. Reprinted by permission of Albert Whitman & Company.

Title . . . . MY NIGHTS AT THE IMPROV
Author. . . . . Jan Siebold
Publisher. . . . . Whitman
Copyright Date 2005
Ages . . . . 10 and up
Read-Aloud Time . . . . 15 minutes per session
Read-Aloud Sessions 11
Themes . . . . New school, friends, family, taking risks, self-confidence, improvisation

Lizzie sits in the projection room while her mother teaches a community education class. She learns about improv from the class conducted on the stage below, but more important, she learns about herself. The author, a public school librarian, took improv classes herself and plays "Think Links" with her classes.

> **PRE-READING FOCUS:** Introducing the book: Show the cover and read the title. Ask: What is "improv" short for? (Improvisation.) What does *improvise* mean? (To make up, invent, or arrange without planning in advance.) Read the the inside flap of the book jacket, in which "Improv" is explained in the context of the story. Ask: Have you ever had the experience of thinking of just the right thing to say after it's too late? Discuss.

Introduction; Chapter 1: "The Projection Booth"; Chapter 2: "Thirty-Second Delay"

> *Pre-reading:* **Let's read to find out** about Lizzie, the character who is mentioned on the inside of the book cover.

> *Follow-up:*
>
> - In the Introduction, Lizzie compares taking risks to climbing a tree and going out on a limb. Discuss.
>
> - What do we learn about Lizzie and the story from the introduction? (There is a character, Ben, from whom Lizzie learned things even though she never met him face to face. Lizzie learned many things from five strangers.) We will return to the introduction after reading the story.
>
> - In "The Projection Booth" we learn the *setting* of the story. Where does this story take place? (Lizzie sits in the projection booth overlooking the school auditorium on Thursday nights while her mother is teaching a class in cake decorating.)

- In "Thirty-Second Delay" we learn some things about Lizzie. What are they? (She is somewhat new in school; she is shy; other students make fun of her because of a pink snakeskin purse she brought to school.)

- Lizzie is learning about alliteration in English class. Ask for examples of alliteration.

If there is a stage with a projection booth in your school, take children on a field trip to see what it is like and the vantage point from inside.

Write Away! Lizzie says, "It's okay to be rare, but not to be odd." Explain what she means.

Chapter 3: "First Class"

Pre-reading: **Let's read to find out** what Lizzie observes from the projection booth.

Follow-up:

- In this chapter we meet the people in a community education class. Make a list of the members and their characteristics. (Ben: bearded, leader of Improv class; Vanessa: student from school who bullies Lizzie; Julian, a muscular man with curly dark hair who is a nurse; a teacher named Mark with short dark hair and glasses; an accountant named Frank is older, balding, and slightly heavy; and Mary, a lawyer with dark skin and a short haircut.) Keep this list available for the duration of the read-aloud of this book to add characteristics about each of these people.

- Note Ben's explanation of improvisational theater, found on page 12.

- What change do we see in Lizzie as a result of the first Improv class? (She is more self-assured in English class.)

- Try the Improv exercise Ben started the class with. Since all listeners are students, have them "be" one of their parents for this exercise.

- Try the "Think Links" activity. Ask each listener to suggest a pair of words for someone else in the group to link.

Write Away! Write about a time when you were called on in class and you felt embarrassed or when you wished you had come up with an answer, one that you thought of later.

Chapter 4: "Mom's Recipe"; Chapter 5: "Comfort Food"

Pre-reading: Read the title of Chapter 4. We meet new characters in this chapter. Ask: Who do you think they might be? (Lizzie's mom; GG, Lizzie's grandmother.) Besides a recipe for a meal, what else might a recipe refer to? (A plan.) **Let's read to find out** what Lizzie's mom's recipe is.

Follow-up:

- In these chapters we meet a few of the people who are important to Lizzie, and we learn about her past. What are Lizzie's problems? (Recent move; her dad died in a rafting accident; her mom will not talk about her dad.)

- What is Mom's recipe? (There's no room for experimenting or straying from the directions.)

Write Away! Write an e-mail from Lizzie to her grandmother, GG, or one of her friends.

Note: In preparation for the next read-aloud session, write down various emotions on pieces of paper and place them in a bag, as described in Chapter 6.

Chapter 6: "Second Class"; Chapter 7: "Smiles and Nods"

Pre-reading: Ask: What is pantomime? (Conveying a story by bodily movements only.) **Let's read to find out** what Lizzie learns in the second class and how she uses it.

Follow-up:

- Review what Ben has taught the group about pantomime.

- Add characteristics of the members of the class to the list.

- In chapter 7 Lizzie uses what she has learned about pantomime to get to know her neighbor better. Discuss.

Write Away! Find out about Marcel Marceau and write a brief report.

Note: In preparation for the follow-up to the read-aloud of Chapter 8, have ready an object with which to try the "Pass the Object" exercise described in the chapter. Also, have an object available for the "Why Is It There?" activity.

Chapter 8: "Third Class"

Pre-reading: **Let's read to find out** what Ben teaches the group in this class and how each member responds.

Follow-up:

- Ask: Why do you think Vanessa was late? Why do you think she was upset?

- Add characteristics of the class members to the list.

- Do the Improv exercises.

Chapter 9: "Elvis Has Left the Building"; Chapter 10: "Fourth Class"

Pre-reading: In Chapter 9 Lizzie uses something she learned from the Improv class. **Let's read to find out** what she does.

Follow-up:

- Ask: Why does Lizzie like Dee?

- What do you notice about Vanessa's behavior in school and her behavior in improv class? (She is nicer in Improv class.)

- Add characteristics of the members of the class to the list.

- Do the Improv exercises.

Chapter 11: "Call a Toe Truck"; Chapter 12: "Fifth Class"

Pre-reading: In Chapter 11 Lizzie is able to make her grandmother feel better by using the "Oh, Yeah?" exercise she learned from the Improv class. **Let's read to find out** what she does.

Follow-up:

- Ask: Why do you think Lizzie loves watching the Improv class? Discuss.

- Add characteristics of the members of the class to the list.

- Do the Improv exercises.

Write Away! Predict how you think this story will end.

Chapter 13: "XYZ"; Chapter 14: "My Father, the Telephone Pole"

Pre-reading: Read the chapter titles. Ask listeners to predict what they might be about. **Let's read to find out**.

Follow-up:

- Ask: What has Lizzie learned from her mother that helps her to understand why her mother hasn't been able to talk about her father? (They fought before he left on the rafting trip in which he was killed.)

- Things are getting better for Lizzie. Discuss.

Write Away! Lizzie is glad to be able to talk about her father. Write an e-mail from Lizzie to her grandmother.

Chapter 15: "First Snow"

Pre-reading: In this chapter Lizzie does something *resourceful*. Ask: What does this word mean? (Able to meet situations.) **Let's read to find out** what she does.

Follow-up:

- Ask: Why do you think Lizzie is happy at the end of this chapter? (Her mom has brought up the subject of her dad and has complimented Lizzie instead of being angry at her for getting locked out of the apartment.)

Write Away! If you were locked out of the house on a cold, snowy day, what would you do?

Chapter 16: "Sixth Class"

Pre-reading: In this chapter Lizzie learns something about Vanessa. **Let's read to find out** what it is.

Follow-up:

- Ask: Knowing what we know about Vanessa and her mom, why do you think Vanessa is so mean to classmates? (Her mother is mean to her and she takes it out on others.)

- Add characteristics of the class members to the list.

- Do the Improv exercise, "Interview the Experts."

Chapter 17: "Point of View"; Chapter 18: "Center Stage"

Pre-reading: In Chapter 17, Lizzie finds a way to reach out to Vanessa. **Let's read to find out** what it is.

Follow-up:

- Ask: Knowing what we know about Vanessa and her mom, do you think this class assignment was hard for Vanessa? Discuss.

- Return to the Introduction. Re-read and discuss.

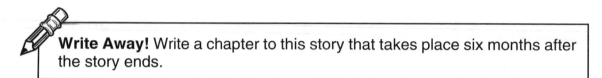

Write Away! Write a chapter to this story that takes place six months after the story ends.

Additional novels by Jan Siebold suitable for this age group include DOING TIME ONLINE, about a boy who must chat online with a nursing home resident as punishment for a mean prank, and ROPE BURN, in which a boy explores his feelings about his parents' divorce and a recent move, among other things, as a result of an English assignment related to proverbs; both novels are published by Whitman.

Notes:

Up Close and Personal

A Note from the Author, Jan Siebold

Playing games . . .

I come from a family that loves games . . . board games, card games, guessing games, word games and more. We're very competitive in that respect. Whenever we get together for holidays or other occasions we end up breaking out a game of some kind.

My husband doesn't quite understand our attraction to playing games, since his family just wasn't the game-playing kind. However, I have found that games provide wonderful opportunities for communication and bonding. They also utilize many different types of higher level thinking skills. They promote sportsmanship and fair play. And they are just plain fun.

Many of the "improv" exercises that I included in MY NIGHTS AT THE IMPROV could be described as games. As a school librarian, I use these types of activities as fillers with my students when we have a few minutes to spare. One of our favorites is "Think Links," as described in Chapter 3. It makes a great car game, too, as Lizzie found out in Chapter 14.

So let the games begin!

For more information on Jan Siebold, visit http://users.adelphia.net/~jansiebold/.

Cover of THE MISSING MANATEE © 2005 by Cynthia DeFelice. Cover Art © 2005 by Wendell Minor. Used with the permission of Farrar Straus Giroux.

Title	THE MISSING MANATEE
Author	Cynthia DeFelice
Publisher	Farrar Straus Giroux
Copyright Date	2005
Ages	10 and up
Read-Aloud Time	15 minutes per session
Read-Aloud Sessions	19
Themes	Manatees, protected refuges, mystery, self-confidence, divorce

Skeet lives in Florida, surrounded by water and fishing guides, one of them his dad. In the midst of trying to figure out his parents' separation, Skeet is also faced with a mystery involving a manatee who was shot. That's not only against the law, it's hard to fathom. Who would purposely harm such a gentle animal? Skeet means to find out.

PRE-READING FOCUS: Introducing the book: Ask: What is a manatee? (A large and gentle aquatic mammal.) Where do manatees live? (In the ocean.) Show the book and read the title. Ask: Where do you think this story takes place? (Coastal Florida.) What kind of story do you think this is? (Mystery.)

Note: Have a map of Florida available for the reading of Chapter One. Also, locate a picture of a manatee to show to listeners. (There is a manatee on the cover of the book, but a photograph might show more detail.)

Chapter One

Pre-reading: **Let's read to find out** about the main character, his problems, and what happens when he's out in the river.

Follow-up:

- In the first chapter the author sets up the story. How does she immediately get our attention? (The narrator overhears his mom telling his dad she doesn't want him back; the narrator comes upon a dead manatee with a bullet wound; the radio in his boat isn't working so he can't call for help.)

- What do we learn about the narrator in this chapter? (He lives in Florida; his dad and mom separated three weeks ago; his dad, Mac, is a fishing guide.)

- Locate the setting of the story on a map of Florida.

Write Away! Read about manatees and list a few facts to share with the class.

Write Away! The narrator offers several comparisons to help the reader imagine what a manatee looks like. After looking at a picture of one, how would you describe a manatee? Which of the narrator's descriptions do you like best? Why?

Note: In preparation for the reading of the next chapter, find a picture of a cormorant.

Chapter Two

Pre-reading: **Let's read to find out** what happens out in the boat with Earl, the deputy from the sheriff's department.

Follow-up:

- In this chapter we learn the narrator's name. What is it? (Skeet.)
- Show the picture of the cormorant.
- How does Skeet feel in this chapter? (Frustrated; annoyed.)
- What do you think will happen next?

Write Away! If you were Skeet, what would you do next?

Write Away! Learn about some of the wildlife common to coastal Florida. Bring in pictures and write a brief introduction about each animal you introduce to the group.

Note: In preparation for the read-aloud of the next chapter, have a picture of a tarpon available.

Chapter Three

Pre-reading: **Let's read to find out** about a few more people who are important to Skeet.

Follow-up:

- In this chapter we learn where Skeet got his nickname. (Skeet is short for Skeeter, which is slang for mosquito.) Mac is Skeet's dad's nickname. Ask: Do you have a nickname? Discuss where it came from and what it means.

- In this chapter we meet another character with a nickname. Discuss what we know about Blink and his dog Blinky. (He is about 30 years old; mentally challenged; he opens his eyes wide and then closes them tightly—thus the nickname.)

- Skeet calls Dirty Dan his hero. Why? (He is a top-notch fisherman.)

- Skeet plays a game with Blink. What does this scene tell us about Skeet? (He is sensitive to Blink's feelings; he is intuitive, kind, and patient.)

- We meet Skeet's grandmother, Memaw, at the end of the chapter. What do we immediately know about her? (She is feisty and full of life.)

Note: In preparation for the read-aloud of the next chapter, have a picture of a hammerhead shark available to show to listeners.

Chapter Four

Pre-reading: **Let's read to find out** more about the characters we've met in this story.

Follow-up:

- In this chapter we learn Skeet's favorite story about Dirty Dan. Look at the picture of the hammerhead shark. Ask: What do his actions and his history tell us about Dirty Dan? (He is adventurous, engages in somewhat risky behavior, and drifts through life.)

- Skeet is annoyed with his mom. He also disagrees with her about a few things. Discuss.

- Explore Skeet's feelings about his parents' separation.

- Have you ever tried karaoke? If so, what was it like?

- If you have access to a karaoke machine, allow children to experience using one!

Write Away! Find out about fly fishing and write a brief report explaining it to the class. Show pictures or photographs, if possible.

Chapter Five

Pre-reading: **Let's read to find out** more about the mystery of the manatee.

Follow-up:

- In this chapter we learn about Skeet's English assignment. What is a pet peeve? (Something that bothers you whenever you encounter it.)

- What does Mr. Giordano mean when he says, "I want to feel the passion in your words"?

- Discuss the contrast between Memaw and Skeet's mom. Review some of the ways Memaw describes Skeet's mom (Fly in the lemonade at a picnic; in a blue funk; sad sack.)

- Skeet remembers from a crime show on TV that police use a formula called MOM to help solve crimes. The letters stand for Means, Opportunity, and Motive. Which of these is the hardest part of this mystery to determine? (Motive.) Do you have any ideas about who might be a suspect?

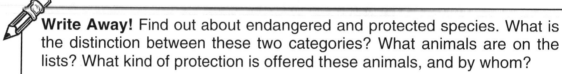 **Write Away!** Find out about endangered and protected species. What is the distinction between these two categories? What animals are on the lists? What kind of protection is offered these animals, and by whom?

Chapter Six

Pre-reading: **Let's read to find out** how Skeet spends his afternoon.

Follow-up:

- Blink and Skeet meet again. What game is Blink playing this time? (He is tossing a tennis ball for Blinky to fetch.)

- In this chapter we learn about Skeet's art class assignment. What does Skeet find in the water? (Milk jug, Dr. Pepper can, tennis ball, motor oil bottle, flip-flop, sandwich bag, and tangled fishing line.)

- Why do you think the author wrote this scene? (She has given readers a clue to the mystery. Note the tennis ball.)

- Create your own Trash Collage!

Write Away! Skeet keeps reminding himself he must be scientific when trying to figure out who would hurt a manatee. What does he mean by this? Use examples from the story.

Chapter Seven

Pre-reading: **Let's read to find out** more about Dirty Dan and fishing for tarpon.

Follow-up:

- What did we learn about the guys Mac hangs out with? (They play poker and drink; they seem to be good friends.)

- How is Skeet feeling at the end of the chapter? (Excited and eager.)

- What does Dan tell Skeet to bring in the morning? (Nothing but himself.) Keep this in mind. Clue listeners in to the fact that this is an example of *foreshadowing,* something that hints at an event that comes later in the story.

> **Write Away!** Find a knot tying book. Learn about the knots mentioned in the chapter and what they are used for (The Bimini twist, the surgeon's loop, and the Huffnagle). Write about them and report to the class. Show pictures of each knot.

In preparation for the read-aloud of this chapter, have pictures of an egret and a heron to show to listeners.

Chapter Eight

Pre-reading: Skeet's big day is here. What do you think will happen in this chapter? **Let's read to find out** what happens when Dirty Dan and Skeet go tarpon fishing.

Follow-up:

- What is a *flat?* (A big area of shallow water.) This is where tarpon often feed.

- What is a *refuge?* (An area that provides shelter or protection.)

- How old is Dan? (Memaw's age.)

- Practice figuring out where various points in the room are, as Skeet figured them out from the boat. Face twelve o'clock. Where is two o'clock? Four o'clock? Eleven o'clock? How far is forty feet? Fifteen feet? Three feet? Estimate distance and then measure.

- At the end of the chapter, the mood changes a bit. Discuss. (Dirty Dan's comment about having to kill Skeet if he tells where the secret spot is makes Skeet a little nervous.)

- At the end of the chapter Dan says, "Some things just oughtta stay secret." What might he be referring to? (The manatee.)

Chapter Nine

Pre-reading: Skeet's big day fishing for tarpon continues. **Let's read to find out** what happens.

Follow-up:

- Discuss the experience Skeet had catching the monster tarpon.

- What do you think will happen next?

Write Away! Have you ever had an experience so amazing you didn't need a photograph to remember it? Write about it.

Chapter Ten

Pre-reading: Review the things that happened out on the boat that would have upset Skeet's mom. Ask: Do you think she has a point in being concerned about Skeet going fishing with Dirty Dan? **Let's read to find out** what happens once Dan and Skeet return to shore.

Follow-up:

- Discuss what Blink says to Dan. Why do you think Blink seems worried?

Write Away! Write Skeet's fish story as he mght write it.

Chapter Eleven

Pre-reading: Skeet and Memaw go out for Chinese food. **Let's read to find out** what happens.

Follow-up:

- Skeet is ready to give up on finding the manatee, but then he decides to go out looking for the manatee again. What causes him to change his mind?

- Do you think Skeet will find the manatee's body?

Write Away! On the boat Dan says tarpon fishing wouldn't be any fun if it was easy. The next morning, Skeet wakes up with sore muscles. He thinks of this as good pain, "a badge of honor." That evening Memaw says, "Nobody ever got anywhere by giving up." Have you ever done something that was really difficult, but you didn't give up? Tell about it.

Chapter Twelve

Pre-reading: Skeet has three days of vacation left. Ask: Do you think he will find the manatee? Do you think he will solve the mystery of who shot the manatee? **Let's read to find out** what happens on Friday and Saturday.

Follow-up:

- Review what Skeet finds. Discuss Skeet's reaction to the evidence.

- Do you think Dirty Dan shot the manatee? If so, why? What would be his motive?

Write Away! Defend your opinion of whether or not Dirty Dan shot the manatee. Support your opinion with evidence from the story.

Chapter Thirteen

Pre-reading: Ask: What do you think Skeet ought to do? Skeet needs to talk to someone about what he's found out. Ask: Who do you think he will talk to? (Memaw.) **Let's read to find out**.

Follow-up:

- What do you think Dirty Dan is going to say?

- Do you think Skeet is going to need Memaw to come to his rescue?

Chapter Fourteen

Pre-reading: **Let's read to find out** what happens when Skeet confronts Dirty Dan.

Follow-up:

Dan tells Skeet that things aren't always what they seem. He mentions looking through the water, not at it. Discuss.

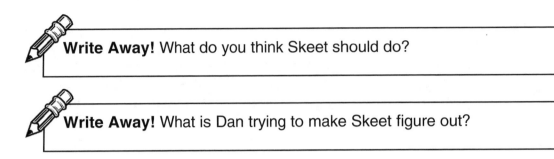

Write Away! What do you think Skeet should do?

Write Away! What is Dan trying to make Skeet figure out?

Chapter Fifteen

Pre-reading: **Let's read to find out** what Skeet does next.

Follow-up:

- Why is Skeet able to talk to Memaw?

- What lie do you think Skeet will tell Memaw?

Write Away! Pretend you are either Skeet's mom or Mac. What advice do you give Skeet? Explain why you advise him as you do.

Chapter Sixteen

Pre-reading: Skeet lies to Memaw. **Let's read to find out** what he lies about and what happens after that.

Follow-up:

- Describe how Skeet must be feeling.

- What do you think will happen next?

Chapter Seventeen

Pre-reading: Skeet and Dan meet out in the channel. **Let's read to find out** what happens.

Follow-up:

- Dan explains what happened to Skeet. How does Skeet feel?

- Skeet makes a decision about what to do. Do you think he is doing the right thing?

Write Away! Skeet learns that there is more than one way to look at something. Have you ever had an experience that made you realize that there is more than one way to look at something? Explain.

Chapter Eighteen

Pre-reading: **Let's read to find out** what happens when Skeet gets back home.

Follow-up:

- Skeet finally learns about how Dirty Dan got his scar. Skeet is so *flummoxed* he hardly knows what to say. What do you think *flummoxed* means? (Confused.)

- The author planted a clue to this revelation earlier in the book. Go back to Chapter 8 and find it. (Memaw is the same age as Dirty Dan.)

- Similarly, the author planted a *red herring* in the scene in which she briefly introduces the tattooed man with the gun rack in his pickup. A red herring is a detail placed in a mystery story to throw off the reader. It is something that distracts attention from the real issue.

- Skeet looks at his art project, trying to *see* each object and its relation to others. Earl tells Skeet that he looks not just at the crime, but at all the circumstances around it before he decides what to do. How do these ideas relate to Skeet and the manatee?

 **Write Away!** What do you think Skeet writes about for his English class?

Epilogue

Pre-reading: **Let's read to find out** what Skeet wrote about for English class.

Write Away! Try the Skeet Waters Golden Moon Menu Method.

For other books by Cynthia DeFelice suitable for fifth and sixth graders, refer to the author index of this resource. For a complete listing of books by Cynthia DeFelice, and to learn more about the author, visit her Web site at www.cynthiadefelice.com, or look for her on the Farrar Straus Giroux Web site at www.fsgkidsbooks.com.

Notes:

Notes:

Up Close and Personal . . . .

A Note from the Author, Cynthia DeFelice

Where ideas come from . . .

Sometimes books seem to spring entirely from my imagination; other times, life hands me experiences that beg to be written about. That was the case with some of my favorite parts of THE MISSING MANATEE. The book came about after several trips my husband and I made to the Everglades and to the Crystal River near Homosassa, Florida. In both places we fly-fished for tarpon. It is an incredibly exciting and challenging activity, one that I hoped my readers would be able to relate to.

At Homosassa, we viewed manatees in the river, went to "All You Can Eat Night" at Fat Boy's Barbeque, and witnessed a karaoke contest at a riverside grill, where all the contestants were *very* senior citizens, leaning on their walkers or canes and singing hard rock classics in quavering voices. Readers of THE MISSING MANATEE will find scenes that I wrote based on these experiences.

It was in Flamingo, in the Everglades, that we fished with a tarpon guide named Dirty Dan, a character I will never forget. He really did have a six-inch long, one inch wide facial scar. When I felt comfortable enough with him to ask how he got it, he took a sip from his bottle of Jack Daniels, which he called his "butterfly milk," and said he'd gotten it in a "hatchet fight over a blonde." Wow! I hoped that someday I'd be able to use this experience in a book, and THE MISSING MANATEE gave me the opportunity.

Skeet Waters and his family are based on no one I know. I wish I *did* know Skeet's grandmother, Memaw, as she is one of my favorite characters I've ever written about. I love her spirit and her humor. I enjoyed writing about Skeet's struggle to figure out who he wants to be, as I think it's a search we all go through when we are the age of my readers, and for the rest of our lives.

It's been my experience that kids are outraged—and rightfully so—when someone harms a defenseless animal. When I had the idea of Skeet coming upon a manatee that had been shot, I knew I was on to something. Aside from the fact that manatees are protected by law, who would want to kill such a defenseless, gentle creature? I knew my readers would want to find out, along with Skeet.

Title	THE PERFECT WIZARD: HANS CHRISTIAN ANDERSEN
Author	Jane Yolen
Illustrator	Dennis Nolan
Publisher	Dutton
Copyright Date	2004
Ages	10 and up
Read-Aloud Time	20 minutes
Read-Aloud Sessions	1
Themes	Biography, fairy tales

Jane Yolen, who has been dubbed "America's Hans Christian Andersen" by *Newsweek,* has pulled together a biography of this great storyteller that exemplifies how fact and fiction are often intertwined. One of several books published in honor of the 200th anniversary of Andersen's birth, this picture book biography spotlights his youth, his singular personality, and the events in Andersen's life that found their way into his fairy tales.

> **PRE-READING FOCUS**: Show the cover of the book. Read the title. Ask: What do we call a book that gives facts about a person's life? (Biography.) **Let's read to find out** why Jane Yolen calls Hans Christian Andersen "the perfect wizard."

> **WHILE READING:** Read the first page of the biography, skipping the material that comes before it. Ask listeners what this tells us about Andersen. (Andersen embellished his experiences for the purposes of story.) Read the next spread. Note how the facts Jane Yolen presents are in black print, and Andersen's words are found below the text in blue script. Ask: What story did Andersen tell? (He said that his childhood was happy and rich.) **Let's read to find out** in what ways it might have been happy and rich, despite his being poor. Read the next two spreads. Ask: In what ways was Andersen rich? (His imagination; his relationship with his father and his mother.) Read the next two spreads. Ask: How was Hans's imagination troublesome for him? (He was taunted by children and considered a pest by neighbors.) Read the next two spreads. Ask: Although Hans was poor, homely, and lonely, he had many gifts. What were some of them? (Imagination, perseverance, tenacity, creativity, and hope.) Read the next two spreads. Ask: Do you think Hans gave up? (No.) **Let's read to find out.** Read the next spread. Ask: Why do you think Andersen refers to his name in the program as "a halo of immortality"? (He feels famous, likening it to being a god or an angel.) Read the next two spreads. Ask: What do you think Hans did next? **Let's read to find out.** Read the next spread. Ask: Why do you think the directors of the Royal Theatre changed their minds and sent Hans to grammar school? Read to the end of the book.

FOLLOW-UP DISCUSSION: Read the quotations found at the front of the book. Discuss the title. Ask: How did Hans use his experiences? (To create stories.) Turn to the back of the book and note the fairy tales from which the passages in blue script at the bottom of each spread were taken. Assign a tale to each child or team of children to read and relate to the group.

Write Away! Read a fairy tale written by Hans Christian Andersen. Tell what parts you think come from Hans's childhood experiences. Illustrate.

Other books about Hans Christian Andersen written for children include THE AMAZING PAPER CUTTINGS OF HANS CHRISTIAN ANDERSEN, by Beth Wagner Brust (Houghton Mifflin), an ALA Notable Book for Children and winner of the Parents' Choice Award; and THE YOUNG HANS CHRISTIAN ANDERSEN, written by Karen Hesse and illustrated by Erik Blegvad (Scholastic).

Notes:

Up Close and Personal · · · · · · · · · · · · ·

A Note from the Author, Jane Yolen

Where the idea for the book came from . . .

THE PERFECT WIZARD: HANS CHRISTIAN ANDERSEN came about the easy way. An editor called me up and said, "We hope you'll be intrigued by the idea of writing a picture book biography of Hans Christian Andersen." And I was. But the editor didn't know that 2005—the year the book was to be published—was actually the 200th anniversary of Hans Christian Andersen's birth until I told him!

Researching the subject . . .

I began the preparation for writing by simultaneously reading through a complete collection of Andersen's tales and his autobiography, and I realized very quickly (I think I already knew this, but the reading confirmed it) that a great many of his stories were little fairy tales about his life. So I began grabbing wonderful quotes from the stories to possibly use in the actual book.

By reading all the stories this way, I—who thought I really knew Andersen's work—came to a new and deeper understanding of his tales, and a new and deeper appreciation of his life's work. But I also realized that I probably wouldn't have liked him a whole lot if I were to meet him today. Andersen was cranky, self-important, and had absolutely no interest in anyone else but himself. How interesting that someone that self-involved should have been so able to write stories that have reached out for two centuries to touch the hearts of millions of readers.

To learn more about Jane Yolen, author of 200+ books for children, visit her Web site at www.janeyolen.com. Offering information for children, teachers, writers, storytellers, and "lovers of children's literature," the site features poems, answers to requently asked questions, a brief biography of Yolen, photos, and links to resources for teachers.

Title	. . . . THE RUMPELSTILTSKIN PROBLEM
Author	. . . . Vivian Vande Velde
Publisher	. . . . Scholastic
Copyright Date	 2001
Ages	. . . . 9 and up
Read-Aloud Time	. . . . 15–20 minutes
Read-Aloud Sessions	 2–7
Themes	. . . . Fractured fairy tales, author's purpose, story elements

In this collection of alternatives to the well-known Grimm brothers' fairy tale, Vande Velde offers listeners funny—and more logical—tales. After all, why would a miller boast that his daughter can spin straw into gold? If it's true, why is the miller poor? Why would a talented little man who can spin straw into gold do it for a miniscule gold ring? The more you question the elements of the original fairy tale, the more you'll enjoy this book. Here are six original tales; choose to read one, a few, or all of them, but don't skip over the Author's Note. It sets the tone for the stories and alerts readers to the author's purpose. Best of all, it introduces listeners to the writing style and winning humor of this talented author of fantasy.

Note: You may want to have on hand a picture book of the story of Rumpelstiltskin so you can briefly review the tale with listeners before reading from this book. A suggestion: the Caldecott Honor book, RUMPELSTILTSKIN, illustrated by Paul O. Zelinsky (Dutton).

PRE-READING FOCUS: Introducing the book: Show the cover and read the title. Review the tale of Rumpelstiltskin. Ask listeners what they like about the story. Ask what parts of the story don't really make much sense. Read the title of Vande Velde's book again. Note that the "problem" in the title refers to those elements of the tale that just don't make much sense.

Author's Note

Pre-reading: Explain what an author's note is. (An author's explanation of why he or she wrote the book, background on the subject of the book, or a brief history of how the book came to be.) **Let's read to find out** from the author why she wrote this book of stories.

Follow-up:

- Review the facts we have learned from the author. (Fairy tales come from an oral tradition; details from the original tale of Rumpelstiltskin)

- Why did the author write these stories? What was her *purpose*? (She feels that some elements of the original tale do not make sense.)

- Discuss the importance of material in a book, such as an author's note, that is ancillary to the main text but provides insight and additional information for readers.

- Play Gossip!

- Read one or more of the stories in subsequent sessions. **Read to find out** what aspect of the tale Vande Velde treats in her story, how she changes that aspect, and whether it makes for a better tale.

Write Away! Choose one of the stories from Vande Velde's THE RUMPELSTILTSKIN PROBLEM. Tell what you liked about it and why.

Write Away! Choose a fairy tale that you feel has elements that don't make much sense. Rewrite the tale.

In addition to Zelinsky's RUMPELSTILTSKIN and his Caldecott Award–winning book, RAPUNZEL, Don't miss RUMPELSTILTSKIN'S DAUGHTER, by Diane Stanley (Morrow). No weepy maiden in a tower here! Her name is Hope, and she's strong and smart. A read-aloud plan for the book can be found in Children's Book Corner, Grades 3–4.

Write Away! Choose one of your favorite fairy tales. Find as many versions of it as you can at the library. Pick the version you like best. Tell why it is your favorite. Prepare to present it to the class.

See also NEWFANGLED FAIRY TALES: CLASSIC STORIES WITH A TWIST, edited by Bruce Lansky (Meadowbrook); a collection of original fairy tales written by well-known and well-loved authors.

For more fractured fairy tales, refer to the Book Notes section of this and other volumes in the Children's Book Corner series.

Notes:

Up Close and Personal

A Note from the Author, Vivian Vande Velde

Here's the thing about fairy tales . . .

I've always enjoyed fairy tales—magic, wishes coming true, younger siblings being revealed as smarter, braver, and purer of heart than their older brothers and sisters (Can you guess my birth order?), and, of course, that traditional ending: "And then they lived happily ever after."

But many times certain elements of the fairy tales I was reading didn't make sense; I especially had trouble with *why* some of the characters acted the way they did. One of the most mixed-up fairy tales—as far as I'm concerned—is the story of Rumpelstiltskin. Every single character in that story does something that strikes me as at least a bit bizarre. For example, I can understand a father being so proud of his daughter that he exaggerates her abilities ("My daughter can spin straw into gold.") ; but I can't understand why a father who has made up such a story would then bring his daughter to the king to demonstrate those made-up abilities—when the king has declared that if she doesn't succeed, he'll have her head chopped off!

How the book came to be . . .

Because there were so many details that needed explaining, I couldn't "solve" all of them in one story, so I had to write several. And since I thought each of the characters acted oddly, it only made sense that I should dedicate at least one story to each of them. Rumpelstiltskin —good guy or bad—is such a fascinating character, I ended up giving him (or, in one case, her) more than one story.

For more about Vivian Vande Velde, her award-winning books, and revelations about where the ideas for her creative and humorous stories came from, visit her Web site: www.vivianvandevelde.com.

Title	FREEDOM ON THE MENU: THE GREENSBORO SIT-INS
Author	Carole Boston Weatherford
Illustrator	Jerome Lagarrigue
Publisher	Dial
Copyright Date	2005
Ages	9 and up
Read-Aloud Time	15 minutes
Read-Aloud Sessions	1
Themes	Discrimination, segregation, civil rights, American history: 1960s

This picture book presents the story of the Greensboro sit-ins from the point of view of a fictional young girl who experiences the events and their effects on her family, her town, and her country. The language is pure and the paintings are lush and evocative, allowing the reader to step back in time and imagine the emotion that surged through the hearts of participants in these historical events.

PRE-READING FOCUS: Show the cover of the book. Ask children what they notice. What is the setting of this story? (Diner.) Read the main title. Discuss what it might refer to. Read the title and subtitle. Ask listeners to predict what this book is about. (An event in American history.) **Let's read to find out**.

WHILE READING: Read the first page. Ask: Why did the narrator and her mother stand as they drank their Cokes? (Segregation; African Americans were not allowed to sit at the counter in many restaurants.) Introduce the word *segregation*. (Separation of a race, class, or ethnic group by discriminatory means.) Read the next two spreads. Ask: Why did the man walk away from the drinking fountain? (He did not want to drink from the fountain after the narrator and her aunt did.) Read the next two spreads. Ask: What can you tell me about Dr. Martin Luther King Jr.? Read the next spread. Ask: Why is voting important? (To have a say in government; to make important changes.) What do you think Connie's dream is? (To sit at the counter.) Read the next three spreads. Ask: How do you think the boys at the counter felt as they sat there for all those hours without being served? Refer back to the subtitle of the book. Discuss the term *sit-in*. Do you think Martin Luther King Jr. would be in favor of a sit-in? (Yes.) Why? (It is an example of peaceful protest.) Do you think sit-ins were effective? Read to the end. Ask: Why do you think the banana split was the best one Connie ever had? Read the quotation on the back cover of the book. Ask: What do you think made people change their minds and allow African Americans to sit and be served in restaurants?

FOLLOW-UP DISCUSSION: Read aloud the factual information in the Author's Note. Discuss. Write on the board report topics suggested by the story (e.g., Martin Luther King Jr.; Greensboro sit-ins; Geneva Tisdale; the Greensboro Four: Joseph McNeil, Franklin McCain, Billy Smith, and Clarence Henderson;

segregation of the 1960s; civil disobedience; NAACP). Have children choose one aspect of the civil rights movement of the 1960s to research and report on to the class.

Write Away! Connie's Dad says, "Sometimes it's important just to try." Explain what he means. Tell about a time when you tried, and why it was important.

Write Away! Write a report on one aspect of the civil rights movement of the 1960s. See Follow-up Discussion above.

For an outstanding biography of Martin Luther King Jr., see MARTIN'S BIG WORDS: THE LIFE OF MARTIN LUTHER KING, JR., written by Doreen Rappaport and illustrated by Bryan Collier (Hyperion) a book for all ages that has garnered a number of prestigious awards. See the read-aloud plan found in Children's Book Corner, Grades 1–2.

See also ROSA PARKS: MY STORY, by Rosa Parks with Jim Haskins (Penguin), the autobiography of the woman who refused to give up her seat on a bus to a white man, an act that eventually led to the end of segregation on buses. Martin Luther King Jr. once wrote that Parks's "creative witness was the great force that led to the modern stride toward freedom."

For other books about the civil rights movement in America, refer to the Book Notes section of this resource.

For information about Carole Boston Weatherford and her books, visit her Web site at www.caroleweatherford.com.

Notes:

Up Close and Personal

A Note from the Author, Carole Boston Weatherford

Where ideas and motivation come from . . .

As an author, I mine the past for family stories, fading traditions, and forgotten struggles. I live just ten miles from Greensboro, North Carolina, where the student sit-ins started in 1960. But I was born and raised in Baltimore, Maryland. Downtown lunch counters there were already integrated by the time I sat on a stool beside my mother and had my favorite meal of a hamburger, French fries and a strawberry ice cream soda.

As a teenager, my first two jobs were at downtown department stores. One store was very upscale. My mother told me that in the early 1950s African Americans were not allowed to try on hats, shoes, or clothes in that store. To determine shoe size, black customers had to trace their feet on paper and compare the tracing to the sole of the shoe.

My mother also told me about my great aunt who refused to drink from fountains designated for blacks. When she visited family down South, she drank from the whites-only fountain in the department store. She always said, "I've never heard of colored water"— just like Connie's Aunt Gertie in FREEDOM ON THE MENU. My great aunt, Gertrude Trigg, was the real Aunt Gertie.

In FREEDOM ON THE MENU, Connie's family boycotted downtown stores during the sit-ins and shopped in the Sears catalog instead. As a girl, I loved leafing through the Sears catalog, especially the annual Wish Book that I used to make my Christmas list. The last Sears catalog was published in 1993.

About being an author . . .

I have been writing since age six when I dictated a poem about the seasons to my mother as she drove me home from school. When I was about seven years old, my mother asked my father, a high school printing teacher, to print a few of my poems on the letterpress in his classroom. In the early 1960s, no one had desktop computers or laser printers, so children rarely saw their work in print. But I did, and it was thrilling! I shared the printed poems with my friends.

I didn't decide that I wanted to be a writer, though, until after I graduated from college. Then, I set out to get published. When I received the inevitable rejection letters, I was disappointed but no less determined. I had the gall to think that my work would be published because my father had already published it years earlier. I dedicated myself to my craft, read all I could, wrote about what interested me, revised my work countless times, and persevered despite rejections. And lo and behold, I have been published — again and again.

Courtesy Harcourt, Inc.

Title . . . . THE LIBRARIAN OF BASRA: A TRUE STORY FROM IRAQ	
Author/Illustrator . . . . Jeanette Winter	
Publisher . . . . Harcourt	
Copyright Date 2005	
Ages . . . . 8 and up	
Read-Aloud Time . . . . 8 minutes	
Read-Aloud Sessions 1	
Themes . . . . War, Iraq, libraries, value of books	

This picture book tells the true story of a librarian in Basra who saved 30,000 books from being destroyed during the bombing of Basra in 2003. Told simply, its impact lies in the courage of one woman to save what matters to her more than "mountains of gold."

Note: Have a map of Iraq available for the read-aloud of this book.

PRE-READING FOCUS: Show the cover of the book. Read the title. Note that the book tells a true story. Note that the book is written and illustrated by the same person. Find Basra on the map. Ask children what they notice about the cover. (Books in sacks; the crates; Alia's dress.) Predict what the story is about. **Let's read to find out**.

WHILE READING: Read the introductory quotation and the first three pages of the story. Ask: What other questions might the people in the library ask? Read the next two spreads. Ask: Alia asks for permission to move the books, and the governor refuses. Why might he have done that? Alia secretly moves the books to her home. She has disobeyed the governor, but she feels she is doing the right thing. Discuss. The author writes, "rumors become reality." What do you think happened next? (Bombs, fires, gunfire.) Read the next three spreads. Ask: Would Alia have been able to save the books herself? (Probably not.) Note that there is more than one hero in this story. Discuss. Read the next two spreads. Ask: What words would you use to describe Alia? (Brave, determined, smart.) Read to the end.

FOLLOW-UP DISCUSSION: Read aloud A Note from the Author, found at the back of the book. Do the math! If Alia was able to save 70 percent of the books in the collection, how many books were there? (We know from the story that she saved 30,000. This means there were about 43,000.) How many did she lose? (About 13,000.) Research the reporter who uncovered the story, Shaila K. Dewan. Read the original story found in the *New York Times*, July 27, 2003.

Write Away! Write imaginary journal entries in Alia's diary for the time when she was saving the books.

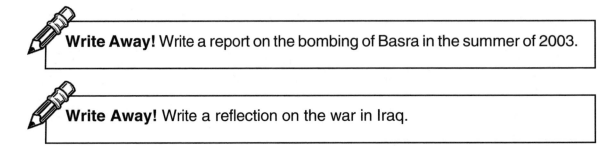

Write Away! Write a report on the bombing of Basra in the summer of 2003.

Write Away! Write a reflection on the war in Iraq.

*For interviews with Jeanette Winter about this book posted on the Web, go to
http://www.bookpage.com/0501bp/jeanette_winter.html and
http://www.harcourtbooks.com/authorinterviews/bookinterview_Winter.asp.*

Notes:

Up Close and Personal

A Note from the Author/Illustrator, Jeanette Winter

Where the idea for the book came from . . .

I was reading the New York Times one Sunday morning in July, 2003, when I came across the story of Alia Baker, and how she saved 70%, (30,000 books) of her library's collection during the war in Iraq. I knew immediately that I wanted to tell this story to children.

Researching the book . . .

I had never been to Iraq, and it was impossible to go there, so I had to find another way to discover how Iraq looked. I wanted the pictures to be as authentic as possible. So I did several things:

- I went to the picture collection of the New York Public Library and checked out many pictures of Iraq, most of them war pictures.

- I studied a book of photographs of the Iraq war.

- I saw an exhibit at the International Center of Photography of photos by war correspondents in Iraq.

- I went to an exhibit, "They Still Draw Pictures," of children's art in wartime, from the Spanish Civil War to the present.

- And I listened to Middle Eastern music while I was painting the pictures.

Among the pictures from the collection of the New York Public Library, there was one that stood out for me. It was an old photo of a man standing in a boat passing through reeds. The image struck me as something from heaven, among all the images of war. So I based my "peace" picture on the photo. After the book was printed, I learned that Saddam had drained all the canals. The painting in the book turned out to be more accurate that I could have imagined.

From research to published book . . .

It usually takes me from six months to a year to write and illustrate a book. I wrote and illustrated THE LIBRARIAN OF BASRA in just four months, and the publisher, Harcourt, produced and published the book in record time. I think we all felt that Alia's story puts a human face on the anonymity of war, and her bravery lights a candle in the dark.

Title	THE PRINCE OF THE POND
Author	Donna Jo Napoli
Illustrator	Judith Byron Schachner
Publisher	Dutton
Copyright Date	1992
Ages	9 and up
Read-Aloud Time	10–15 minutes
Read-Aloud Sessions	11
Themes	Fantasy, frogs and other pond life, family

In this fantasy of a prince turned into a frog and then back again, we are treated to all sorts of facts about frogs, toads, pond life, and even how to stump a snapping turtle —if you ever get caught on his back. This tale is delightful, fact-infused, and wise—sort of like the Frog Prince himself.

Note: Copy the hag's words and description for the Write Away! assignment.

PRE-READING FOCUS: Show the cover of the book. Ask: What kind of story do you think this is? (Fantasy.) Read the dedication. Ask: Have you ever read a book, magazine article, or poem that changed the way you looked at things? Discuss.

Chapter One: "The Hag"

Pre-reading: Read the title of the chapter. Ask: What is a *hag*? (An ugly or evil-looking old woman; a witch.) Show the picture of the hag in the first chapter. **Let's read to find out** the setting of this story, and what it is about.

While Reading:

- Read through the first section. Stop at the point where it is revealed that the narrator is a frog. Ask: Who did you think the narrator might be up to this point? (A boy or girl.) Discuss what we now know. (It is a frog.)

- As you read the hag's words, use expression and a hag-like voice!

Follow-up:

- Discuss how the author helps us to see the frog in the first scene and the hag later in the chapter. Point out a few of the sensory images she uses. (See the Write Away! assignment below.)

- Where does this chapter take place? (Along a path in a royal kingdom.)

- Who are the characters we have met so far? (Narrator, prince turned into a frog, hag.)

- What is the problem, or conflict? (The hag has turned the prince into a frog.)

> **Write Away!** Find out about the differences between toads and frogs. Write a brief explanation.

> **Write Away!** Using the excerpt of the hag's description and words, highlight the images, using a different color for each sense they appeal to. For example, use a yellow highlighter for visual images, a blue highlighter for those images that appeal to the sense of smell, and so on. Then choose the image Napoli uses that you like best. Tell why.

Chapter Two: "Water"

Pre-reading: Review the information gathered on frogs and toads from the Write Away! assignment above. We will learn more about these animals in this next chapter. Read the title of the chapter. Ask: What do you think will happen in this chapter? **Let's read to find out.** Listen for more facts about frogs and toads.

While Reading: Ask: What is a predator? (One that preys, destroys, or devours.)

Follow-up:

- As we read this story we are learning facts about frogs. We also learn a bit about toads in this chapter. Let's list facts as we learn them. Refer back to Chapter One for facts. (Frogs eat aphids; they have mucus glands that keep their bodies moist; they look with one eye, not both; they leap.) Add facts from Chapter Two. (Frogs hibernate; they like the sun; they have folds of skin instead of bumps; they eat slugs and snails as well as aphids; they absorb water through their skin; their skin is sensitive; bullfrogs are "boorish and gluttonous"; special green frogs have two vocal sacs located on each side of the head instead of one located on the throat.)

- What did we learn about toads? (They are brown and bumpy; their skin is poison, dry, and warty; toads have bean-shaped bumps behind the eyes and in other places; they like dark places; they are short and fat with squat, little legs.)

- What do you think the strange frog was trying to tell the narrator to call him? (Prince.)

Note: In preparation for the reading of the next chapter, find a picture of a sow bug to show to listeners.

Chapter Three: "The Turtle"

Pre-reading: Read the title of the chapter. Ask: What do you know about snapping turtles? **Let's read to find out** what the Frog Prince learns about turtles in this chapter.

While Reading:

- Show the picture of the sow bug.

- As you read the Frog Prince's words, use expression!

Follow-up:

- Add to the facts on frogs. (They eat sow bugs; they are amphibians; they live in fresh water; they do not live in salt water; they feel the slightest movements; they are no friend of the snapping turtle.)

- Where does this chapter take place? (In the pond.)

- What do we learn about the Frog Prince in this chapter? (He is mad that he is a frog; he can outsmart the turtle; he is cunning and funny.)

> **Write Away!** What makes this story fun to read? Explain and support with examples from the story.

Note: Find pictures of a caecilian and a glass worm to share with listeners during the reading of this chapter.

Chapter Four: "Food"

Pre-reading: Read the title of the chapter. Ask: What do you think we will learn about frogs in this chapter? (What frogs eat.) What do you think we will learn about the Frog Prince? **Let's read to find out**.

While Reading:

- Show the picture of the caecilian (si-**sil**-yen). Explain that this is a tropical, burrowing amphibian that resembles a worm.

- As you read the Frog Prince's words in the opening pages of the chapter, occasionally stop to allow listeners to figure out what he is saying before the narrator does.

- What letters does the prince have trouble pronouncing?

Follow-up:

- Add to the facts list. (Green frogs eat dragonflies, insects, minnows, gnats, mosquitoes, and glass worms; jaw is wide but not hinged like a snake's; some frogs have little teeth; frogs eat only live things; stomach acids dissolve hard matter; bullfrogs eat small mammals and turtles; the tongue is long and fat and attached to the front of the mouth; the green frog's enemies include toads, raccoons, turtles, water birds, bullfrogs, and snakes.)

- The narrator notices the ripple in the water. What do you think the narrator was concerned it might be? (A snake.)

- What changes in this chapter? (The Frog Prince snaps to when the narrator admits to wanting the Frog Prince to stay.)

> **Write Away!** The prince is not happy with being changed into a frog. Write about a time when something in your life changed, and tell how you gradually got used to it.

Note: Find a picture of a green frog to show to listeners.

Chapter Five: "Singing"

Pre-reading: Read the title of the chapter. Ask: Do frogs sing? **Let's read to find out** what this chapter is about.

While Reading:

- Read through the revelation that the narrator is a female frog. Ask: Did you think the narrator was a boy or a girl? Discuss how the author slyly left that fact out until this chapter. Look for clues the author hid in previous chapters that hint that the narrator is a female. (She often comments on what a fine frog the Frog Prince is.)

- Read to the point just before the Frog Prince lands on the head of the water snake. Ask listeners what they think the Frog Prince is trying to say. (Snake.) before reading on.

Follow-up:

- Add to the frog facts list. (Male frogs sing to mate; they mate in June; they become pale when frightened.)

> **Write Away!** Choose one of the pond specimens mentioned in this chapter. Find out more about it and write a brief report. Be sure to find pictures of the animal to show to the group.

Chapter Six: "Eggs"

Pre-reading: Read the title of the chapter. Ask: What do you think happens next? **Let's read to find out**.

Follow-up:

- Add to the frog facts list. (Tadpoles eat algae; frog eggs are black masses while toad eggs are long and loopy; frog stay in calm waters; frogs don't know their fathers.)

- Where has the Frog Prince taken the narrator? (To his palace.) Discuss.

- Where will she lay the eggs? Use the story clues to figure it out. (In the well.)

Write Away! The Frog Prince has taken the narrator to a safe place to lay the eggs even though this is unfroglike. What does this tell us about him?

Chapter Seven: "Tadpoles"

Pre-reading: Read the title of the chapter. The tadpoles hatch in the palace well. Do you think this was a good spot to lay the eggs? Discuss. Ask: What do you think will happen next? **Let's read to find out**.

While Reading:

- Read to the point just before the Frog Prince and the narrator discuss the wisdom of bringing the tadpoles to the pond. Ask: Do you think it was wise for them to lay the eggs in the well? Wouldn't it have made more sense just to go to the pond first? What are the benefits of each environment?

Follow-up:

- Add to the frog facts list. (Eggs sink before rising; tadpoles hatch in seven days; frog and toad tadpoles look the same; special green frogs mature in a month, while common green frogs take a year to grow into adult frogs.)

- Discuss the Frog Prince's reaction to and delight in his offspring. Compare with the narrator's response. What does this tell us about the Frog Prince? (He is a human in frog form.) Discuss.

Write Away! The narrator tells the Frog Prince, "Sometimes you seem to know nothing and other times you know everything." This may be true of all of us. Is it true about you? Explain, using an example from your own experience.

Chapter Eight: "Jimmy"

Pre-reading: Read the title of the chapter. We meet a new character in this chapter. Ask: Who do you think it will be? **Let's read to find out**.

While Reading:

- Read to the point where the Frog Prince names the narrator. Ask: Why do you think he named her Jade? (Jade is a green gem.) Read on to the end.

Follow-up:

- Jade and Pin (Frog Prince) have a conversation about Jimmy. Who do you agree with, Jade or Pin?

- Discuss what happens at the end of the chapter. What do you think will happen next?

Write Away! List the skills Jimmy might have learned that will help him in his predicament. Use examples from the story to support your opinion.

Note: In preparation for the reading of this chapter, find pictures of a wood frog and a squid.

Chapter Nine: "Battle"

Pre-reading: Read the title of the chapter. Ask: What do you think will happen next? Let's not waste another moment! This is an action-packed, suspenseful chapter. **Let's read to find out** why!

While Reading:

- Jade is acting differently than she has acted before. Ask: What is she doing? (She is insulting Pin.) Why? (She is angry and afraid for her son.)

- Show the squid and wood frog pictures at appropriate places in the chapter. Note that squids shoot ink to protect themselves.

- Use expression when you read the hag's lines!

Follow-up:

- Discuss the pace and suspense of the chapter. What made this chapter so exciting? Could you have put down this book in the middle of the scene with the hag? Discuss.

- What have the frogs done in this chapter that is very froglike, that helped them? (The froglets disobeyed; Pin clutched the hag's nose with a fierce grip.)

- What have the frogs done in this chapter that is very unfroglike? (Jade is feeling emotions for her son; the froglets help save Jimmy; Pin jumps in all directions to avoid the hag.)

Chapter Ten: "Bullfrog"

Pre-reading: Read the title of the chapter. What do we know about bullfrogs from this book? (They are fearsome and unlikable.) **Let's read to find out** what a bullfrog has to do with this chapter.

Follow-up:

- Add to the frog facts list. (Frogs have goggle-like lids that help keep the water out and allow them to see underwater; frogs breathe through their skin; frogs go underwater to the bottom of the pond when in danger.)

- Note the pond life mentioned in this chapter while the family is underwater. (Protozoa, bristle worms, hydra, and a diving beetle.)

Write Away! Consider the last scene in the chapter. The author uses the word *gibbous.* What does it mean? Where have we seen that word before? Return to the dedication. Write about why you think the author chose to close this chapter in this way.

Chapter Eleven: "Back to the Well"

Pre-reading: Read the title of the chapter. Review where the well is located. (In the palace gardens.) Ask: What do you think will happen next? **Let's read to find out**.

Follow-up:

- What quality does Pin have that is human? (He is stubborn and insistent when he makes up his mind about something.)

- Just before the princess meets Jimmy, something funny and very froglike happens. What is it? (The froglets disobey.)

- How does Jade feel when they come upon the princess? (She is afraid, then jealous because of the way Pin looks at the woman.)

- Why doesn't Jade understand what has happened? (She is a frog, after all.)

- What about Jimmy? (He seems to understand.)

- What makes this story so vivid? (The author's writing style and imagery.)

• What makes this story believable despite the fact that it is a fantasy? (The facts Napoli wove into the story.)

Be sure to share with listeners Napoli's Up Close and Personal piece, which immediately follows this read-aloud plan.

Do not reveal the other titles in this trilogy until the Write Away! assignment is complete. Then have available copies of the second and third books in the trilogy for listeners to look at and borrow.

Write Away! If you were going to write a sequel to this book, what would it be about?

The titles of the other books in this trilogy are JIMMY, THE PICKPOCKET OF THE PALACE and GRACIE, THE PIXIE OF THE PUDDLE.

See also UGLY, written by Donna Jo Napoli and illustrated by Lita Judge (Hyperion), the story of an ugly duckling's search for self.

Notes:

Up Close and Personal · · · · · · · · · · · ·

A Note from the Author, Donna Jo Napoli

Telling stories . . .

When my children were little, all five shared one bedroom. So we had two bunk beds and a crib in there, which later was replaced by a junior bed. We used to read in a small room next to the bedroom. Then we'd all go into their bedroom and the children would climb into their beds while I turned off the light and my husband and I sat on the rug in the center of the room. In the dark like that, we'd tell stories.

Sometimes my husband told stories. His were often long, so they went on for many nights, in serial form. Sometimes I told stories. Mine were short. And often we went around the room and whoever wanted to told stories. We did a lot of cooperative story-telling, where one person would start a story and the next person would continue it, and so on around the room. And we often told the same story from different points of view. That's how I got into telling fairy tales from unusual points of view. And I do mean "telling" tales, not just writing them. When I write, I talk out loud. That way, I can hear my characters and I can listen to make sure their dialogue rings true to my ear.

THE PRINCE OF THE POND is the first book in a trilogy, which also includes JIMMY, THE PICKPOCKET OF THE PALACE and GRACIE, THE PIXIE OF THE PUDDLE. To make these stories, I had to learn a lot about frogs. So I went to our local public library and checked out every book on amphibians and pond life. After I'd read them, I went to the science library at the college where I work and I read as many books on amphibian anatomy as I could stand to read. (They got quite tedious after a while.)

Reading what other people have found out is called doing secondary research. And I did plenty of it. But I urge you, if you want to write stories, to please do as much primary research as you can. Primary research will give your story vividness. So, because I wanted vividness, I had to go out and learn some things about frogs on my own.

I went to two ponds. One is a small, concrete pond in my back yard. It is full of frogs and goldfish and all sorts of little creatures and plants (including lilies and iris). The other is a large pond that is in the neighboring town. I would sit in front of them for hours, just watching. You'd be surprised at what does not happen when you do that; ponds are very quiet places. But because I'd done my secondary research first, I could understand more about what I was seeing. For example, if a dragonfly swooped down and laid eggs on the water's surface and flew off again, I knew that something dramatic had happened from a frog's point of view because dragonfly larvae eat tadpoles. So the enemy had invaded. As I watched the ponds, scenes formed in my head for the three books.

I hope you enjoy the story that the lovely frog Jade tells. And I hope you'll hop happily from this pond to the others awaiting you.

To learn more about this intriguing, award-winning author of a number of memorable books for children and young adults, visit her Web site at www.donnajonapoli.com.

Cover of DON'T TELL THE GIRLS, A FAMILY MEMOIR by Patricia Reilly Giff.
Published by Holiday House. Reprinted by permission.

Title	DON'T TELL THE GIRLS: A FAMILY MEMOIR
Author	Patricia Reilly Giff
Publisher	Holiday House
Copyright Date	2005
Ages	10 and up
Read-Aloud Time	10–15 minutes
Read-Aloud Sessions	10
Themes	Memoir, family, storytelling, intergenerational connections, genealogy

Patricia Reilly Giff is a storyteller. Those fortunate enough to have read her fiction books know this. What readers may not know is that Giff credits her Nana with shaping this talent. Environment, Giff calls it. In 10 loosely connected chapters, Giff introduces the reader to her relatives by way of warm, nostalgic remembrances and suggests ways of researching genealogy. Gather around the hearth of her childhood and listen. What you hear will lead you to look within your own family for stories of who you are and where you may have gotten your special gifts.

Note: The read-aloud of this memoir will be most meaningful to listeners if they are familiar with other books written by Patricia Reilly Giff. Have on hand a selection of her books throughout the read-aloud of DON'T TELL THE GIRLS. Encourage listeners to get to know the author who penned this memoir through her fiction and to consider how her life experiences contributed to her books.

PRE-READING FOCUS: Briefly review a selection of Giff's books, from the perennially popular Polk Street School series for young readers to her fascinating, award-winning historical fiction. Introduce DON'T TELL THE GIRLS by showing the cover and reading the title. Ask: What do we know about this book from its cover? (This is the story of specific events in the lives of people who were important in the author's life. The photo gives us a clue to the time period. Note the print font, which gives the book an "old-fashioned" feel. Note the size of the book, which gives the impression of a diary.) Ask if anyone knows what a memoir is. (The story of the author's personal experiences as he or she remembers it.) Discuss the differences between a memoir and a biography or autobiography. (Biography: the factual story of a person's life; autobiography: the story of a person's life told by that person; memoir: the remembrance of meaningful parts of a person's life.) Encourage listeners to think about these differences as you read the book.

1. "Nana's Stories"

Pre-reading: Read the title of the chapter. Find Nana on the family tree at the front of the book. Trace her relation to Patricia Reilly Giff (PRG). **Let's read to find out** what Nana was like.

Follow-up:

- Discuss what we have found out in this first chapter. (Nana was a wonderful storyteller; she was happy-go-lucky; PRG was close to her grandmother; PRG had two aunts; her mother and the aunts were referred to by Nana as "the girls"; the time period of the memoir is the 1940s.)

- PRG is like her grandmother in some ways. Discuss. (She loses things; she likes to tell stories.) PRG is unlike her grandmother in other ways. Explain. (Nana is neat; she is not.)

- Discuss Nana's *characteristics.*

- At the end of the chapter, PRG says she wishes she had known her other grandmother, Jennie. Ask: Do you know one set of grandparents better than you know others? Discuss.

Write Away! Describe one of your extended family members, or an older person with whom you have a close relationship (excluding parents).

Write Away! Tell a story you've heard from one of your grandparents or an older relative. Include plenty of details to keep your story interesting.

Note: In preparation for the reading of the next chapter, ask children to find an old photo of their relatives and ask a parent to explain who the people in the photograph are and what was happening when the photo was taken. Ask children to bring in their photos to share with the class.

2. "Mary's Picture"

Pre-reading: Ask children to relate their experiences gathering photos. Save the sharing of photos until after the read-aloud of this chapter. **Let's read to find out** about Mary's photo.

Follow-up:

- At the beginning of the chapter PRG regrets something she has done (Cutting her hair.) At the end of the chapter, she regrets something else (Never asking Nana who Mary Redfern was.) Discuss.

- What was Nana's reaction to PRG cutting her hair and the box tumbling down the attic stairs? What do her reactions tell us about her? (She was wise and insightful and not easily agitated.)

Write Away! Describe something you once did that you then regretted.

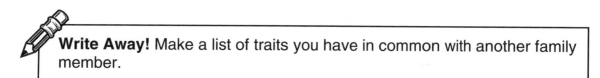

Write Away! Do you have a memory box in which you keep special things? Describe what's in your box. Draw a picture.

Note: In preparation for the reading of the next chapter, ask children to bring in something from a memory box, or something that evokes a memory, to "show and tell." Bring in a persimmon for children to sample.

3. "Mary's Sketches"

Pre-reading: Show and tell memory box items the children have brought in. Read the title of the chapter. Ask: What do you think this chapter might be about? **Let's read to find out** about Mary's sketches.

Follow-up:

- Discuss what PRG learned about Mary and what the two have in common.

- Try the persimmon! Use adjectives to describe the taste.

Write Away! Make a list of traits you have in common with another family member.

Note: In preparation for the reading of the next chapter, have children ask their parents to tell them two things about the year, month, or day they were born. Ask children to write down what they find out and bring it to class. Find photos of Coney Island, from the 1940s and more recent times, to share with children.

4. "Jennie's Shawl"

Pre-reading: Ask: Do you own something special that once belonged to an older relative? Describe it. How do you feel when you wear or use this item? **Let's read to find out** what PRG treasures that once belonged to her grandmothers.

While Reading: Define *mules*. (Shoes without backs.)

Follow-up:

- Discuss what PRG learned about Jennie and what they have in common.

- Show children photos of Coney Island. Ask children to describe their amusement park adventures.

- Share what children have learned from their parents about the year, month, or day they were born.

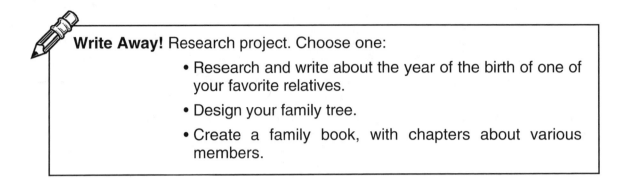

Write Away! Research project. Choose one:

- Research and write about the year of the birth of one of your favorite relatives.
- Design your family tree.
- Create a family book, with chapters about various members.

5. "Jennie's Storm"

Pre-reading: Ask: Is there something that happened to you a long time ago that you remember very well? Discuss. **Let's read to find out** what PRG discovered in her research about the time when Jennie was a child.

Follow-up:

- What did PRG learn about the time when Jennie was a child? How did she learn about it?
- Contrast PRG's cemetery visits with typical spooky graveyard stories.

Write Away! Interview a relative to find out about one of his or her vivid memories.

Write Away! Continue to work on research projects.

6. "Michael's Story"

Pre-reading: Close your eyes. Think about something that happened this morning before you came to school. Picture the details. What did it look like? Feel like? Smell like? Taste like? **Let's read to find out** about Michael's story and the details PRG remembers from early mornings when she was a child.

Follow-up:

- List the details of PRG's memories of her father.
- Contrast PRG's memories with what those of her grandmother, Jennie, must have been.
- Do you think PRG finds out the facts about Michael Monahan?

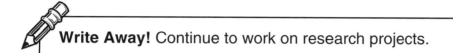

Write Away! Continue to work on research projects.

7. "Michael's Horses"

Pre-reading: Do you think PRG finds out what happened to Michael? **Let's read to find out!**

Follow-up:

- Discuss what PRG learned about searching for clues about Michael. (Gather as many facts as possible; don't guess; use maps; piece clues together.)

- How do you think PRG felt when she wasn't able to find Michael in the ship's records?

Write Away! Continue to work on research projects.

Note: In preparation for the reading of the next chapter, have available a large map of Ireland for use with the follow-up activity.

8. "Margaret's Birth Certificate"

Pre-reading: **Let's read to find out** who Margaret is.

Follow-up:

- How does PRG feel when she discovers her grandmother's sister's name in the birth records?

- On a map of Ireland, trace PRG's journey from Dublin to Cornacullew.

Write Away! Continue to work on research projects.

9. "Endings"

Pre-reading: **Let's read to find out** what the title means.

Follow-up:

- How does PRG feel when she learns the truth about Michael?

- Who has helped PRG understand what's important and valuable? (Nana.) Discuss.

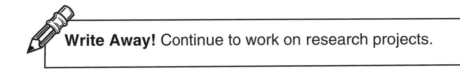

Write Away! Continue to work on research projects.

10. "Nana's Cup"

Pre-reading: **Let's read to find out** about Nana's cup.

Follow-up:

- How is PRG passing along what she has learned from Nana to her grandchildren?

- What has the relative you are researching passed along to you?

Write Away! Conclude work on research projects.

For information about Patricia Reilly Giff's other outstanding books, visit www.patriciareillygiff.com, http://www.randomhouse.com/features/patriciareillygiff/, and http://www.randomhouse.com/teachers/authors/results.pperl?authorid=10018. For an interview with Giff, visit http://www.kidsreads.com/authors/au-giff-patricia-reilly.asp.

Notes:

Up Close and Personal

A Note from the Author, Patricia Reilly Giff

In another book, NORY RYAN'S SONG, I described a winding road as a ball of twine let loose. Writing DON'T TELL THE GIRLS was certainly that: the winding road resembling a ball of yarn tossed across the floor, twisting and turning, becoming something I'd never expected.

It began as a book about genealogy, about research, about finding family history. My own family's part in it was supposed to be minor, a brushstroke or two. I started with Mary Redfern. In fact, the original title was WHO WAS MARY REDFERN? For years I'd tried to find her place in our family and never could.

But something happened as I wrote. And that something was Nana. I could see her beautiful hands, her smiling face. I found a picture of the two of us, Nana and baby Pat, on a swing in her garden in Lynbrook, Long Island. On the back she had written: *My Pet*. It brought tears to my eyes. My editor saw that, too. "The book is about Nana," she said. "It comes alive when you write about her."

The ball of yarn skittered in a new direction. I stacked the notes on genealogy, the advice on census finding, and library research into neat piles. They became the brushstrokes; Nana and my childhood memories became the focus of the book.

How lucky I was to have had Nana, to share secrets, to hear stories, to know that she loved me as much as I loved her. Today I still find her everywhere: her lovely glasses with the gold rims are in my china closet, her wedding ring is on the third finger of my right hand, a prayer she wrote out for me is on my desk, and the original picture of her taken on that hot summer day in Belford, New Jersey, which you see in the book, is in my bedroom.

So the book became Nana's book. In large measure it was because of Nana that I wanted to find out more about my other grandmother, Jennie Monahan Reilly. How unfair, I realized, that I'd missed knowing Jennie the way I knew Nana. And so the ball of yarn turned again. I studied Brooklyn to see what it must have been like in Jennie's growing up years. I went to Ireland where she was born, found her house, her cousins, and even the sweet little cemetery where her father rests.

And maybe that's what a book about genealogy is really all about after all: a story of the past, a story of memories, a joy to think about, a joy to write.

Cover of NEW YORK IS ENGLISH, CHATTANOOGA IS CREEK. by Chris Raschka. Copyright © 2005. Used with permission of Richard Jackson Books/Atheneum Books for Young Readers, an imprint of Simon & Schuster Children's Publishing.

Title	NEW YORK IS ENGLISH, CHATTANOOGA IS CREEK
Author/Illustrator	Chris Raschka
Publisher	Atheneum
Copyright Date	2005
Ages	8 and up
Read-Aloud Time	10 minutes
Read-Aloud Sessions	1
Themes	Origins of names of cities, word study, poetry

Chris Raschka is a Caldecott Award–winning illustrator with a distinctive style. (Refer to the indexes for other books illustrated by Raschka that are featured in this resource.) In this book, which he wrote and illustrated, Raschka offers a light and creative look at how cities were named. The map of the United States found on the inside cover will be useful in the read-aloud of this book and the follow-up activity.

Note: Have dictionaries available for the read-aloud of this book.

PRE-READING FOCUS*:* Show the cover of the book. Read the title. Note that the book is both nonfiction and fiction, and that it is written and illustrated by the same person. Ask: What is the subject of the book? (Origins of city names.) **Let's read to find out** what we learn about how some cities got their names.

WHILE READING: Note the "Guest List" but do not read the information. Read the first two spreads. Ask: What does *boastful* mean? (Prideful; bragging.) Listen carefully for the words used to describe the cities as we read this next section. Read the next three spreads. Ask: What does *steadfast* mean? (Firmly fixed in place; faithful.) What does *lofty* mean? (Elevated in status; superior; noble.) What does *adventuresome* mean? (Full of adventure or spirit.) Use dictionaries to look up the meanings of these words. Note how Raschka's illustrations complement the meaning of the cities' names. Ask: What other cities might New York invite? **Let's read to find out.** Read the next two spreads. Use dictionaries to define *fiasco* (Complete failure.), *sensitive* (Highly responsive; easily hurt.), *fearsome* (Causing fear.), and *ferocious* (Fierce, violent, brutal; intense.) Read to the end of the book.

FOLLOW-UP DISCUSSION: In the party section of this book the author gives the reader clues to the names of the cities invited to New York's party. Assign one city to each child. Research the city names and prepare to report back to the class. Consult the "Guest List" at the front of Raschka's book. (See Write Away! below.) Compare Raschka's artwork in this book with art in other books he has illustrated. See especially YO? YES! (Orchard), for which Raschka won a Caldecott Honor Award, and A POKE IN THE I: A COLLECTION OF CONCRETE POEMS, selected by Paul B. Janeczko (Candlewick), in which Raschka has illustrated 30 delightful poems.

Write Away! Write a report on a city's name. Illustrate, using your drawing to help explain where the name comes from.

Write Away! Read the poem, "Song of Hiawatha," by Longfellow. Write down your impressions of it.

Write Away! Research your city's name or the name of another city you have lived in.

Notes:

Up Close and Personal

A Note from the Author/Illustrator, Chris Raschka

Where the idea for the book came from . . .

It struck me one day as I was leaning against a light pole in San Francisco, that in this country we are blessed with a great abundance of wonderful, unusual, many-tongued names for our cities, which in themselves tell us something about the cities they name, and about our big rambling country all together. For instance, take San Francisco. San Francisco is named for St Francis of Assisi. Assisi is a city in Italy. St. Francis was a man who left his old way of life behind. He was a rich nobleman who gave away all of his money and then began his life anew as a helper of the poor, a beggar, and a mystic who believed in the holiness of all of creation. That sounds a lot like the lives of many people who have lived in San Francisco. Not everyone in San Francisco gave away all of their money or spent their lives helping the poor, of course. But some did. And since the city was founded, a lot of San Franciscans went there to start anew life, that's for sure.

So I thought, if San Francisco, the name, fits San Francisco, the city, so well, maybe it's true with other cities too, like Chicago, New York, Kankakee, Albany, and other names. So I started to root around in books about the names of things and discovered that the United States of America has cities named in many wonderful ways, in dozens of different languages. Sometimes the reasons are clear, such as in the name, Anchorage, a good place for a boat. Sometimes, though, the name is unclear, like Baton Rouge, which means "red stick" in French. Whatever the reason, once a place was named, it seems as if the name itself gave that place a certain flavor, which may have helped to determine the sort of place it was to become. Because this country is named in so many ways in so many different languages, you know that this country has to be a place where people live and talk and think in all kinds of different ways, too, and that's one of the best things about this country.

Right now I'm sitting in a house in Huntingdon, Pennsylvania. That's a good name. Where are you sitting? What kind of a good name does it have?

Cover of THE SEVEN WONDERS OF SASSAFRAS SPRINGS by Betty G. Birney, illustrated by Matt Phelan. Copyright © 2005. Used with permission of Atheneum Books for Young Readers, an imprint of Simon & Schuster Children's Publishing.

Title	THE SEVEN WONDERS OF SASSAFRAS SPRINGS
Author	Betty G. Birney
Illustrator	Matt Phelan
Publisher	Atheneum
Copyright Date	2005
Ages	9 and up
Read-Aloud Time	10 minutes
Read-Aloud Sessions	19
Themes	Values, perspective, home, dreams, Seven Wonders of the World

This delightful story takes place in rural Missouri. Memorable characters and their wonders populate the pages. Come along; search Sassafras Springs with Eben McAllister for seven wonders just beyond his doorstep. You will marvel at what he finds. You will applaud, laugh, sigh, ponder, and be thankful for this gem of a read.

Note: Have a map of the United States available for the first read-aloud session.

PRE-READING FOCUS: Introducing the book: Show the cover and read the title. Ask: What does the title of this book bring to mind? (The Seven Wonders of the World). Can you name the Seven Wonders of the World? (Great Pyramid of Giza, Colossus of Rhodes, Statue of Zeus, Giant Lighthouse at Alexandria, Mausoleum at Halicarnassus, Temple of Artemis at Ephesus, and The Hanging Gardens of Babylon.) What does the name, Sassafras Springs, bring to mind? (Rural area.)

"How It Started"

Pre-reading: **Let's read to find out** about the characters, the setting, and the problem, or *conflict* in this story.

Follow-up:

- Describe the setting of the story. (A farm in rural Missouri; "smack dab in the center of the country.") Find where this might be on a map of the United States.

- Who are the characters we meet in this chapter? (Eben McAllister, the narrator; Pa; Aunt Pretty, Eben's aunt and Pa's sister; Sal, the dog.)

- What other pieces of information have we learned from this chapter? (Eben is interested in faraway places; his mother died four years ago, and his aunt moved in to help out; it is the beginning of summer.)

- Pa says he can't believe there aren't "a few Wonders around here somewhere." This *foreshadows* events to come. What do you think might happen in this story? (Consider the title.)

- The book Eben is reading describes a wonder as, "a marvel: that which arouses awe, astonishment, surprise, or admiration." Ask listeners to name wonders that come to mind.

- What is the problem or conflict in this story? (Eben must find seven wonders in Sassafras Springs to earn a trip to Colorado; the internal conflict is that Eben doesn't value Sassafras Springs.)

- Eben's pa challenges him to find seven wonders in Sassafras Springs in a week. Ask: Do you think he will do it? What might be some of the wonders he will find?

> **Write Away!** Choose one of the Seven Wonders of the World and research it. Write a brief report to present to the class.

Note: In preparation for this read-aloud session, find pictures of sassafras and cockleburs. Have an example of a diorama to show children. As the story progresses, teams will make dioramas of the different places Eben visits in Sassafras Springs.

Day One: "I Go Searching"

Pre-reading: Read the chapter title. **Let's read to find out** what Eben finds.

Follow-up:

- What facts have we learned in this chapter? (It is 1923; Yellow Dog Road is a wide strip of dirt that goes down the middle of Sassafras Springs; Eben's best friend is Jeb, the oldest of nine children.)

- Draw a map of Sassafras Springs based on Eben's description.

- Make an applehead doll!

> **Write Away!** Mrs. Pritchard tells Eben to read the parable of the mustard seed in the Bible (Mark: 4:30). Read it and write a summary.

Note: Consider making "Eben tablets" out of about 15 pages of lined paper for each listener to use to complete the Write Away! assignments as you progress through the read-aloud of this book.

"Mrs. Pritchard's Story: Miss Zeldy's Message"

Pre-reading: **Let's read to find out** about the story Mrs. Pritchard tells Eben and why it is a Wonder.

Follow-up:

- Why does Mrs. Pritchard consider Miss Zeldy a Wonder? (She believes the doll called her back to this world.)

- Do you agree with Mrs. Pritchard that Miss Zeldy is a Wonder? Discuss.

- Choose a team to make a diorama of Mrs. Pritchard's home.

Write Away! Eben picked up his tablet and began to write at the end of Mrs. Pritchard's story. Write the entry you imagine Eben wrote.

Day Two: "Jeb Joins In"

Pre-reading: Ask volunteers to read their "Eben entries" from yesterday's Write Away! assignment. Read the title of the chapter. **Let's read to find out** what the boys find.

Follow-up:

- Jeb does not agree with Eben about Mrs. Saylor's "wonders." Why? (Jeb says the jewelry is worth more than anything else in Sassafras Springs.)

- Do you agree with Eben or with Jeb about Mrs. Saylor's "wonders"? Discuss.

- Choose a team to make a diorama of Mrs. Saylor's home.

- Why do you think Cully Pone considers his bookcase a Wonder?

"Cully Pone's Story: The Rainmaker's Revenge"

Pre-reading: **Let's read to find out** about Cully Pone's bookcase.

Follow-up:

- How would you describe Cully Pone's Wonder?

- Choose a team to make a diorama of Cully Pone's shack.

Write Away! Eben wrote in his tablet at the end of Cully Pone's story. What do you imagine he wrote? Write the entry as if you were Eben.

Day Three: "Disappointments"

Pre-reading: **Let's read to find out** why this chapter is titled, "Disappointments."

Follow-up:

- What does the title mean? (Eben is disappointed with Jeb.)

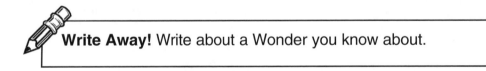

Write Away! Eben and Jeb are best friends, but they don't share all the same views. Do you have a good friend like this? Explain.

Day Three Continued: "Difficulties and Discoveries"

Pre-reading: At the end of the last chapter, Eben and Sal were going on a search. **Let's read to find out** why this chapter is titled, "Difficulties and Discoveries."

Follow-up:

- We meet Rae Ellen Hubbell in this chapter. What do you think of this character? What does Eben think of her?

- We also meet Violet Rowan. Contrast Eben's opinion of her with his opinion of Rae Ellen.

- We also meet Calvin Smiley. Describe his characteristics.

Write Away! Write about a Wonder you know about.

Note: In preparation for the read-aloud of the next chapter, find an instrumental rendition of "Amazing Grace."

"Calvin Smiley's Story: Amazing Grace"

Pre-reading: In the last chapter we learned about Calvin's saw. **Let's read to find out** about his story.

Follow-up:

- Play the recording "Amazing Grace."

- How is Eben's dad helping him with his task? (He is relieving him of his chores here and there throughout the week.)

- How does Aunt Pretty feel about this deal Eben's pa has struck with him? (She disapproves.)

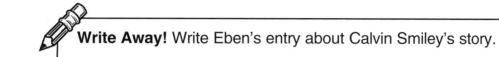

Write Away! Write Eben's entry about Calvin Smiley's story.

Day Four: "Smells and Spells"

Pre-reading: Ask: How many Wonders has Eben collected in three days? (Three.) How many days does he have left? (Four.) Do you think he will make his goal? (Not in seven days.) Read the title of the chapter. What do you think this chapter might be about? **Let's read to find out** about smells and spells.

Follow-up:

- In this chapter we meet a new character. Describe Junior Watkins. (Shorter and squatter than Eben; a school friend; a prankster.)

- What qualities does Eben mention a Wonder must have? (Natural, not manmade; something important.)

- What is the "stink" of the chapter title? (Eben's refusal to count the rotten eggs as a Wonder causes a stink with Junior. Also, rotten eggs stink.)

- We learn more about Violet Rowan. Describe her characteristics. (Smart, tall, bright blue eyes, older than Eben, appealing to Eben.)

- Choose a team to make a diorama of the Rowans' home.

"Eulie Rowan's Story: The Four-Legged Haint"

Pre-reading: In the last chapter we met Eulie and went into her home with Eben. Ask: What did she call her Wonder? (A table.) Read the title of the chapter. Ask: Does anyone know what a *haint* is? (A ghost.) **Let's read to find out** what Eulie's story is.

Follow-up:

- What does *superstitious* mean? (Swayed by belief or practice resulting from ignorance or fear of the unknown; trust in magic, chance, or a false conception of causation.)

- What does *suspicious* mean? (Distrustful.)

- If you lived in Sassafras Springs, do you think you would be more superstitious or suspicious?

- Look up the origin of the saying "Take it with a grain of salt." (Don't believe the story entirely.)

- Be sure to note the author's reference to the table in the Up Close and Personal piece following this read-aloud plan.

- What do you think Aunt Pretty was thinking about?

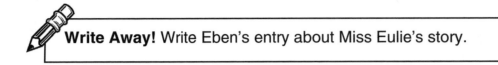

Write Away! Write Eben's entry about Miss Eulie's story.

Day Five: "Into the Woods"

Pre-reading: It's Sunday in Sassafras Springs. **Let's read to find out** how Eben spends his day.

Follow-up:

- We meet Coogie in this chapter. Do you know anyone like Coogie? Discuss.

- What is a *chigger*? (A six-legged mite that sucks blood and causes irritation.)

- Eben calls the outhouse a calamity. What is a *calamity*? (Some thing or event that causes deep distress or misery.)

"Coogie Jackson's Story: Flight from Georgia"

Pre-reading: In the last chapter we met Coogie. **Let's read to find out** his story.

Follow-up:

- Discuss how Eben treats Rae Ellen.

- Do you think Rae Ellen's story will be Eben's fifth Wonder?

Write Away! Write a conversation between Coogie and the other kids after they leave Eben in the outhouse.

"Rae Ellen's Story: Dark Seas"

Pre-reading: In this chapter we finally learn about Rae Ellen's "Wonderful." **Let's read to find out** her story.

Follow-up:

- Do you agree with Eben that Rae Ellen's story is a Wonder?

- Do you have time, patience, and parent volunteers? Make a ship in a bottle!

Write Away! Write Eben's entry about Rae Ellen's story.

Days Six and Seven: "I Start Again"

Pre-reading: Read the title of the chapter. Ask: What do you think it means? **Let's read to find out.**

Follow-up:

- Discuss the boys' experiences with townspeople's wonders.

> **Write Away!** Mayor Peevey says, "Sometimes you can have a Wonder right under your nose, but if you don't know the meaning of it, it's worthless." What do you think Mayor Peevey means by this?

"Mayor Peevey's Story: Song of the Loom"

Pre-reading: **Let's read to find out** about the cloth with BUDDY woven across it.

Follow-up:

- Have you ever done something that might surprise people if they found out about it?

> **Write Away!** Mayor Peevey says, "There are some things you can't hide, so you might as well be honest." Write about that.

> **Write Away!** Tell a parent about Mayor Peevey. Interview one of your parents about something he or she did as a child and learned from. Write about it.

Day Eight: "A Setback and a Surprise"

Pre-reading: Ask: What is a setback? (Defeat; reverse.) What do you think the setback might be for Eben? **Let's read to find out.**

Follow-up:

- Do you think Eben has come upon his seventh Wonder?

- What do you think will happen next?

> **Write Away!** Interview someone who might have a Wonder to tell you about. Write about it on your Eben tablet.

Uncle Alf's Story: "Graven Images"

Pre-reading: Ask: What is a graven image? (Idol; an item of worship, usually carved from wood or stone.) What do you think Uncle Alf's story might be? **Let's read to find out**.

Follow-up:

- Do you think Eben will leave Sassafras Springs someday? Discuss.

- Uncle Alf says, "[N]ow that you've found seven Wonders, I'll bet you'll be noticing new ones every day." What do you think he means? (Eben will come to appreciate Sassafras Springs.)

- What are the things that Eben appreciates but may take for granted? (Pa's kind and wise manner; Aunt Pretty's great cooking; a solid and stable home; a true friend; Sal.)

> **Write Away!** Eben says to Uncle Alf, "I was only looking for big things, but a small thing can be a prize too." Explain what he means.

Day Nine: "Change of Plans"

Pre-reading: Ask: What do you think the title of this chapter means? (A change of plans for Eben.) **Let's read to find out**.

Follow-up:

- Eben is off to St. Louis. What do you think that will be like for him?

"The Beginning"

Pre-reading: Ask: What do you think the title of this chapter means? (A start for Eben exploring the world.) **Let's read to find out**.

Follow-up:

- What have we learned about Eben and Sassafras Springs from this last chapter? (Eben is ready for his adventure; the town supports and is happy for Eben.)

- Eben is different at the end of the story from what he was like when we met him at the beginning of the book. How has he changed?

- How would you describe a Wonder after reading about Eben and Sassafras Springs?

- What is wonder-ful about Sassafras Springs?

Write Away! What is wonder-ful about your town, school, or neighborhood?

Notes:

Notes:

Up Close and Personal · · · · · · · · · ·

A Note from the Author, Betty G. Birney

Where the idea for the book came from . . .

THE SEVEN WONDERS OF SASSAFRAS SPRINGS, a book about a Missouri boy growing in the country, began with two Missouri girls in the city. My sister, Janet, and I lived in the St. Louis suburbs, but we spent a lot of time at my grandparents' house in the city. Over the years, we were entertained, captivated, and delighted by the stories Grandma told us about growing up on a farm in Lonedell, Missouri around the turn of the last century.

While some children might object to hearing the same stories being repeated, Janet and I actually begged our grandmother to tell hers again and again. "Tell us about the time you were riding your horse and got caught in the quicksand," we'd ask. That was our favorite. We also thrilled to hear how the baby she heard crying in the woods turned out to be a panther! And there was the eerie but true tale of the table that haunted a graveyard. (That one made it into the book.)

These stories were firmly tucked away in my brain but didn't come to the fore until many years later. At an early age, my son, Walshe, announced his intentions to travel the planet, so I wasn't surprised to find him engrossed in a book about the seven ancient wonders of the world. That sight triggered the idea of a boy who longs to visit exotic places but must first discover the wonders in his own rural town. Grandma's stories seemed to call out, "Write us!" so I combined my son's longing to travel with the rural Missouri setting I imagined from Grandma's tales and the book was born.

I worked on the book on and off for years and when it was finally published, my son was spending his junior year of college in far-off Thessaloniki, Greece. Somehow, I wasn't surprised.

For more information on Betty G. Birney, visit her Web site at http://bettybirney.com.

Title	. . . . THE JOURNEY THAT SAVED CURIOUS GEORGE
Author	. . . . Louise Borden
Illustrator	. . . . Allan Drummond
Publisher	. . . . Houghton Mifflin
Copyright Date	 2005
Ages	. . . . 9 and up
Read-Aloud Time	. . . . 15 minutes
Read-Aloud Sessions	 2
Themes	. . . . Nazi invasion of Paris, refugees, biography, time line

This picture book tells the true story of the wartime escape on bicycle of Margret and H. A. Rey from the Nazi invasion of Paris in June 1940, with the manuscript that would become CURIOUS GEORGE tucked safely in the few belongings they carried with them.

Note: The maps found on the inside covers of the book will be useful in the read-aloud of this book. You may also want to have available a map that shows France, Spain, and Portugal.

Have copies of Curious George titles available for listeners to peruse.

PRE-READING FOCUS: Hold up a Curious George book. Ask: Who is this? (Curious George.) How many of you have read Curious George books or had them read to you? Talk about the character and his nature. Show the cover of Borden's book. Read the title and subtitle of the book. Note that the book tells a true story about the team that created Curious George and how there almost wasn't a CURIOUS GEORGE for us to read.

"Two Artists: Part I"

Pre-reading: You've heard about Curious George. Have you ever heard about a monkey named Fifi? **Let's read to find out** about the Reys' true adventure, which also involved a monkey named Fifi.

While Reading:

• Show the photographs and pictures as you read along.

Follow-up:

• Review what life was like for this creative couple.

• The Reys' life was about to change as history moved forward. Note that the Reys were Jewish. Review the history of the time period.

• Begin a time line of the Reys' lives. Consider adding in significant events from the history of that time.

> **Write Away!** What do you like about the Curious George books? Give details and use examples from the stories.

> **Write Away!** Write about what you have learned thus far about the Reys.

"Escape From Paris: Part II"

Pre-reading: **Let's read to find out** about the Reys' escape from danger with their treasured manuscripts safe in the basket of the bikes they were riding.

While Reading:

- Show the photographs and pictures as you read along.

- Trace their path to safety on the map.

- Note how fortunate the Reys were to escape.

Follow-up:

- What is a refugee? (A person who flees a country or authority to escape danger or persecution.)

- Contrast the Reys' early life with their life in 1940.

- Read "After the Escape". Discuss.

- Complete the time line.

- Read CURIOUS GEORGE.

- If time allows, read WHITEBLACK THE PENGUIN.

> **Write Away!** Read about June 14, 1940, a terrible day in the history of Paris, France. Write about what you find out.

> **Write Away!** Write a book report about one of the Curious George books!

Write Away! Why do you think Curious George is still so popular after all these years?

For another book about World War II, see the read-aloud plan for THE FLAG WITH FIFTY-SIX STARS: A GIFT FROM THE SURVIVORS OF MAUTHAUSEN, written by Susan Goldman Rubin and illustrated by Bill Farnsworth (Holiday House). See also the Book Notes section of this resource for additional suggestions.

For other biographies suitable for fifth and sixth graders, refer to the Book Notes section of this resource.

<u>Notes:</u>

Up Close and Personal

A Note from the Author, Louise Borden

Where the idea for the book came from . . .

In 1995 I read a few sentences in an article in *Publishers Weekly* stating that H. A. and Margret Rey fled from Paris on bicycles in June 1940 carrying with them the original manuscript for CURIOUS GEORGE, I immediately pictured the Reys in a sea of refugees. I already knew about the great exodus from wartime Paris because years ago, while in college, I had studied this time period of World War II (I majored in history). Also, I had just finished writing a book called THE LITTLE SHIPS which takes place in June 1940.

On that day in 1995, I didn't know anything about Margret and Hans Rey. I didn't even know what the H. and the A. stood for in H. A. Rey. I didn't know that the Reys both had been born in Hamburg, or that they later lived in Brazil. But I did have a strong image of them as refugees on bicycles leaving in the great exodus, and I found that image amazing. This was the beginning of my own journey of researching and writing the book—a journey that would take seven years and lead me on many adventures.

Researching the book . . .

Much of my research was groundbreaking. First I located the name of the hotel where the Reys lived in Paris. I visited the hotel several times and talked to the present owner, Jean Max Hurand, who was ten years old when the Germans took control of Paris. He fled with his parents by car and headed south, as millions of others did.

I also found the Chateau Feuga, a place where the Reys stayed over 60 years ago. I learned about the Chateau by reading an old newspaper article from the 1950's in which Hans mentioned the house in an interview. He stated that he set up a studio and worked on the art for CURIOUS GEORGE while living at the chateau. When I later found letters with Chateau Feuga as the return address in the Rey archives at the de Grummond Collection in Mississippi, I began to gather more clues that I could use to locate this house. I was dusting off history and a long ago story full of Rey adventures. I had to find the clues and piece the story together—a story no one else had had the energy to look for or the curiosity to tell. I had to believe in myself and in my ability to find answers to questions.

Adventures along the way to publishing the book . . .

I had so many adventures during my research travels! These included having my suitcase lost by the airlines, so that on one trip, like the Reys, all I had with me was my backpack—and my curiosity and perseverance. Yes, I can write this book, I had to tell myself many times. Many friends were my encouragers along the way. I even called up my high school French teacher (now 80 years old) and she helped me translate many letters as I could read only about half of the diaries and letters.

Interest, curiosity, connection . . .

I have long held an interest in World War II. I was born in 1949 in the shadow of the war that had just ended. My dad served in the Pacific as a weatherman on a reconnaissance plane in the Air Force. My uncle was killed in World War II. So I grew up with those stories and also an interest in the countries of Europe that began when I was in elementary school. As a kid, I loved Social Studies and maps. Now, when I open the book and see the endpaper with the wonderful map drawn by Allan Drummond, I'm thrilled that I was able to find the pieces of this long ago journey and share them with fans and readers of CURIOUS GEORGE books. I feel a deep kinship with the Reys even though they are no longer living because, like Hans and Margret, I love creating books for children. It is my lifework, just as it was theirs.

Find subjects that interest you, use your own curiosity, and you will be able to create stories that will fascinate others.

For more about Louise Borden and her books, including "the stories behind the stories," visit her Web site at http://www.louiseborden.com/index2.html.

For more books by Louise Borden recommended in this volume, refer to the author index. See also references to other books by Borden in other volumes of the Children's Book Corner series.

Title	LOCOMOTION
Author	Jacqueline Woodson
Publisher	G. P. Putnam's Sons
Copyright Date	2003
Ages	10 and up
Read-Aloud Time	10 minutes
Read-Aloud Sessions	10
Themes	Poetry, foster homes, loss, friendship, school

These poems tell the heart-wrenching story of an 11-year-old boy navigating through the tragedy of his parents' death due to a fire in their apartment several years previously. Through the poems he writes in a variety of forms over the course of a year, Lonnie moves from despair to hope.

Note: Prepare to have a poetry notebook to distribute to each listener in the third session of the read-aloud of this book. Children will use these notebooks to experiment with poetry of their own. This notebook can be a small, simple journal.

Have a variety of poetry books available for listeners to browse and borrow throughout the read-aloud of this book. For a list of poetry anthologies and collections suitable for fifth and sixth graders, refer to the Tips and Techniques section of this resource. See also the list of recommended teacher resources, which will be useful in exploring poetry forms.

Note the images of nature, and especially the sky, throughout the reading of this book. Keep a running list of these images on chart paper or the chalkboard, available for listeners to see and add to as you progress through the book.

> **PRE-READING FOCUS:** Introducing the book: Show the cover and read the title. Note the blurriness of the character on the photo. Ask: What do the cover and title of this book bring to mind? (Movement.) What does the word *locomotion* mean? (The act of moving from place to place.) Take a closer look at the photos. What is the boy doing in the third photo? (Hugging himself.) Turn to the back cover and note the photograph there. Ask: What might this book be about? Note that this story is told through poems. Discuss what that means and why the author might have chosen this format. Ask listeners to pay attention to how a novel in verse differs from a prose novel. Read the opening poem, found before the title page. Ask: Have you ever heard of the poet, Lonnie C. Motion? You are about to.

"Poem Book," "Roof," "Line Break Poem," "Memory," "Mama," "Lili," and "First"

> *Pre-reading:* **Let's read to find out** who the main character is, who is telling the story, and why the story is written in poems.

While Reading:

- After reading "Poem Book," ask: What do we know from this opening poem? (Main character is Lonnie, age 11; Miss Edna yells at him often; Ms. Marcus encourages him to write down what's going on in his mind before he loses it; Lonnie seems to get in trouble often.)

- Lonnie creates a powerful image in this poem. What is it? (The ideas in his head are like a candle that goes out when Miss Edna yells at him to be quiet. He continues the image with the string of smoke.)

- What are *line breaks*? (Where a poem is broken up to form lines.) We'll find out more about line breaks from Lonnie soon.

- Who do you think Miss Edna and Ms. Marcus are?

- Read "Roof."

- What do we know from this poem? (Lonnie's parents are deceased.)

- Now who do you think Miss Edna is? (Foster parent.)

- Read "Line Break Poem," "Memory," "Mama," and "Lili."

- Discuss what we have learned about Lonnie. (He has a younger sister named Lili. He was close to his mother.)

- Do you get the feeling Lili is still near? (No.)

- How do you think Lonnie felt when he was in the drugstore? Discuss the reactions of the adults with whom he came in contact. (Suspicious, impatient, annoyed.)

- Discuss the tone of Lonnie's poems. (Somber.)

- Read "First." What do we know from this poem? (Lonnie's spirit is broken.) Discuss.

Follow-up:

- What do you think this story is about? What is the *conflict*? (Lonnie's search for healing from his loss.) Discuss. Note that this story is mainly about a character's internal conflict as opposed to an external conflict. Ask: Is there any other conflict in this story? (Yes; the conflict between Lonnie and Miss Edna.) Is this an internal or external conflict? (External.) Ask for examples of internal and external conflicts from other books you have read aloud to the group or that they have read independently.

Write Away! Do you like stories told in poems? What do you like or not like about them? Explain, using examples.

"Commercial Break," "Haiku," "Group Home Before Miss Edna's House," "Halloween Poem," "Parent's Poem," and "Sonnet Poem"

Pre-reading: What characters are you curious about? Today we will learn more about Lonnie and his life through the poems that he writes. **Let's read to find out** more about Lonnie and Ms. Marcus.

While Reading:

- After reading "Commercial Break," show the pages on which it is written. Note that this segment is written in prose, not in verse. Discuss how it is different. (There are full sentences and paragraphs.) Note the title. Ask: Why do you think the author chose to do this?

- What do we know from this segment? (Lonnie is African American; Ms. Marcus is his favorite teacher in the world; Ms. Marcus's remark discourages him)

- Discuss Lonnie's reaction to Ms. Marcus's comments.

- What else have we learned in this segment? (Miss Edna's couch is scratchy; what Lonnie longs for.)

- Do you think Ms. Marcus missed what Lonnie was trying to say?

Follow-up:

- Read "Haiku."

  - Explain what haiku is. (Three lines; 5–7–5 syllables in each line; usually about nature).

  - Is Lonnie's poem haiku? (Lonnie's poem follows the form but it is not about nature.)

  - What do we know from this poem? (Lonnie's having a bad day.)

- Read "Group Home Before Miss Edna's House."

  - Discuss what we have learned about Lonnie. (He lived in a group home before moving to Miss Edna's, and it was not a pleasant experience.)

  - Discuss the details of the group home that Lonnie gives us. (Bullies; hand-me-down clothing, beat-up books, unappetizing food; lots of rules; loud.)

  - What else is revealed in this poem? (Lonnie does not know where Lili is.)

- What is a Throwaway Boy?

- Read "Halloween."

  - In an earlier poem we learn that Lonnie does not steal. Here we learn that he feels it isn't right to snatch a younger child's trick or treat bag. Ask: What do we know about Lonnie from these details? (Lonnie has values and morals.) Discuss.

- Read "Parents Poem."

  - What have we learned in this poem? (Lonnie's parents died in a fire. He still has vivid, happy memories of his family. His dad referred to him as Loco-motion.)

- Lonnie sometimes doesn't tell the details of what happened to his parents to others. Discuss.

- Refer back to the first poem in the book. Note the images of fire, candle, and smoke.

- Read "Sonnet."

  - What do we know about sonnets from Lonnie's poem? (It rhymes; it's about love; it comes from the word *sonetto* which means "little song.")

  - Note that Ms. Marcus tells Lonnie you have to "write things a lot of times before they come out sounding the right way."

  - Teach the sonnet form.

  - Study Lonnie's sonnet.

> **Write Away!** Lonnie sometimes doesn't tell the details of what happened to his parents. Have you ever had an experience in which you found it was easier to shrug it off with a simple explanation rather than go into all the details? Tell about it.

> **Write Away!** Try writing a sonnet.

Note: In preparation for the read-aloud of the next set of poems, have a recording of the song, "Come on, Baby, Do the Locomotion" to play for listeners.

Pass out poetry notebooks at the end of this read-aloud session.

"How I Got My Name," "Describe Somebody," "Epistle Poem," "Roof Poem II," "Me, Eric, Lamont & Angel;" and "Failing"

Pre-reading: Play the recording of "Come on, Baby, Do the Locomotion." **Let's read to find out** about how Lonnie got his name.

While Reading:

- Read through "Describe Somebody." Ask: Why do you think Ms. Marcus is Lonnie's favorite teacher?

- Pass out poetry notebooks.

- Read "Epistle Poem."

    - To whom is this poem addressed? (His dad.)

    - What do we know from reading this poem? (Lonnie's having a bad day.)

- Read "Roof Poem II" and "Me, Eric, Lamont & Angel." Discuss what we have learned about Lonnie's friends from this poem and "Describe Somebody." (Eric is mean, can sing beautifully; Lamont's "just regular" and can draw well; Angel's chubby, has light brown hair, and is good at science.)

    - Would you say these boys are really friends? Discuss.

- Read "Failing." This poem is both about math and not about math. Here we learn that Lonnie feels that sometimes people lie. To what or whom might he be referring? Discuss.

Follow-up:

- Discuss the purpose of the poetry notebooks and encourage children to use them to experiment with writing different kinds of poems about things they are thinking or feeling, as Lonnie does, so their thoughts don't go up in smoke like Lonnie's candle in the first poem we read.

Write Away! Write an occasional poem.

"New Boy," "December 9th," "List Poem," "Late Afternoon in Halsey Street Park," Pigeon," "Sometimes Poem," "War Poem" and "Georgia"

***Pre-reading:* Let's read to find out** about how Lonnie came to be in a foster home.

While Reading:

- Read through "December 9th." Discuss what we have learned in this poem. (Lonnie was seven when the fire occurred; he and Lili were passed around for a while before they landed in group homes and foster care.)

    - What is the setting of this story? (City) Cite clues.

- Read "List Poem," "Late Afternoon in Halsey Street Park," and "Pigeon."

- Read "Pigeon" without pausing (as much as possible) to emphasize the lack of punctuation.

    - What do you notice about "Pigeon"? (There is no punctuation.) This is known as stream of consciousness and makes us feel as if we are in the character's thoughts. Discuss.

- What other time in the story did we read about pigeons? (When Lonnie was remembering Lili as a baby in the poem, "Memory.")

- Read "Sometimes Poem"

  - We see a different side of Miss Edna here. Discuss.

- Read "War Poem" and "Georgia"

- Note how Lonnie observes the things that happen around him. Discuss.

- Ask for reactions to "War Poem" and its message.

- Do you know anyone fighting a war? Discuss.

- What war is Lonnie fighting? (An internal one.)

> **Write Away!** Write in your poetry notebook.

"New Boy Poem II," "Tuesday," "Visiting," "Just Nothing Poem," and "God Poem"

Pre-reading: Read the title, "New Boy Poem II." Ask: What do you think this poem is about? (The new boy in school, from the South.) Review what we know about him. Make note of how the author, through Lonnie, describes him so that we have a picture of this boy in our minds. **Let's read to find out** more about Clyde.

While Reading:

- After reading "New Boy Poem II" discuss what causes Lonnie to become emotional. (Clyde's sister reminds him of Lili. The relationship between the new boy and his sister reminds him of his relationship with Lili.)

- Read "Tuesday."

- Why does Lonnie like to write? (It helps him remember his family.) Discuss.

- Why do you think Lonnie doesn't tell Eric what he is doing? (Eric is not a true friend.) Discuss.

- Read "Visiting"

- Discuss.

- Read "Just Nothing Poem" and "God Poem."

- Lonnie is upset with Ms. Marcus. His mood is dark. Why is Lonnie so angry? (He has been asked to write a poem about his family.) Discuss.

- This is the second time Ms. Marcus does something that upsets Lonnie. Sometimes people do things they don't realize are hurtful to others. Discuss.

> **Write Away!** Lonnie is upset when he is told to write about his family. Have you ever been asked to write about something that was hard for you to face? Tell about it.

> **Write Away!** Write in your poetry notebook.

"All of a Sudden, The Poem," "Hey Dog," "Occasional Poem," "Haiku Poem" and "Poetry Poem"

Pre-reading: **Let's read to find out** how things are going for Lonnie.

Follow-up:

- Discuss revision.

> **Write Away!** Write an occasional poem.

In preparation for the next read-aloud session, have a book or two of Richard Wright and Langston Hughes's poetry on hand, or find a poem or two by these poets in an anthology. See the Tips and Techniques section of this resource for suggested anthologies.

"Eric Poem," "Lamont," "Hip Hop Rules the World," "Photographs," "New Boy Poem III," and "Happiness Poem"

Pre-reading: Read the title, "Eric Poem." Ask: What do you think this poem is about? Review what we know about Eric. **Let's read to find out** what Lonnie writes about Eric.

- Read "Eric Poem."

- After reading the poem, discuss what Ms. Marcus tells the class.

- Discuss what listeners know about sickle cell anemia. Review what Ms. Marcus has told the class members.

  – How does Lonnie feel? (Upset.)

- Read "Lamont."

  – Why do you think Lamont is angry? (He's upset about Eric.)

- Discuss what haiku and free verse poetry is.

- Read a Richard Wright haiku to the class.

- Read "Hip Hop Rules the World."

    – Note that the author has lightened the mood a bit with "Hip Hop." Why do you think she does this? Discuss.

- Read "Photographs," "New Boy Poem III," and "Happiness Poem."

> **Write Away!** Learn a few facts about sickle cell anemia that were not mentioned in the book. Write them down. Be prepared to share the facts with the group.

> **Write Away!** Write in your poetry notebook.

"Birth," "Lili's New Mama's House," "Church," "New Boy Poem IV," "Teacher of the Year," and "Easter Sunday"

Pre-reading: **Let's read to find out** more of Lonnie's memories.

While Reading:

- Read "Birth." Before reading "Lili's New Mama's House," ask listeners to close their eyes and think about what the words make them see.

    – Discuss the imagery in this poem.

- Read "Church."

    – Discuss what Lonnie writes on his hand and what it might mean.

- Read "New Boy Poem IV" and "Teacher of the Year."

    – What do you think the newsman thought of the poem? How do you know?

- Read "Easter Sunday."

> **Write Away!** Write in your poetry notebook.

"Rodney," "Epitaph Poem," "Firefly," "The Fire," and "Almost Summer Sky"

Pre-reading: Ask: Who is Rodney? (Miss Edna's son.) **Let's read to find out** why Lonnie's poem is titled "Rodney."

Follow-up:

- Read "Rodney."

    - How does Lonnie feel? (He feels wanted; he feels part of a family.) Discuss.

- Read "Epitaph Poem."

    - What is an *epitaph*? (A brief statement commemorating a deceased person.)

    - How does this poem about his mother differ from some of the other poems Lonnie has written? (It seems to indicate more acceptance of what has happened.)

- Read "Firefly," "The Fire," and "Almost Summer Sky."

    - How does Lonnie sound in these poems? (Hopeful.)

    - Who seems to be making a big difference in Lonnie's life? (Rodney.) Why? (He is accepting and affirming. He calls Lonnie his brother.) Discuss.

    - Note the change of seasons. Note the change in Lonnie. Do you think the author has gone from fall to spring on purpose?

    - Look over the list of nature images. Note how they have evolved. Compare to Lonnie's growth through the book. Do this again at the end of the book.

> **Write Away!** Write a nature poem.

"Clyde Poem I: Down South," "First Day of School," "Dear God," "LeTenya II," and "June"

Pre-reading: Read the title of "Clyde Poem I: Down South." Ask: Who is Clyde? (The new boy.) What do you notice about the title of this poem? (New Boy has become Clyde.) **Let's read to find out** how things are going for Lonnie.

Follow-up:

- How does Lonnie feel at the end of the story? Discuss.

- Compare the opening poem of the book with this poem. Note the differences in mood and tone.

- Review the nature images you have collected from this story.

- Which type of poems do you seem to like best?

- Delve into the poetry forms used in this book.

- Explore the poems in this book by theme or subject. For example, review all the poems about the new boy, Clyde. Or, review all the epistle poems, sonnets, rhyming poems, haiku, etc., and discuss why the author may have chosen to use the form she did for the subject treated in the poem.

- Re-read the poem by Lonnie found before the title page. Discuss the author's placement of this poem by a fictional character here.

Write Away! Write in your poetry notebook.

Notes:

Up Close and Personal

A Note from Jacqueline Woodson

How the book came to be . . .

I started writing Locomotion because I wanted to challenge myself – to see if I could write a book that only had poems in it. As the poems started flowing, I realized I wasn't just writing a collection of poetry, I was writing a novel and the main character was a young boy.

Since I never outline when I write, I never know where a book is going. The first poem I wrote in LOCOMOTION was "Pigeon Poem." That ended up being toward the middle of the book instead of at the opening. The last poem I wrote was "Clyde Poem 1: Down South." I had originally thought there'd be only one poem about the new boy, Clyde, but then his character stayed in my head and I wanted to know more and more about him. By the end of writing LOCOMOTION, I liked Clyde as much as I liked Lonnie.

Where the characters came from . . .

People always ask if my books are autobiographical. To some extent, they are. Locomotion—Lonnie—is a lot like I was in the fifth grade. I loved writing; I was always watching people and thinking about things. But Clyde is also like me. I spent a lot of my childhood in South Carolina and I know what it feels like to walk into the room and be "the new kid."

A writing tip . . .

Write with your heart. Tell the story that matters to YOU and don't be afraid of what others may think or say about it. Everybody has a story. Ask yourself: *What is mine?*

Jacqueline Woodson won both a Newbery Honor (for SHOW WAY, illustrated by Hudson Talbott; see the Book Notes section of this resource) and the Margaret A. Edwards Award for lifetime contribution in writing for young adults, announced at the 2006 ALA midwinter conference. For more information about Jacqueline Woodson's award-winning collection of books, visit her Web site at www.jacquelinewoodson.com.

Notes:

Cover of ENCYCLOPEDIA PREHISTORICA: DINOSAURS: THE DEFINITIVE POP-UP.
Copyright © 2005 by Robert Sabuda and Matthew Reinhart. Candlewick Press, Inc.

Title	ENCYCLOPEDIA PREHISTORICA: DINOSAURS
Author/Illustrator	Robert Sabuda and Matthew Reinhart
Publisher	Candlewick
Copyright Date	2005
Ages	7 and up
Read-Aloud Time	10 minutes
Read-Aloud Sessions	1
Themes	Dinosaurs, pop-ups

Sabuda is the king of pop-ups. From fantasies (ALICE'S ADVENTURES IN WONDERLAND; THE WONDERFUL WIZARD OF OZ) to Christmas wonders (A WINTER'S TALE; THE TWELVE DAYS OF CHRISTMAS; THE NIGHT BEFORE CHRISTMAS) to tributes (AMERICA THE BEAUTIFUL), his creations are amazing. Sabuda calls opening a pop-up the "wow moment." He's a paper engineer with a vision. ENCYCLOPEDIA PREHISTORICA: DINOSAURS not only presents wondrous moving paper models of beastly prehistoric creatures, but also offers an amazing number of little known facts about the featured dinosaurs. This book is simply a treat: "eye candy," as a preteen might say.

Note: If possible, have available other pop-up books created by Robert Sabuda to show to listeners.

PRE-READING FOCUS: Show the book. Ask: Why do you think this book is so fat? (It's a pop-up!) Read the title. Tickle listeners' interest by opening to one pop-up. Tell listeners that the creators, Robert Sabuda and Matthew Reinhart, and their assistants work with their hands, building paper models that not only pop up, but pop down. Demonstrate with a page from the book. Sabuda says this is the hard part but also the fun part of creating his books. He believes making something happen with your hands is satisfying and interesting work. Discuss. Ask: What other careers involve making something with your hands? Ask listeners what they know about dinosaurs. List facts on the board or easel. **Let's read to find out** other facts about these prehistoric animals.

WHILE READING: Read the information and enjoy the magnificent pop-ups. Don't forget the cute little ones tucked into the corners!

FOLLOW-UP DISCUSSION: List facts learned from this book. Add them to the list. Ask listeners to vote on which pop-up is their favorite! Ask: Do you think making pop-ups would be fun? Do you think it would be easy? Sabuda says he loves making pop-ups, but that it's hard. Why do you think he does it? Sabuda uses scissors and X-Acto knives more than computers. He begins with the words, or the *text* of the book. Then he sketches. Next he builds designs from card stock and uses tape to hold them together. Sabuda's goal is to design pop-ups that work in four dimensions—height, width, depth, and time. This last one may be the neatest of all—things move and change when you first open the page. Look again at a few of the pop-ups in the book. If you have other books by Sabuda, study the pop-ups he has created in them.

Write Away! Choose one of the dinosaurs depicted in Sabuda's book. Learn more about it. Write about what you find out.

Write Away! Learn more about Sabuda. Write about three interesting things you find out.

Write Away! Read about how to make pop-ups. (Several books are listed on Sabuda's Web site.) Make a pop-up and write out the directions. Be specific and clear.

Fascinate dinosaur aficionados even more with the outstanding biography, THE DINOSAURS OF WATERHOUSE HAWKINS, written by Barbara Kerley and illustrated by Brian Selznick (Scholastic), a Caldecott Honor book about the artist and sculptor who, in the mid-1800s, showed the world what a dinosaur looked like. See the read-aloud plan found in Children's Book Corner, Grades 1–2.

Up Close and Personal

A Note from Robert Sabuda

Where the idea for the book came from . . .

I've always been interested in dinosaurs and have been getting more and more requests to create pop-up books that can be used in the classroom.

DINOSAURS was written by Matthew Reinhart, and he did a great deal of the research for the book. One of the problems with researching dinosaurs is that the information we have about them is always changing. Who would have thought ten years ago that we would be talking about dinosaurs that have feathers?!

About pop-ups . . .

Making pop-ups is challenging! You never know if they'll work until you make them. With DINOSAURS, one of the greatest challenges was making sure that the dinosaurs moved correctly according to their anatomy.

If you're interested in making pop-ups or some other form of paper craft, there's no better time to start than now! I started making pop-ups when I was eight years old after seeing pop-up books at the dentist's office, and I am forever thankful that I did!

For more information about Robert Sabuda and his books, visit his Web site at http://robertsabuda.com/. Included on the site is an extensive list of books on how to make pop-ups, from easier to more challenging.

Tips and Techniques for Teachers and Librarians

Reading Aloud to Fifth and Sixth Graders: The Justification

A book should always be a celebration of life.—Leo Lionni, children's author

Teachable moments abound during read-aloud sessions. When a teacher or librarian reads with expression, pauses, considers, laughs out loud, or wells up with emotion, the power of the written word is demonstrated as essential reading behaviors are being modeled.

CHOOSING WHAT TO READ ALOUD

Your teaching time and your students' learning time are valuable. Choose books to read aloud that are outstanding examples of literature. Consult the list of awards bestowed on children's books and refer to the list of Web sites later in this section for handy references to the awards that interest you. Choose classics that have withstood the test of time as well as new books that blaze trails for today's youth. Read short stories (see "Shorties") newspapers, and magazines (see "Glossy Grabbers"). Build poetry pauses into every school day (see "Thirty-second Snapshots").

Introduce historical fiction, fantasy, biography, memoirs, and nonfiction, and you enrich students' knowledge and familiarity with the breadth of books available to them. Offer a perspective on other cultures, other times, feelings, ethics, morals, and you enable children to witness vicariously the strength of the human spirit. Through books, children visit other nations, view the world through a different set of eyes, and walk a while in another's shoes. By choosing to read aloud books that enhance and extend the curriculum, you deepen students' understanding of key concepts and of themselves while nurturing and developing an interest in reading.

You know your students, their needs, their abilities, and their interests. Consider the curriculum and long-range objectives. Choose to read aloud books that enhance your study of subject matter. Only you can determine if a book is suitable and age appropriate for your class or group, and if reading it aloud will be of value to your students. Take a few moments to familiarize yourself with a book in its entirety so you can choose read-aloud selections wisely.

Strategies for Reading Aloud

Preview books you intend to read aloud. Review content carefully so you can be confident that your selection augments your classroom study and that there is nothing in the book that may be unsuitable for your students. Reading a book before presenting it to children enables you to choose those books that best fit into your overall teaching plan: You will have an understanding of the overarching themes in the book, you will be equipped to generate discussion points, you can determine the pacing of the read-aloud, and you can plan for the length of time necessary to complete the book.

Begin read-alouds the first day of school. Establish a tradition and set expectations. Your behavior will give students the message that here is a place where books are honored and cherished; here is an adult who loves to read. Students will come to know that your classroom or library is a haven for those who love books and a nurturing environment for those who are reticent readers.

As you follow the read-aloud plans, note the three steps consistent in all of them. Preview the book with listeners. When reading longer works over a period of days, review what happened in the last chapter as a warm-up to each subsequent read-aloud session. Build on prior knowledge and make predictions before reading. Keep the pre-reading segment short. Read with expression. Note difficult vocabulary as you read. Encourage use of context to determine meaning. Question or comment throughout the read-aloud, but do so judiciously. Don't lose the thread or momentum of the chapter or the book. In the follow-up to fiction, consider the story elements, the author's techniques, the pacing of the story. With nonfiction, discuss the author's point of view, consider the author's "expert" status, and explore the slant or angle from which the author chose to present the material. What facts were offered, and what was not discussed?

For simple but effective read-aloud techniques, refer to the Parent Pull-Out Pages.

Where to Read Aloud

Create an inviting read-aloud area. Bring in an area rug, a table lamp, a comfy chair. If feasible, gather listeners around you rather than having them sit at their desks during read-aloud sessions. Make reading and books valued and special in your learning space.

When to Read Aloud

Each and every day! There are so many opportunities to bring children and the written word together. Read to the group as part of your opening exercises. This offers a calming, focusing, affirming activity with which to begin the instructional day. Upon the conclusion of a difficult lesson that stretched your students' brain power, read a poem, a joke, or a riddle. (For recommended poetry on all sorts of topics, see the anthologies and collections listed elsewhere in this section.) Following lunch, read a pertinent news clip or magazine article to reconnect your students to the instructional setting, initiate discussion, or reinforce a current unit of study. Choose a specific time of the day that suits you and your students to read daily from riveting novels, nonfiction accounts, and picture books. Read aloud for the purpose of pure pleasure and to connect to curricular study. (See the Book Notes section of this resource for suggestions cross-referenced by content area subjects.) End the day by reading something warm and fuzzy, lighthearted and whimsical, action-packed, or hilarious. Send them out the door eager to hear more of the story tomorrow.

Picture Books for Preteens?!?: Reading Aloud to Older Children

There are shelves crammed with thought-provoking, multifaceted picture books written especially for older children. The fact that these books happen to be lustrous and glossy, brimming with illustrations that augment the text, only makes them more valuable and appealing to preteens navigating complex concepts.

Picture books designed for older students feature longer text, with elaborate story lines in fiction and denser concept loads in nonfiction. It is the engaging art that enhances the reader's comprehension of the material. Although illustrated, the text could stand alone (which distinguishes these books from those written primarily for the primaries, in which the simple text and the illustrations are dependent upon one another).

Enhance, enrich, and extend curricular study with picture books related to the themes of the content area units you present. In 15 minutes or less, the time it takes to read one of these books aloud, you can deepen an understanding of a concept. Because well-executed picture books engage multiple senses, they make even the driest subject appealing. How can a child resist a clearly drawn map in full color, an illustrated explanation of an abstract theory, or a vivid pictorial portrayal of a figure in history? When you want to ease a stressful situation, what's better than an uproarious picture book? The best of illustrated books make classroom study lively, accessible, and memorable. Lucky for kids, and lucky for adults who have their audience mesmerized from page one

So invest 15 minutes. Indulge your listeners' senses; tempt preteens with a luscious treat-of-a-book that's certain to make a tough subject easier to digest. Sit back, gather your students in, and clinch their comprehension of a difficult concept with a picture book!

In addition to the Read-Aloud Plans, consult the Book Notes section of this resource for recommendations of nonfiction picture books suitable for upper elementary grade students. Conveniently listed by subject according to general content area themes, books are briefly summarized, and bibliographical information is provided. In addition, subject, title, author, and illustrator indexes are included at the back of this resource.

Thirty-Second Snapshots: Otherwise Known As Poetry Pauses

Poetry should be read every single day of the year, at all times, for all times.
—Lee Bennett Hopkins

When the troops are restless, when you're shifting gears from one subject to the next, when you need your tired 23 to snap-to, pull a poem out of your pocket. Delight your students with *poetry pauses* throughout the day, week, month, and year when they least expect it, when they've come to anticipate it, or for closure on a topic. And don't forget those times when you need to punch up your own fading energy. Strive for five a week. Short, sweet, and neat, the just-right poem is powerful and pretty. Deep or witty, poetry can't be beat. Get to know a few poetry collections, and you're on your way. You've got rhythm at your fingertips and words dancing from your lips. Guaranteed.

Hint: As you collect poetry books, use sticky notes to mark poems that relate to units of study, celebrate seasons, explore common issues, or are simply perky pieces that just plain appeal to you. When you need to locate that poem, you'll have no trouble putting your finger on the perfect verse. *Another idea:* Jot down on lesson plans or in your notes the book titles and page numbers of poems that complement lessons or seasons of the year. Then offer the kids 30-second snapshots to cap a concept or jump-start their afternoon.

Recommended Poetry Collections

- A JAR OF TINY STARS: POEMS BY NCTE AWARD-WINNING POETS, edited by Bernice E. Cullinan and illustrated by Andi MacLeod, with portraits by Marc Nadel (Wordsong/Boyds Mills Press); poems by 10 award-winning poets, field-tested and chosen as favorites by more than 3,500 children across the United States; includes a brief biography of each of the featured poets and their reflections on poetry.

A JAR OF TINY STARS: POEMS BY NCTE AWARD-WINNING POETS, by Bernice E. Cullinan, illustrated by Andi MacLeod. Copyright © 1996. Published by Wordsong, an imprint of Boyds Mills Press. Reprinted by permission.

- A FAMILY OF POEMS: MY FAVORITE POETRY FOR CHILDREN, selected by Caroline Kennedy with illustrations by Jon J. Muth (Hyperion). Selecting from poems her family enjoyed when she was a child, Kennedy has arranged classic gems into child-centered categories, including silly, seasonal, adventure, and bedtime. At the back of the book, foreign poems that were translated in the body of the book appear in their original languages. Accompanied by gorgeous paintings, this collection of poems written by e. e. cummings, Marianne Moore, Emily Dickinson, William Wordsworth, Robert Frost, William Carlos Williams, Richard Wilbur, and others explores emotions, values, and everyday experiences.

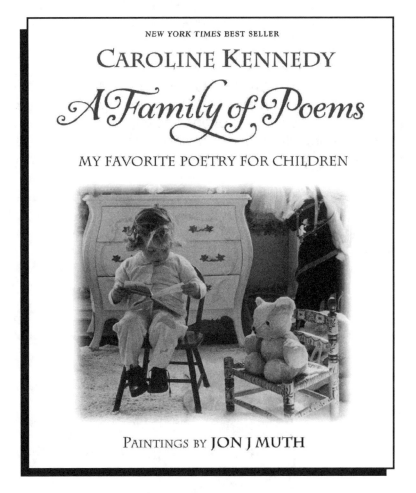

Hyperion Books for Children.

- SING A SONG OF POPCORN: EVERY CHILD'S BOOK OF POEMS, selected by Beatrice Schenk de Regniers, Eva Moore, Mary Michaels White, and Jane Carr and illustrated by nine Caldecott Medal artists (Scholastic); a hefty treasury compiled in memory of Arnold Lobel.

- TAKE SKY, written by David McCord and illustrated by Henry B. Kane (Little, Brown); 48 poems reflect on everyday subjects, such as a "Spelling Bee" and "The Importance of Eggs"; a classic collection.

- MY AMERICA: A POETRY ATLAS OF THE UNITED STATES, selected by Lee Bennett Hopkins and illustrated by Stephen Alcorn (Simon & Schuster); outstanding illustrations accompany the work of well-known poets and worthy newcomers.

- LIVES: POEMS ABOUT FAMOUS AMERICANS, selected by Lee Bennett Hopkins and illustrated by Leslie Staub (HarperCollins); 16 men and women, from Paul Revere to Rosa Parks, are honored in poems and full-page art; includes biographical information on each subject at the back of the book.

- WE THE PEOPLE, written by Bobbi Katz and illustrated by Nina Crews (Greenwillow); 65 first-person poems portray five centuries of American life; the poet conducted in-depth research to find and fuel the voices of her subjects—both real and imagined. Quotations and a time line augment the presentation.

- A POEM OF HER OWN: VOICES OF AMERICAN WOMEN YESTERDAY AND TODAY, edited by Catherine Clinton and illustrated by Stephen Alcorn (Abrams). This collection of both classic and contemporary poems reflects on the history and strength of American women and the issues they have faced. Brief biographies of the poets are included at the back of the book.

A POEM OF HER OWN: VOICES OF AMERICAN WOMEN YESTERDAY AND TODAY by Catherine Clinton, illustrated by Stephen Alcorn. Reprinted with permission of Abrams Books for Young Readers (www.abramsyoungreaders.com).

- HEROES AND SHE-ROES: POEMS OF AMAZING AND EVERYDAY HEROES, written by J. Patrick Lewis and illustrated by Jim Cooke (Dial); celebrates heroes from Martin Luther King Jr. and Lady Godiva to a 13-year-old Pakistani child-labor crusader.

- HERE IN HARLEM: POEMS IN MANY VOICES, by Walter Dean Myers (Holiday House); 54 poems profiling people who live and work in Harlem, from a mail carrier and a mechanic to a student and a hairdresser; in the style of SPOON RIVER ANTHOLOGY. This handsome volume is illustrated with photographs from Walter Dean Myers's personal collection.

HERE IN HARLEM: POEMS IN MANY VOICES by Walter Dean Myers.
Published by Holiday House. Reprinted by permission.

• GOOD LUCK GOLD AND OTHER POEMS, by Janet S. Wong (McElderry); reflections on the ups and downs of growing up Asian American.

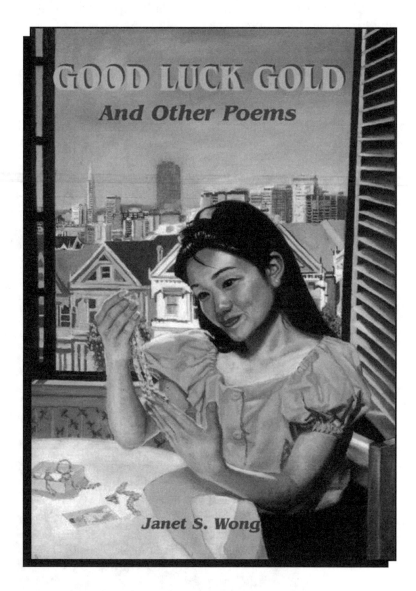

GOOD LUCK GOLD AND OTHER POEMS by Janet S. Wong. Copyright © 1994. Used with permission of Margaret K. McElderry Books, an imprint of Simon & Schuster Children's Publishing.

• TALKING DRUMS: A SELECTION OF POEMS FROM AFRICA SOUTH OF THE SAHARA, edited by Veronique Tadjo (Bloomsbury); traces African history; arranged in chapters, from the "Animal Kingdom and People" to "Pride and Defiance." Poems such as "Friendship" speak universally on common themes.

- NOT A COPPER PENNY IN ME HOUSE: POEMS FROM THE CARIBBEAN, written by Monica Gunning and illustrated by Frané Lessac (Wordsong/Boyds Mills Press); lyrical portrayal of a girl's life in the Caribbean.

NOT A COPPER PENNY IN ME HOUSE: POEMS FROM THE CARIBBEAN, by Monica Gunning, illustrated by Frané Lessac. Copyright © 1993. Published by Wordsong, an imprint of Boyds Mills Press. Reprinted by permission.

- LET THERE BE LIGHT: POEMS AND PRAYERS FOR REPAIRING THE WORLD, compiled and illustrated by Jane Breskin Zalben (Dutton). Reflecting a cross-section of faiths, these timely poems offer comfort and hope; illustrated with collages.

- FESTIVALS, poems by Myra Cohn Livingston and illustrated by Leonard Everett Fisher (Holiday House); a collection of poems about festivals celebrated by people of different faiths and cultures.

- WINTER LIGHTS: A SEASON IN POEMS & QUILTS, by Anna Grossnickle Hines (Greenwillow). Poems illustrated with quilts celebrate the winter holidays. Back material offers information on how the quilts were made and photographs of the process. See also PIECES: A YEAR IN POEMS & QUILTS, winner of the 2002 Lee Bennett Hopkins Award for Children's Poetry.

- PLEASE BURY ME IN THE LIBRARY, written by J. Patrick Lewis and illustrated by Kyle M. Stone (Harcourt). Super-duper poems celebrate reading, libraries, and books in an entertaining way; my favorite: "Great, Good, Bad," pithily explains the differences among books that fit each category.

Courtesy Harcourt, Inc.

- KNOCK ON WOOD: POEMS ABOUT SUPERSTITIONS, written by Janet S. Wong and illustrated by Julie Paschkis (McElderry); touches on superstitions, from the common one of the title and black cats, to lesser known beliefs, such as potatoes in your pocket and ear itches. Brief information about each superstition can be found at the back of the book.

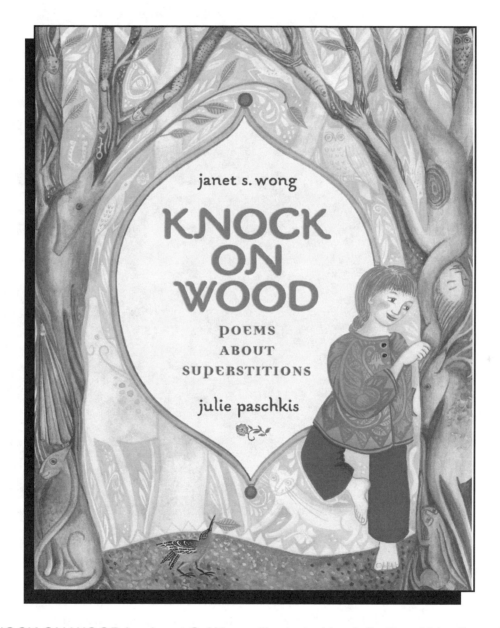

KNOCK ON WOOD by Janet S. Wong, illustrated by Julie Paschkis. Copyright © 2003. Used with permission of Margaret K. McElderry Books, an imprint of Simon & Schuster Children's Publishing.

- NIGHT GARDEN: POEMS FROM THE WORLD OF DREAMS, written by Janet S. Wong and illustrated by Julie Paschkis (McElderry); lovely illustrations accompany poems about dreams; winner of the NCTE Notable Children's Book in the Language Arts Award and a New York Times Best Illustrated Book.

NIGHT GARDEN by Janet S. Wong, illustrated by Julie Paschkis. Copyright © 2000. Used with permission of Margaret K. McElderry Books, an imprint of Simon & Schuster Children's Publishing.

- JOYFUL NOISE: POEMS FOR TWO VOICES, written by Paul Fleischman and illustrated by Eric Beddows (HarperCollins); poems intended for two to read aloud together; Newbery Medal.

- HONEY, I LOVE AND OTHER LOVE POEMS, by Eloise Greenfield and illustrated by Diane Dillon and Leo Dillon (HarperCollins). Daily happenings in a girl's life make for beautiful, evocative poetry.

• ALL THE SMALL POEMS AND FOURTEEN MORE, written by Valerie Worth and illustrated by Natalie Babbitt (Farrar Straus Giroux); short wonders about common objects, from telephone poles to lawn mowers.

ALL THE SMALL POEMS AND FOURTEEN MORE © 1994 by Valerie Worth; illustrated by Natalie Babbitt. Used with the permission of Farrar Straus Giroux.

• FARMER'S DOG GOES TO THE FOREST: RHYMES FOR TWO VOICES, written by David L. Harrison and illustrated by Arden Johnson-Petrov (Wordsong/Boyds Mills); fun poems in two voices; this picture book collection serves as a great introduction to this collaborative format.

- A MAZE ME: POEMS FOR GIRLS, written by Naomi Shihab Nye and illustrated by Terre Maher (Greenwillow); poems written especially for girls in their preteen years and beyond.

- FEARLESS FERNIE: HANGING OUT WITH FERNIE AND ME, poems by Gary Soto and illustrated by Regan Dunnick (Putnam); a collection of about 40 poems that chronicles the friendship from birth between two sixth-grade boys.

- MY MAN BLUE, poems by Nikki Grimes and illustrated by Jerome Lagarrigue (Penguin); poems form the story of a boy without a father and a man who has lost his son and the friendship they forge that helps them both heal.

- SQUEEZE: POEMS FROM A JUICY UNIVERSE, written by Heidi Mordhorst with photographs by Jesse Torrey (Wordsong/Boyds Mills); rhythmical reflections on the ups and downs of everyday life; these poems are like the days of childhood: "Some . . . sting and others pour like sugar."

SQUEEZE: POEMS FROM A JUICY UNIVERSE, by Heidi Mordhorst, photographs by Jesse Torrey. Copyright © 2005. Published by Wordsong, an imprint of Boyds Mills Press. Reprinted by permission.

- SILVER SEEDS, written by Paul Paolilli and Dan Brewer and illustrated by Steve Johnson and Lou Fancher (Penguin); simple, lovely, evocative poems about ordinary things in which the first letter of each line forms a word; sweet, soothing illustrations.

- WONDERFUL WORDS: POEMS ABOUT READING, WRITING, SPEAKING, AND LISTENING, selected by Lee Bennett Hopkins and illustrated by Karen Barbour (Simon & Schuster); a celebration of words, wonderful words, in poems by Emily Dickinson, Nikki Grimes, Lee Bennett Hopkins, and other poets. Don't miss "How to Say a Long, Hard Word" by David McCord, "The Word Builder" by Ann Whitford Paul, or "The Period" by Richard Armour, which is aptly the last poem in the collection.

WONDERFUL WORDS: POEMS ABOUT READING, WRITING, SPEAKING, AND LISTENING by Lee Bennett Hopkins, illustrated by Karen Barbour. Copyright © 2004. Used with permission of Simon & Schuster Books for Young Readers, an imprint of Simon & Schuster Children's Publishing.

- IN THE LAND OF WORDS: NEW AND SELECTED POEMS, written by Eloise Greenfield and illustrated by Jan Spivey Gilchrist (HarperCollins). Written and illustrated by Coretta Scott King Award winners, this book of poetry celebrating words includes "In The Land of Words", "Nathaniel's Rap", "Books", and 18 other sprightly poems.

- A POKE IN THE I: A COLLECTION OF CONCRETE POEMS, selected by Paul B. Janeczko and illustrated by Chris Raschka (Candlewick); 30 delightful poems in which words are arranged in special ways, depicted with distinctive type, or spaced to add meaning beyond the actual words. For this reason, the poems must be seen as well as heard to be understood and appreciated. Take Robert Carola's "Stowaway", for example, or "Pattern Poem with an Elusive Intruder" by Reinhard Döhl.

A POKE IN THE I: A COLLECTION OF CONCRETE POEMS.
Illustrations © 2001 Chris Raschka. This Collection © 2001
Paul B. Janeczko. Candlewick Press, Inc.

- READ A RHYME, WRITE A RHYME, selected by Jack Prelutsky and illustrated by Meilo So (Knopf). Poems on 10 themes chosen to delight children are paired with "poemstarts" (opening lines of poems that children are encouraged to finish) and plenty of creative Prelutsky-esque suggestions.

- SEEING THE BLUE BETWEEN: ADVICE AND INSPIRATION FOR YOUNG POETS, compiled by Paul B. Janeczko (Candlewick); poetry and advice from 32 poets, including Lee Bennett Hopkins, Jack Prelutsky, Nikki Grimes, J. Patrick Lewis, and Douglas Florian.

SEEING THE BLUE BETWEEN: ADVICE AND INSPIRATION FOR YOUNG POETS. Jacket Illustration Copyright © 2002 Jeffrey Fisher. This Collection Copyright © 2002 Paul B. Janeczko. Letters Copyright © 2002 by individual authors. Poems copyright year of publication as indicated in Acknowledgments. Candlewick Press, Inc.

- THE PLACE MY WORDS ARE LOOKING FOR, selected by Paul B. Janeczko (Simon & Schuster); poems, reflections, and photos of 39 poets, including Nancy Willard, Eve Merriam, Cynthia Rylant, and Naomi Shihab Nye.

THE PLACE MY WORDS ARE LOOKING FOR: WHAT POETS SAY ABOUT AND THROUGH THEIR WORK by Paul B. Janeczko. Copyright © 1990. Used with permission of Simon & Schuster Books for Young Readers, an imprint of Simon & Schuster Children's Publishing.

- DIRTY BEASTS, written by Roald Dahl and illustrated by Quentin Blake (Penguin). Beginning with the pig and ending with "The Tummy Beast", this riotous collection of irreverent verse is sure to sweep the dirty doldrums right out the door.

- RUNNY BABBITT: A BILLY SOOK, by Shel Silverstein (HarperCollins). Read these koems to the pids; Silverstein wrote this thook especially for bem! See also WHERE THE SIDEWALK ENDS, FALLING UP, and A LIGHT IN THE ATTIC.

- NO MORE HOMEWORK! NO MORE TESTS! KIDS' FAVORITE FUNNY SCHOOL POEMS, selected by Bruce Lansky and illustrated by Stephen Carpenter (Meadowbrook). what kid can resist a book of poetry with a title like this?

NO MORE HOMEWORK! NO MORE TESTS! © 1997.
(www.meadowbrookpress.com).

- THE GOOF WHO INVENTED HOMEWORK AND OTHER SCHOOL POEMS, by Kalli Dakos and illustrated by Denise Brunkus (Dial). Traipse through the ups and downs of a typical year in elementary school with these 36 poems, some of which encourage reading aloud by two or more voices.

- DIRTY LAUNDRY PILE: POEMS IN DIFFERENT VOICES, selected by Paul B. Janeczko and illustrated by Melissa Sweet (Greenwillow). Animals and inanimate objects, from a mosquito to a vacuum cleaner and the dirty laundry pile, tell it like it is from their perspective; ideal for a study of point of view.

- I INVITED A DRAGON TO DINNER AND OTHER POEMS TO MAKE YOU LAUGH OUT LOUD, illustrated by Chris L. Demarest (Philomel); hilarious collection of poems by a number of poets.

- IF KIDS RULED THE SCHOOL, edited by Bruce Lansky and illustrated by Stephen Carpenter (Meadowbrook); giggly poems on the topics of detention, school lunches, and other school-related subjects.

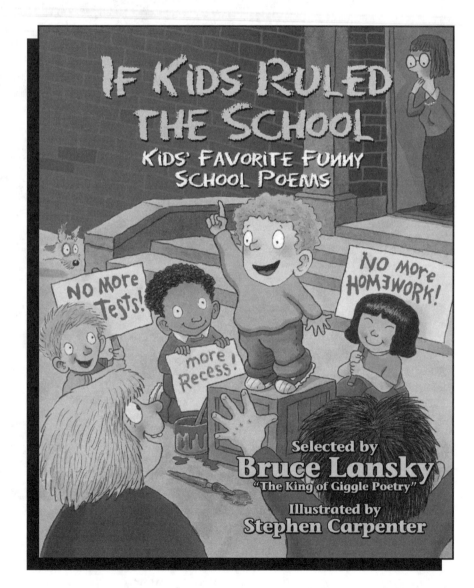

IF KIDS RULED THE SCHOOL © 2004. (www.meadowbrookpress.com).

• ROLLING IN THE AISLES: A COLLECTION OF LAUGH-OUT-LOUD POEMS, collected by Bruce Lansky and illustrated by Stephen Carpenter (Meadowbrook); includes poems by Shel Silverstein, Jack Prelutsky, Bruce Lansky, and others.

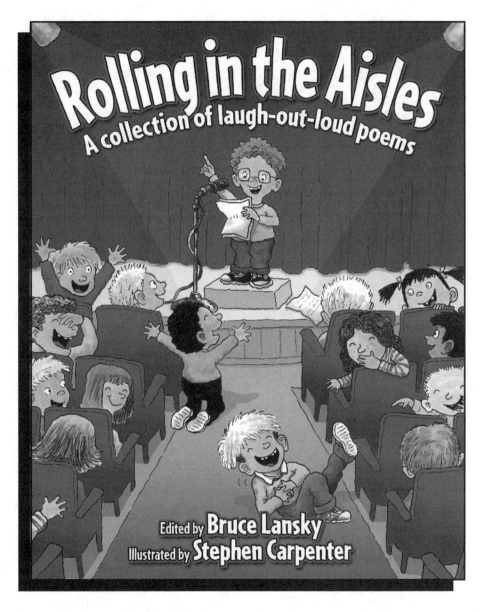

ROLLING IN THE AISLES © 2004. (www.meadowbrookpress.com).

• SCRANIMALS, poems written by Jack Prelutsky and illustrated by Peter Sis (Greenwillow). The subjects of these poems are animal-veggie combos that populate Scranimal Island. Look out for "porcupineapple" and "radishark" as you explore the island!

- MY DOG ATE MY HOMEWORK, collected by Bruce Lansky and illustrated by Stephen Carpenter (Meadowbrook); another funny collection kids most certainly will enjoy.

MY DOG ATE MY HOMEWORK! © 1996, 2002.
(www.meadowbrookpress.com).

- IF NOT FOR THE CAT, haiku by Jack Prelutsky and illustrated by Ted Rand (Greenwillow); stunningly illustrated; Parents' Choice Gold Award; see the read-aloud plan in *Children's Book Corner, Grades 3–4*.

- HOOFBEATS, CLAWS & RIPPLED FINS: CREATURE POEMS, edited by Lee Bennett Hopkins and illustrated by Stephen Alcorn (HarperCollins). In this collection of poems by 13 poets, Alcorn's animal portraits inspired the words.

• PAINT ME A POEM: POEMS INSPIRED BY MASTERPIECES OF ART, by Justine Rowden (Wordsong/Boyds Mills); 14 poems and the art that inspired them, snappily presented in varying typefaces and word configurations.

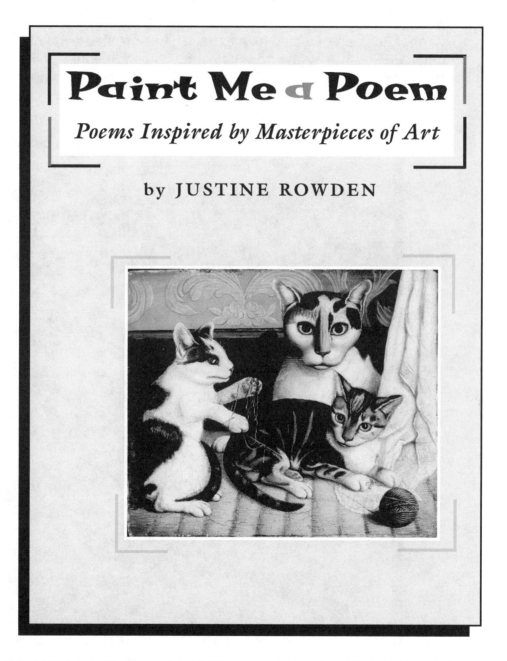

PAINT ME A POEM: POEMS INSPIRED BY MASTERPIECES OF ART, by Justine Rowden, cover image © National Gallery of Art, Washington. Copyright © 2005. Published by Wordsong, an imprint of Boyds Mills Press. Reprinted by permission.

- A VISIT TO WILLIAM BLAKE'S INN: POEMS FOR INNOCENT AND EXPERIENCED TRAVELERS, written by Nancy Willard and illustrated by Alice and Martin Provensen (Harcourt). This book of poems was awarded both the Newbery Medal and a Caldecott Honor Award. Willard, who was introduced to Blake's poetry at the age of seven by a sitter (whose phone number any parent would love to have), has created a set of poems about an imaginary inn run by the poet himself. Delightful alone, Willard's poems also make for a memorable study of Blake when paired with the poems that inspired them.

Courtesy Harcourt, Inc.

- WHEN I HEARD THE LEARN'D ASTRONOMER, written by Walt Whitman and illustrated by Loren Long (Simon & Schuster). See the read-aloud plan found elsewhere in this resource.

- PAUL REVERE'S RIDE, written by Henry Wadsworth Longfellow and illustrated by Ted Rand (Dutton); illustrates the moonlit journey that was immortalized by Longfellow's epic poem, told in its entirety.

- STOPPING BY WOODS ON A SNOWY EVENING, written by Robert Frost and illustrated by Susan Jeffers (Dutton); lovely presentation of the well-loved poem.

- LEWIS CARROLL'S JABBERWOCKY, illustrated by Jane Breskin Zalben with annotations by Humpty Dumpty (Boyds Mills Press). Originally published in 1872 as part of THROUGH THE LOOKING GLASS AND WHAT ALICE FOUND THERE, the classic poem is imaginatively illustrated by Zalben in this edition. Other illustrated editions include JABBERWOCKY, written by Lewis Carroll and illustrated by Stephane Jorisch (Kids Can Press), and JABBERWOCKY, written by Lewis Carroll and illustrated by Joel Stewart (Candlewick). For more poetry by Lewis Carroll, look for the collection, POETRY FOR YOUNG PEOPLE: LEWIS CARROLL, edited by Edward Mendelson and illustrated by Eric Copeland (Sterling).

LEWIS CARROLL'S JABBERWOCKY, illustrated by Jane Breskin Zalben. Illustrations copyright © 1977. Published by Boyds Mills Press. Reprinted by permission.

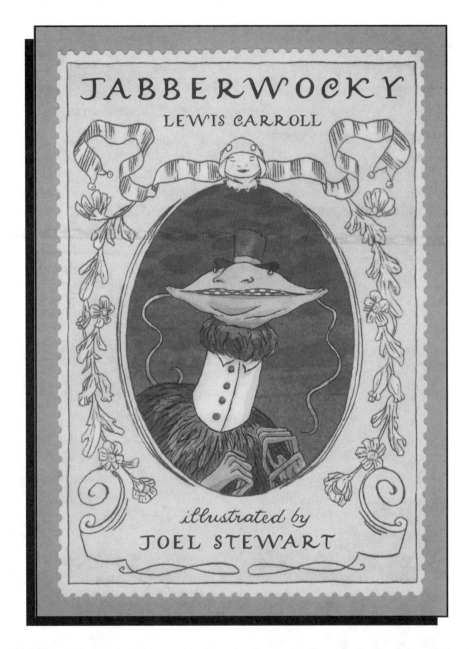

JABBERWOCKY. Written by Lewis Carroll. Illustrations Copyright © 2003 Joel Stewart. Candlewick Press, Inc. on behalf of Walker Books Ltd.

- A SWINGER OF BIRCHES: POEMS OF ROBERT FROST FOR YOUNG PEOPLE, illustrated by Peter Koeppen (Stemmer House); a collection of Frost's best-loved poems.

- POETRY FOR YOUNG PEOPLE: RUDYARD KIPLING, edited by Eileen Gillooly and illustrated by Jim Sharpe (Sterling); a great collection for the poetry shelf. See also KITTY AND MR. KIPLING: NEIGHBORS IN VERMONT, written by Lenore Blegvad and illustrated by Erik Blegvad (McElderry), the historical novel based on fact about the friendship between a young girl and the famous author in the late 1800s.

- POETRY FOR YOUNG PEOPLE: EMILY DICKINSON, edited by Frances Schoonmaker Bolin and illustrated by Chi Chung (Sterling); some of Dickinson's best-loved poems illustrated in this volume intended for children.

- POETRY FOR YOUNG PEOPLE: ROBERT BROWNING, edited by Eileen Gillooly and illustrated by Joel Spector (Sterling); thoughtfully selected; nicely illustrated.

- CARL SANDBURG: ADVENTURES OF A POET, written by Penelope Niven with poems and prose by Carl Sandburg and illustrated by Marc Nadel (Harcourt). Biographical sketches on one side of the page face pieces of Sandburg's writing that serve to illustrate the key points in Sandburg's life. From "Vagabond" to "Pen Pal" to "Dreamer," readers trace the life of this American icon. A time line of Sandburg's life and illustration notes make for insightful backmatter.

- POETRY FOR YOUNG PEOPLE: CARL SANDBURG, edited by Frances Schoonmaker Bolin and illustrated by Steven Arcella (Sterling); illustrated collection of selected poems.

- CARVER: A LIFE IN POEMS, by Marilyn Nelson (Front Street); a biography in poems that garnered the poet a National Book Award Finalist distinction, the Newbery Honor Award, the Coretta Scott King Honor Award, and the Boston Globe-Horn Book Award.

- SCIENCE VERSE, written by Jon Scieszka and illustrated by Lane Smith (Penguin). Wacky poems about science topics are take-offs on well-known poems; see the read-aloud plan in *Children's Book Corner, Grades 3–4*.

- HERE'S WHAT YOU CAN DO WHEN YOU CAN'T FIND YOUR SHOE: INGENIOUS INVENTIONS FOR PESKY PROBLEMS, written by Andrea Perry and illustrated by Alan Snow (Atheneum). Zany suggestions for useful inventions in poetry form will delight readers of all ages; see the read-aloud plan in *Children's Book Corner, Grades 1–2*.

- LANGSTON'S TRAIN RIDE, written by Robert Burleigh and illustrated by Leonard Jenkins (Orchard); tells about the inspiration for Hughes's famous poem, "The Negro Speaks of Rivers" and how it led to his life as a writer.

- LOVE THAT DOG, by Sharon Creech (HarperCollins); story told in poems; poetry helps Jack overcome his grief over the loss of his dog; poems from authors such as Robert Frost, William Carlos Williams, and Walter Dean Myers are woven into the telling of this wonderful story.

Helpful Guides for Young Writers:

- A KICK IN THE HEAD: AN EVERYDAY GUIDE TO POETIC FORMS, selected by Paul B. Janeczko and illustrated by Chris Raschka (Candlewick); lively picture book of poems illustrating poetic forms.

A KICK IN THE HEAD: AN EVERYDAY GUIDE TO POETIC FORMS. This Collection Copyright © 2005 Paul B. Janeczko. Illustrations Copyright © 2005 Chris Raschka. Candlewick Press, Inc.

- HOW TO WRITE POETRY, by Paul B. Janeczko (Scholastic); a useful, usable guide.

- POETRY FROM A TO Z: A GUIDE FOR YOUNG WRITERS, compiled by Paul B. Janeczko (Simon & Schuster); handy handbook.

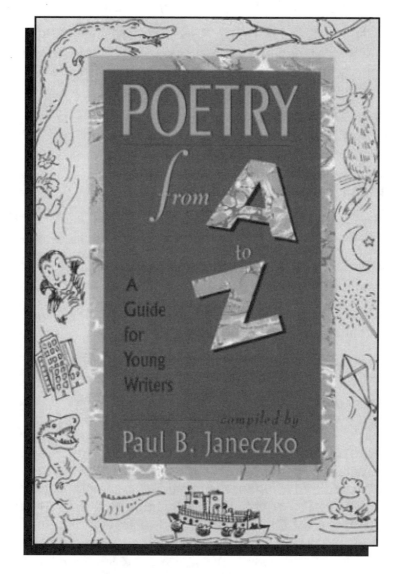

POETRY FROM A TO Z: A GUIDE FOR YOUNG WRITERS compiled by Paul B. Janeczko, illustrated by Cathy Bobak. Copyright © 1994. Used with permission of Simon & Schuster Books for Young Readers, an imprint of Simon & Schuster Children's Publishing.

- POETRY MATTERS; WRITING A POEM FROM THE INSIDE OUT, by Ralph Fletcher (HarperCollins); the how and why of writing poetry.

- POEM-MAKING: WAYS TO BEGIN WRITING POETRY, by Myra Cohn Livingston (HarperCollins); advice from a pro in language kids will understand and appreciate.

- READ A RHYME, WRITE A RHYME, selected by Jack Prelutsky and illustrated by Meilo So (Knopf). Poems on 10 themes chosen to delight children are paired with "poemstarts" (opening lines of poems that children are encouraged to finish) and plenty of creative Prelutsky-esque suggestions.

- SEEING THE BLUE BETWEEN: ADVICE AND INSPIRATION FOR YOUNG POETS, compiled by Paul B. Janeczko (Candlewick); poetry and advice from 32 poets, including Lee Bennett Hopkins, Jack Prelutsky, Nikki Grimes, J. Patrick Lewis, and Douglas Florian.

- THE PLACE MY WORDS ARE LOOKING FOR, selected by Paul B. Janeczko (Simon & Schuster); poems, reflections, and photos of 39 poets, including Nancy Willard, Eve Merriam, Cynthia Rylant, and Naomi Shihab Nye.

References for Teachers and Librarians

- WISHES, LIES, AND DREAMS: TEACHING CHILDREN TO WRITE POETRY, by Kenneth Koch and Ron Padgett (HarperCollins).

- PASS THE POETRY, PLEASE! 3rd edition, by Lee Bennett Hopkins (HarperCollins).

- ROSE, WHERE DID YOU GET THAT RED?: TEACHING GREAT POETRY TO CHILDREN, by Kenneth Koch (Vintage).

- FOR THE GOOD OF THE EARTH AND SUN: TEACHING POETRY, by Georgia Heard (Heinemann).

- AWAKENING THE HEART: EXPLORING POETRY IN ELEMENTARY AND MIDDLE SCHOOL, by Georgia Heard (Heinemann).

- www.readwritethink.org; offers resources for teaching poetry. Click on "Instructional Resources" in the drop-down box in the Web Resources section. Look in "Calendar" under the Highlights heading on the home page, and peruse the "Lessons." A couple to note: "Shape Poems: Writing Extraordinary Poems About Ordinary Objects" and "In the Poet's Shoes: Performing Poetry and Building Meaning." Interactive poetry tools can be found in the "Student Materials" section. Useful poetry Web site links are listed in the Web Resources section.

- www.poets.org; Academy of American Poets; sponsor of National Poetry Month; click on "For Educators" on the home page.

- www.favoritepoem.org; Favorite Poem Project site; click on "For Teachers" on the home page.

- www.poetryteachers.com; site for teachers includes information on how to teach poetry, poetry theater, poetry activities, and more; linked to Meadowbrook Press.

• www.gigglepoetry.com/; site where kids are invited to "read and rate" hundreds of funny poems collected by Bruce Lansky of Meadowbrook Press; includes other activities designed to bring kids and poetry together.

Did You Know?

April is National Poetry Month in the United States, and the third week in April is designated **Young People's Poetry Week**. The Children's Book Council, in collaboration with the American Academy of Poets (sponsor of National Poetry Month) and the Center for the Book in the Library of Congress, sponsors Young People's Poetry Week. Visit the Children's Book Council at www.cbcbooks.org for details, teaching suggestions, book lists, and other free materials.

The **National Council of Teachers of English (NCTE) Award for Poetry for Children** was established in 1977 to honor a living American poet for his or her body of work for children ages 3–13. The award is given every three years. For more information and a list of previous winners, go to http://www.ncte.org/elem/awards/poetry/.

The **Lee Bennett Hopkins Award for Children's Poetry**, administered by The Pennsylvania Center for the Book and Penn State University Libraries, is a national award granted annually to an anthology of poetry or a single-volume poem published for children in the previous calendar year by a living American poet or anthologist. Go to http://www.pabook.libraries.psu.edu/activities/hopkins/criteria.html for more information.

The **Lee Bennett Hopkins Promising Poet Award** is a US$500 award given every three years by the International Reading Association to a promising new poet who writes for children and young adults and who has published no more than two books of children's poetry. A book-length single poem may be submitted. Go to http://www.reading.org/association/awards/childrens_hopkins.html for a list of winners.

Tantalizing Tidbits: First Chapters Sure to Jump-Start Independent Reading

The books listed below contain outstanding first chapters that are sure to tickle the fancy and rouse the interest of the most jaded anti-bookster in the group. Consider occasionally reading the first chapter of a great book aloud. Follow up with a brief booktalk, and then make available a copy or two (or three or four) to lend to interested students. Reading the first chapter of a recommended book is perfect for the last day of the week, before a vacation, or in preparation for the assignment of book reports.

THE TEACHER'S FUNERAL: A COMEDY IN THREE PARTS, by Richard Peck (Dial)

BUD, NOT BUDDY, by Christopher Paul Curtis (Delacorte)

THE BOY WHO SAVED BASEBALL, by John H. Ritter (Penguin)

BECOMING JOE DIMAGGIO, by Maria Testa (Candlewick)

MY LOUISIANA SKY, by Kimberly Willis Holt (Random House)

HARRIET BEECHER STOWE AND THE BEECHER PREACHERS, by Jean Fritz (Penguin)

BOY: TALES OF CHILDHOOD, by Roald Dahl (Farrar Straus Giroux)

JUST ELLA, by Margaret Peterson Haddix (Simon & Schuster)

JUST ELLA by Margaret Peterson Haddix, illustrated by Rene Milot. Copyright © 1999. Used with permission of Simon & Schuster Books for Young Readers, an imprint of Simon & Schuster Children's Publishing.

NEWFANGLED FAIRY TALES: CLASSIC STORIES WITH A TWIST, edited by Bruce Lansky (Meadowbrook)

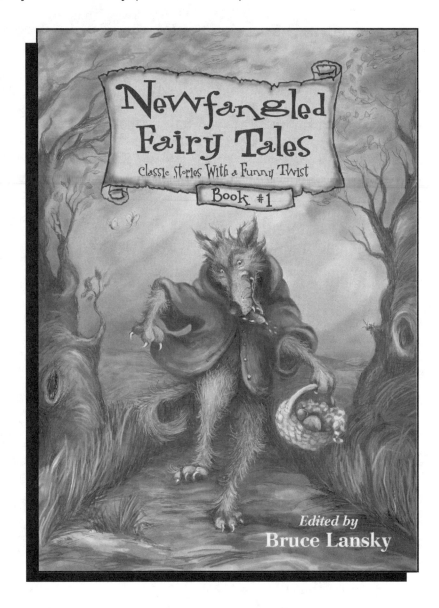

NEWFANGLED FAIRY TALES #1 © 1997. (www.meadowbrookpress.com).

STEVEN SPIELBERG: CRAZY FOR MOVIES, by Susan Goldman Rubin (Abrams)

STEVEN SPIELBERG: Crazy for Movies by Susan Goldman Rubin. Reprinted with permission of Abrams Books for Young Readers (www.abramsyoungreaders.com).

LEONARDO DA VINCI, written by Kathleen Krull and illustrated by Boris Kulikov (Viking)

For additional suggestions, see the Parent Pull-Out Pages and "More! Additional Fiction Choices for Read-Alouds, Read-Alongs, and Read-Alones".

More!: Additional Fiction Choices for Read-Alouds, Read-Alongs, and Read-Alones

In books I have traveled, not only to other worlds, but into my own. I learned who I was and who I wanted to be, what I might aspire to, and what I might dare to dream.
—Anna Quindlen, author

Listed here according to genre, with brief summaries and approximate reading levels, are additional premium, shelf-space-worthy titles of fiction books sure to interest a cross-section of fifth and sixth graders. Whether they are chosen to be read aloud, read together, or read alone, these books stand tall.

Titles are listed in each section in descending order of general reading difficulty and are cross-referenced according to major themes.

Natalie Babbitt once said that children, like all are people, are, "[s]eparate, distinct, with different dreams and different sorrows." As with all books featured in this resource, it is the responsibility of the person recommending the book to become familiar with its content to determine whether it is suitable for the student(s) to whom it is recommended.

For a listing of recommended books related to content-area subjects, refer to the Book Notes section of this resource.

Historical Fiction

• JOHNNY TREMAIN, by Esther Forbes (Houghton Mifflin); fast-paced, action-packed story set in Boston on the cusp of the Revolutionary War; one of my all-time favorite historical fiction novels; Newbery Medal. Reading level: upper sixth grade.

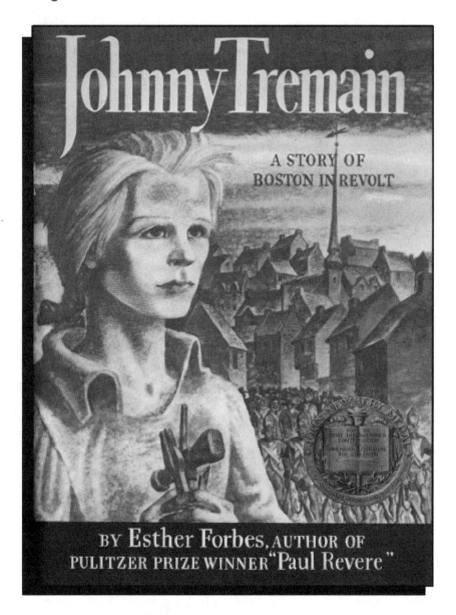

Cover from JOHNNY TREMAIN by Esther Forbes, with illustrations by Lynd Ward. Copyright © 1943 by Esther Forbes Hoskins, renewed 1971 by Linwood M. Erskine, Jr., Executor of the Estate of Esther Forbes Hoskins. Reprinted by permission of Houghton Mifflin Company. All rights reserved.

- YANKEE GIRL, by Mary Ann Rodman (Farrar Straus Giroux). Set in the mid 1960s, this riveting fictional story is based on the author's own experience with school integration in Mississippi, raw prejudice, and the Ku Klux Klan, all while facing more mundane issues, such as being new in the neighborhood in sixth grade and trying to find a place in the peer group. Reading level: sixth grade.

YANKEE GIRL © 2004 by Mary Ann Rodman. Cover Art © 2004 by Douglas Jones. Used with the permission of Farrar Straus Giroux.

- CATHERINE, CALLED BIRDY, by Karen Cushman (HarperCollins), Set in the Middle Ages, this is the diary of a spunky 14-year-old girl who is determined to make her own choices in a time when it just wasn't done! Newbery Honor. Reading level: sixth grade.

- THE MIDWIFE'S APPRENTICE, by Karen Cushman (HarperCollins). Memorably and evocatively set in England in the Middle Ages, this is the witty story of preteen Alyce, who rises from nameless waif to experienced midwife, and her personal growth along the way; Newbery Award. Reading level: sixth grade.

- OUT OF THE DUST, by Karen Hesse (Scholastic); novel in verse set in Oklahoma during the Depression about the physical and emotional battles of 14-year-old Billie Jo; winner of the Newbery Medal and numerous other awards. Reading level: sixth grade.

- GHOSTS I HAVE BEEN, by Richard Peck (Penguin). Blossom Culp's ability to see into the future is often humorous, but not when she foresees the sinking of the *Titanic*; award-winning tale by an award-winning author. See also THE GHOST BELONGED TO ME, THE DREADFUL FUTURE OF BLOSSOM CULP and BLOSSOM CULP AND THE SLEEP OF DEATH. Reading level: sixth grade.

- WEASEL, by Cynthia DeFelice (Atheneum). Set in Ohio in the 1800s, this riveting adventure handles hatred of Native Americans and the morality of vengeance with great skill; a well-crafted, award-winning novel. Reading level: sixth grade.

- FEVER 1793, by Laurie Halse Anderson (Simon & Schuster); multiple award-winning novel about the yellow fever epidemic in Philadelphia; 16-year-old Mattie grows up as she tries to escape the city and the disease. Reading level: sixth grade.

FEVER 1793 by Laurie Halse Anderson. Copyright © 2000. Used with permission of Simon & Schuster Books for Young Readers, an imprint of Simon & Schuster Children's Publishing.

- THE GHOST IN THE TOKAIDO INN, by Dorothy Hoobler and Thomas Hoobler (Philomel). Set in Japan in 1735, this gripping tale centers around the theft of a ruby and the sharp investigative work of 14-year-old Seikei, who dreams of being a samurai despite his merchant class status; an Edgar Allan Poe Award finalist, and winner of numerous other awards. Reading level: sixth grade.

- MY BROTHER SAM IS DEAD, by James Lincoln Collier and Christopher Collier (Simon & Schuster); set in the time of the American Revolution; two brothers must choose between their family loyalty and their beliefs; Newbery Honor. Reading level: sixth grade.

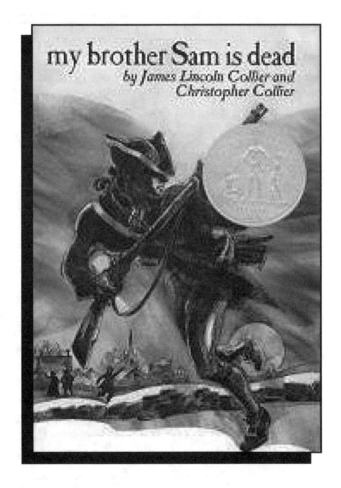

MY BROTHER SAM IS DEAD by James Lincoln Collier and Christopher Collier. Copyright © 1984. Used with permission of Simon & Schuster Books for Young Readers, an imprint of Simon & Schuster Children's Publishing.

- SOUNDER, by William H. Armstrong (HarperCollins); the heartrending story of a sharecropper and his experiences with prejudice; a classic; Newbery Medal winner. Reading level: sixth grade.

- FRIEDRICH, by Hans Peter Richter (Penguin); first published in German; the touching story of a Jewish boy's harrowing experiences during the Nazi regime, as told by his German friend. Reading level: sixth grade.

- ANNE OF GREEN GABLES, by L. M. Montgomery (various editions available: illustrated, unabridged, abridged, and boxed sets); the classic tale of Anne Shirley, an 11-year-old, red-headed orphan, who comes to live with Matthew and Marilla Cuthbert (a brother and sister who had hopes for a boy to help on the farm) on the island of Prince William; an unforgettably winning character. See also ANNE OF THE ISLAND, ANNE OF AVONLEA, and the other titles of the further adventures of the character who has won the hearts of readers for 100 years. Reading level: sixth grade.

- REBECCA OF SUNNYBROOK FARM, written by Kate Douglas Wiggin and illustrated by Barbara McClintock (Houghton Mifflin). A cheerful young lass comes to live with her two elderly aunts; reissue of the 1903 classic, with illustrations. Reading level: sixth grade.

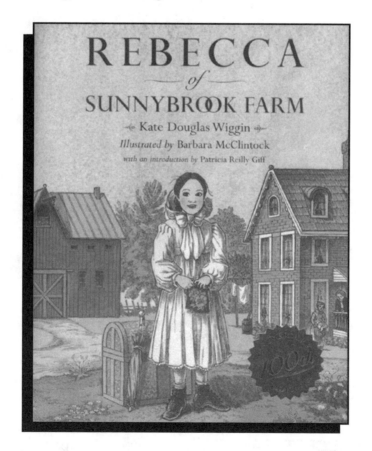

Cover from REBECCA OF SUNNYBROOK FARM by Kate Douglas Wiggin, illustrated by Barbara McClintock (Boston: Houghton Mifflin, 1938).

- THE TRUE CONFESSIONS OF CHARLOTTE DOYLE, by Avi (Scholastic); adventure on the high seas in 1832 involves mutiny, murder, and a 13-year-old girl who comes out of her shell as a result; Newbery Honor. Reading level: sixth grade.

- A SINGLE SHARD, by Linda Sue Park (Clarion); set in twelfth-century Korea; a tightly crafted story of the perseverance and passion of 12-year-old Tree-Ear, a potter's apprentice who has a dream of making a pot of his own; Newbery Award. Reading level: sixth grade.

Cover from A SINGLE SHARD by Linda Sue Park. Jacket and case cover copyright © 2001 by Jean and Mousien Tseng. Reprinted by permission of Clarion Books, an imprint of Houghton Mifflin Company. All rights reserved.

- BY THE GREAT HORN SPOON!, by Sid Fleischman (Little, Brown); hilarious tale of adventure set in the time of the California Gold Rush. Reading level: sixth grade.

- THE SECRET GARDEN, by Frances Hodgson Burnett (HarperCollins); classic tale of the friendship between an unlikely pair who blossom in the garden they share. Reading level: sixth grade.

- THE CAY, by Theodore Taylor (Delacorte); tale of survival with themes of prejudice and friendship set in 1942 on a deserted island; award-winning classic. Reading level: sixth grade.

- NUMBER THE STARS, by Lois Lowry (Houghton Mifflin); set in 1943; an affecting story about 10-year-old Annemarie Johansen and her best friend, Ellen Rosen, whose life is threatened when the Nazi soldiers come to Copenhagen; based on a true account; Newbery Medal. Reading level: fifth–sixth grades.

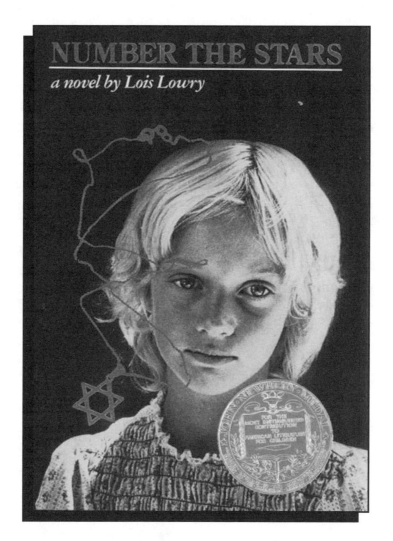

Cover from NUMBER THE STARS by Lois Lowry. Copyright © 1998 by Lois Lowry. Reprinted by permission of Houghton Mifflin Company. All rights reserved.

- THE TEACHER'S FUNERAL: A COMEDY IN THREE PARTS, by Richard Peck (Dial). It's August 1904, and the teacher who rules the one-room schoolhouse has died. Thus begins a memorable, comic tale about Russell Culver and his cronies. Reading level: fifth–sixth grades.

- A LONG WAY FROM CHICAGO: A NOVEL IN STORIES, by Richard Peck (Dial); Newbery Honor book set in the 1930s, about eight hilarious and wonderful experiences Joey and Mary Alice have when they visit Grandma Dowdel. See also A YEAR DOWN YONDER, a Newbery Award winner that focuses on Mary Alice and Grandma Dowdel's escapades. Reading level: fifth–sixth grades.

- LETTERS FROM RIFKA, by Karen Hesse (Penguin); the story of 12 year-old Rifka, whose plan to flee Russia for America is squashed when she is refused passage because of illness, and the ensuing events that ultimately lead to her reunion with her family; told in letters to a relative; National Jewish Book Award. Reading level: fifth -sixth grade.

- AL CAPONE DOES MY SHIRTS, by Gennifer Choldenko (Penguin). Set in 1935 on Alcatraz Island (when Al Capone was a resident), this is the humorous, appealing story of the family of a prison guard; Newbery Honor. Reading level: fifth–sixth grades.

- NORY RYAN'S SONG, by Patricia Reilly Giff (Random House); chronicles the struggles of a 12-year-old girl hoping to survive the Great Potato Famine in Ireland in the mid-1800s. See also the sequel, MAGGIE'S DOOR, in which Nory sets sail for America a few days after her brother. Reading level: fifth–sixth grades.

- Shakespeare Stealer series, by Gary Blackwood (Dutton). Widge, an orphan in Elizabethan England, solves Shakespeare-related mysteries in stories that also happen to teach about the era and its main drama man. Titles include THE SHAKESPEARE STEALER, SHAKESPEARE'S SCRIBE, and SHAKESPEARE'S SPY. Reading level: fifth–sixth grades.

• BELLE PRATER'S BOY, by Ruth White (Farrar Straus Giroux). Virginia in the 1950s is the setting for this story about cousins and best friends, Gypsy and Woodrow, and the losses they face together in their sixth-grade year; Newbery Honor. See also the acclaimed sequel, THE SEARCH FOR BELLE PRATER. Reading level: fifth–sixth grades.

BELLE PRATER'S BOY © 1996 by Ruth White. Cover Art © 1996 by Elizabeth Sayles. Used with the permission of Farrar Straus Giroux.

- A GATHERING OF DAYS: A NEW ENGLAND GIRL'S JOURNAL, 1830–32, by Joan W. Blos (Simon & Schuster). Journal entries chronicle major as well as everyday events in the life of a farm girl after the loss of her mother; Newbery Medal. Reading level: fifth–sixth grades.

A GATHERING OF DAYS: A NEW ENGLAND GIRL'S JOURNAL, 1830-32 by Joan W. Blos. Copyright © 1979. Used with permission of Atheneum Books for Young Readers, an imprint of Simon & Schuster Children's Publishing.

- A HOUSE OF TAILORS, by Patricia Reilly Giff (Random House); memorable story of the immigrant experience in the 1870s, told by the talented two-time Newbery Honor Award–winning author. Reading level: fifth–sixth grades.

- STOWAWAY, written by Karen Hesse and illustrated by Robert Andrew Parker (McElderry); fictional account of a boy's experiences in the mid-1700s aboard James Cook's ship bound for an unknown continent; based on Hesse's research of the journey of Nicholas Young, an 11-year-old boy who was a stowaway on Cook's extraordinary voyage south of the equator. Reading level: fifth–sixth grades.

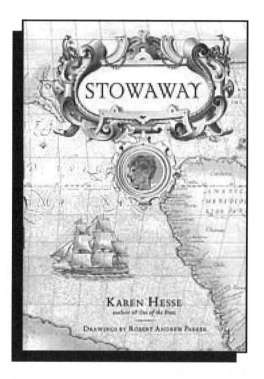

STOWAWAY by Karen Hesse, illustrated by Rodica Prato. Copyright ©
2000. Used with permission of Margaret K. McElderry Books, an imprint of
Simon & Schuster Children's Publishing.

- THE BORNING ROOM, by Paul Fleischman (HarperCollins); events in the life of Ohioan Georgina Caroline Lott and her family between 1851 and 1918 that revolve around the borning room, a room off the kitchen reserved for births and deaths. Reading level: fifth–sixth grades.

- MY DANIEL, by Pam Conrad (HarperCollins); a grandmother's remembrance of her life with and loss of her brother and their quest for a dinosaur on their farm in Nebraska. Reading level: fifth–sixth grades.

- BECOMING JOE DIMAGGIO, by Maria Testa (Candlewick). New York City in the 1930s and 1940s is the setting for this novel in verse about a boy and his Italian grandfather and the dreams they hold in their hearts. Reading level: fifth–sixth grades.

- KIRA-KIRA by Cynthia Kadohata (Atheneum). *Kira-kira* means "glittering" in Japanese. Narrator and first-generation American Katie Takeshima learns this and more from her dying sister as this glimmering story set in the 1950s evolves; 2005 Newbery Award. Reading level: fifth grade.

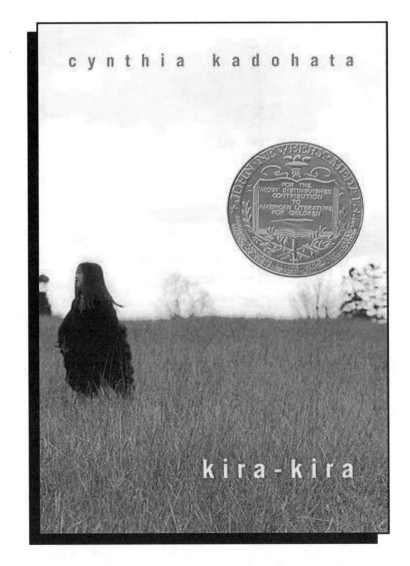

KIRA-KIRA by Cynthia Kadohata. Copyright © 2004. Used with permission of Atheneum Books for Young Readers, an imprint of Simon & Schuster Children's Publishing.

- LILY'S CROSSING, by Patricia Reilly Giff (Random House); Newbery Honor book set in the summer of 1944 about the friendship between an American girl whose father has gone overseas to fight the war and a Hungarian refugee who has escaped the Nazis. Reading level: fifth grade.

- BULL RUN, by Paul Fleischman (HarperCollins); 60 deeply affecting narratives written as journal entries, offering the points of view of 16 people from all walks of life about the first battle of the Civil War, war in general, and life in the mid-1800s. Reading level: fifth grade.

- DAVE AT NIGHT, by Gail Carson Levine (HarperCollins); story set in Harlem in the 1920s about a Jewish boy's experiences in an orphanage; based on Levine's father's childhood; winner of numerous awards. Reading level: fifth grade.

- BUD, NOT BUDDY, by Christopher Paul Curtis (Delacorte), On the run from abusive foster care situations, 10-year-old Bud (not Buddy) is in search of the man he believes is his father; laugh-out-loud funny, yet also sensitive; Newbery Medal and Coretta Scott King Award. Reading level: fifth grade.

- FROM THE LIGHTHOUSE, by Liz Chipman (Dutton). In this story set in the late 1930s in a lighthouse on the Hudson River, Weezie, her brothers, and her father cope with Ma's leaving and the impact this loss (and later the death of the middle sibling) has on the family over the course of a year; although sad, the story, beautifully written, offers hope and celebrates the strength of family—a unit of related individuals. Reading level: fifth grade.

- MY LOUISIANA SKY, by Kimberly Willis Holt (Random House); set in 1957; the multiple award–winning debut novel of 12-year-old Tiger Ann Parker, who is bright, athletic, and shunned by her peers because her parents are "slow"; when she is offered the chance to leave the small Southern town in which she has lived with her parents and grandmother, Tiger Ann comes to realize what she values most. Reading level: fifth grade.

- THE WATSONS GO TO BIRMINGHAM—1963, by Christopher Paul Curtis (Delacorte); debut novel that won a slew of awards, including the Newbery Honor and the Coretta Scott King Honor; at once funny and deeply moving; 10-year-old Kenny Watson and his warm-hearted, everyday family embark on an unforgettable road trip to visit their grandmother in Birmingham—the site of the bombing of the Sixteenth Avenue Baptist Church with four children inside. Reading level: fifth grade.

- BELLE TEAL, by Ann M. Martin (Scholastic). Set in the rural South in the 1960s, this powerhouse of a story about a poor girl's experiences with racial hatred and social injustice also explores the themes of judging individuals rather than their appearances, the strength of family bonds, and the inevitability of change. Reading level: fifth grade.

- THE LIBERATION OF GABRIEL KING, by K. L. Going (Putnam). Set in 1976 in a small town in Georgia, this comically serious novel explores racism, friendship, and family, as fourth-grader Gabe, who is white, and his feisty African American pal, Frita, confront fears, bullies, moving up to the "big kids' " wing of the school, and lists. Reading level: fifth grade.

- SOME FRIEND, by Marie Bradby (Atheneum). Set in the 1960s with the Civil Rights movement as the backdrop, this is the story of 11-year-old African American Pearl and what she learns about friendship and peer groups from the hip and popular Lenore and the newcomer Artemesia, whose migrant status and secondhand clothes cause her to be shunned, even by Pearl, who secretly admires this new girl in the neighborhood and comes to regret her behavior toward her. Reading level: fifth grade.

SOME FRIEND by Marie Bradby. Copyright © 2004. Used with permission of Richard Jackson Books/Atheneum Books for Young Readers, an imprint of Simon & Schuster Children's Publishing.

- ALMOST FOREVER, by Maria Testa (Candlewick); a young child waits for her father's return from Vietnam; spare novel in verse explores feelings with tenderness and poignancy.

- RIDING FREEDOM, written by Pam Muñoz Ryan and illustrated by Brian Selznick (Scholastic); based on true events in the life of Charlotte Parkhurst, a skilled equestrian, well-known stagecoach driver, and the first woman to vote in the state of California—all things she accomplished before it was legal for her to do them. Reading level: fourth–fifth grades.

- STARRING SALLY J. FREEDMAN AS HERSELF, by Judy Blume (Bradbury); set in 1947 with World War II as the backdrop; the story of a girl who manages life events, from an absent father and an ill brother, to a new home, with the help of a vivid and therapeutic imagination. Reading level: fourth–fifth grades.

- SARAH, PLAIN AND TALL, by Patricia MacLachlan (HarperCollins); courage, pluck, and wisdom in a hugely entertaining, slim novel about a mail-order bride who comes to live with a family on the prairie; Newbery Award; see also the sequel, SKYLARK. Reading level: fourth grade.

- Little House on the Prairie series; written by Laura Ingalls Wilder and illustrated by Garth Williams (HarperCollins). This classic historical fiction series has been loved and cherished since it was first published in the 1930s and 1940s. Reading level: fourth grade.

- MR. MYSTERIOUS & COMPANY, written by Sid Fleischman and illustrated by Eric von Schmidt (Little, Brown; Greenwillow). There's magic and wizardry on this journey out West. Reading level: fourth grade.

• PEDRO'S JOURNAL: A VOYAGE WITH CHRISTOPHER COLUMBUS, written by Pam Conrad and illustrated by Peter Koeppen (Boyds Mills Press); fictional journal of a cabin boy traveling with Columbus. Reading level: fourth grade.

PEDRO'S JOURNAL: A VOYAGE WITH CHRISTOPHER COLUMBUS, by Pam Conrad, illustrated by Peter Koeppen. Copyright © 2005. Published by Boyds Mills Press. Reprinted by permission.

- KITTY AND MR. KIPLING: NEIGHBORS IN VERMONT, written by Lenore Blegvad and illustrated by Erik Blegvad (McElderry). Based on fact, this is the story of the friendship between a young girl and the famous author in the late 1800s. Reading level: fourth grade.

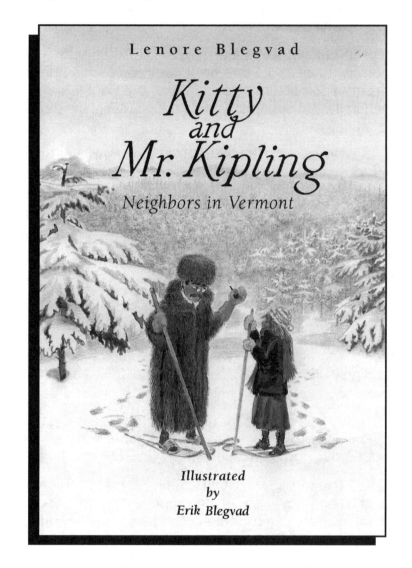

KITTY AND MR. KIPLING: NEIGHBORS IN VERMONT by Lenore Blegvad, illustrated by Erik Blegvad. Copyright © 2005. Used with permission of Margaret K. McElderry Books, an imprint of Simon & Schuster Children's Publishing.

Realistic Fiction

- OLIVE'S OCEAN, by Kevin Henkes (Greenwillow). The journal entry of a classmate who was suddenly killed by a car begins 12-year-old Martha's journey toward understanding herself and life; Newbery Honor. Reading level: sixth grade.

- WALK TWO MOONS, by Sharon Creech (HarperCollins); a story within a story about loss and acceptance. Of Native American ancestry, 13-year-old Salamanca Tree Hiddle's mom has disappeared, and so has the mom of her new friend, Phoebe Winterbottom. On Sal's journey with her grandparents to retrace her mother's path, she tells Phoebe's story and travels an emotional journey toward acceptance; Newbery Medal. Reading level: sixth grade.

- SURVIVING THE APPLEWHITES, by Stephanie S. Tolan (HarperCollins); humorous novel about the misadventures of this uproarious family, told from the alternating points of view of Jake, the troublemaker, and E. D. a member of the family that accepts Jake into their clan; Newbery Honor. Reading level: sixth grade.

- THE BOY WHO SAVED BASEBALL, by John H. Ritter (Penguin); the highly praised novel about a town and a team full of legendary characters who come together to save a ball field; memorable in every way. Reading level: sixth grade.

- STRIKE TWO, by Amy Goldman Koss (Penguin). Cousins and best friends face family tension, an aborted softball season, and more when the newspaper that employs both their fathers and sponsors the team is embroiled in a strike. Reading level: sixth grade.

- PARK'S QUEST, by Katherine Paterson (Penguin). Park's father was killed in Vietnam, but Park intends to "find" him in this multilayered novel with themes of family, secrets, human weakness, prejudice, and war, written by one of the most highly acclaimed authors in the field. Reading level: sixth grade.

- THE MUSIC OF DOLPHINS, by Karen Hesse (Scholastic). A teen who has been raised by dolphins is "rescued" and learns what it means to be human; intriguing use of typefaces further enhances a haunting, poetic, and thought-provoking story. Reading level: sixth grade.

- A DAY NO PIGS WOULD DIE, by Robert Newton Peck (Knopf); coming-of-age novel set in Vermont; a moving and memorable story of the relationship between a Shaker man and his son; somewhat violent. Reading level: sixth grade.

- GRACE HAPPENS, by Jan Czech (Viking). Grace, 15-year-old daughter of a gorgeous but distant movie star, longs for a normal life and to know who her father is. Her summer on Martha's Vineyard turns out to be a dream come true. Reading level: sixth grade.

- SHAPER, by Jessie Haas (Greenwillow). Fourteen-year-old Chad has no intention of forgiving his grandfather for the part he played in the loss of his dog, Shep, or of bonding with the new dog, Queenie. How his new neighbor, a "shaper" who trains animals, and his daughter help Chad learn about himself makes for a thoughtful read. Reading level: sixth grade.

- THE BOY WHO OWNED THE SCHOOL, by Gary Paulsen (Scholastic). In this slim, farcical novel about a hapless teen and first love, the laughs are as fast-paced as the plot. Reading level: sixth grade.

- THE VACATION, by Polly Horvath (Farrar Straus Giroux). Left in his persnickety aunts' care, Henry embarks on a cross-country venture that is at once real and symbolic of his journey toward maturity—because of and in spite of—the adults. Reading level: fifth–sixth grades.

THE VACATION © 2005 by Polly Horvath. Cover Art © 2005 by Miles Hyman. Used with the permission of Farrar Straus Giroux.

- EVERYTHING ON A WAFFLE, by Polly Horvath (Farrar Straus Giroux). Funny, self-reliant, and wise, 11-year-old Primrose Squarp waits for her parents' return, even though most everyone else in town seems convinced they were lost at sea. In the meantime, the reader is treated to a delightfully memorable cast of characters who inhabit the small Canadian town of Coal

Harbour, including Kate Bowzer, the lovable proprietor of The Girl on the Red Swing restaurant, where everything comes on a waffle—from lasagna to, well, waffles. Newbery Honor. Reading level: fifth–sixth grades.

- MIRACLE'S BOYS, by Jacqueline Woodson (Putnam); poignant story of three brothers who must rely on themselves and each other as they struggle with life after the death of their parents; Coretta Scott King Award. Reading level: fifth–sixth grades.

- HEARTBEAT, by Sharon Creech (HarperCollins); story told in poems that is simple yet deep, about 12-year-old Annie, who loves to run, and her changing relationships with her friend, Max, her ailing grandfather, the new baby her mother is carrying, and her interest in art. Reading level: fifth–sixth grades.

- LOVE THAT DOG, by Sharon Creech (HarperCollins); humorous yet touching story told in poems; poetry helps Jack overcome his grief over the loss of his dog; poems from authors such as Robert Frost, William Carlos Williams, and Walter Dean Myers are woven into the telling of this wonderful story. Reading level: fifth–sixth grades.

- SOMETHING ABOUT AMERICA, by Maria Testa (Candlewick); story in poems from a young teen's perspective, about an immigrant family's gradual assimilation into American culture after fleeing war-torn Kosova (Kosovo), Yugoslavia. Reading level: fifth–sixth grades.

- THE WISH, by Gail Carson Levine (HarperCollins). Wilma is an eighth grader who, like many, is smart but wishes to be popular. When she is granted her wish, the fun and the education begin for this girl, who knows the wisdom of the famous words, "To thine own self be true." Reading level: fifth–sixth grades.

- EACH LITTLE BIRD THAT SINGS, by Deborah Wiles (Harcourt). Ten-year-old Comfort, the daughter of the owner of a funeral home, learns about death when her dear great-great aunt Florentine dies suddenly—and about life, friendship, family, and herself—with the help of a wonderfully singular cast of characters with unique names, such as Dismay (Comfort's loyal dog), Peaches Shuggars (her annoying cousin), and Declaration (her not-so-true friend); letters, lists, and recipes further enhance the storytelling. Reading level: fifth–sixth grades.

- CON-FIDENCE, by Todd Strasser (Holiday House); middle-school girls and the quest for popularity are central to this story about friendship, self-confidence, and manipulation; told in the second person. Reading level: fifth–sixth grades.

- THE YEAR MY PARENTS RUINED MY LIFE, by Martha Freeman (Holiday House). The move from sunny, surfin' California to a small town in Pennsylvania drives the story of 12-year-old Kate's struggle to adjust; entertaining, endearing story about change, friendship, and family. Reading level: fifth–sixth grades.

THE YEAR MY PARENTS RUINED MY LIFE by Martha Freeman. Published by Holiday House. Reprinted by permission.

- THE TROLLS, by Polly Horvath (Farrar Straus Giroux). Aunt Sally comes to stay while the parents are off on vacation and regales the Anderson kids with hilarious, memorable stories she swears are true; National Book Award finalist; Boston Globe-Horn Book Honor Award. Reading level: fifth–sixth grades.

- ONE-EYED CAT, by Paula Fox (Simon & Schuster). Eleven year-old Ned knew he shouldn't shoot the rifle; how he lives with his guilt and eventually makes things right won this riveting novel a Newbery Honor. Reading level: fifth–sixth grades.

- Alice series, by Phyllis Naylor Reynolds (Atheneum); funny, realistic travails of Alice, the sole female in her family, beginning with her sixth-grade year and advancing through common high school angst. Numerous titles, the first of which is THE AGONY OF ALICE; prequels cover Alice's younger years. Reading level: fifth–sixth grades.

THE AGONY OF ALICE by Phyllis Naylor Reynolds. Copyright © 1985. Used with permission of Atheneum Books for Young Readers, an imprint of Simon & Schuster Children's Publishing.

- STEALING THUNDER, by Mary Casanova (Hyperion); well-paced, satisfying adventure about a girl who sets out to save an abused horse from its owner. Reading level: fifth–sixth grades.

- TRACKER, by Gary Paulsen (Atheneum). Hunting for deer and the meaning of life, a boy grapples with the end of his grandfather's life. Reading level: fifth–sixth grades.

- DOGSONG, by Gary Paulsen (Simon & Schuster); dog-sledding adventure/survival story; Newbery Honor Award. Reading level: fifth–sixth grades.

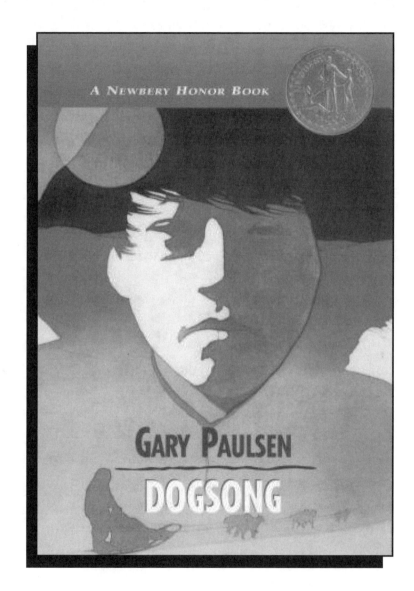

DOGSONG by Gary Paulsen. Copyright © 1985. Used with permission of Richard Jackson Books/Atheneum Books for Young Readers, an imprint of Simon & Schuster Children's Publishing.

- HOW I BECAME A WRITER AND OGGIE LEARNED TO DRIVE, by Janet Taylor Lisle (Penguin). Adventure, writing, and even driving enter into this story about 11-year-old Archie, who writes stories to help his little brother, Oggie, cope with their parents' separation; when his life begins mirroring his stories, the suspense begins. Reading level: fifth grade.

- BECAUSE OF WINN-DIXIE, by Kate DiCamillo (Candlewick). Opal's mother deserted her and her preacher dad seven years ago, but it's not until a tail-wagging stray comes to stay that the healing begins; Newbery Honor. Reading level: fifth grade.

- FRINDLE, by Andrew Clements (Simon & Schuster). Nick is an irascible fifth grader who, on a lark, decides to coin a new word for *pen*. The events that ensue make this multi-million-copy best seller and modern classic a memorable, satisfying must-read. Reading level: fifth grade.

FRINDLE by Andrew Clements, illustrated by Brian Selznick. Copyright © 1996. Used with permission of Simon & Schuster Books for Young Readers, an imprint of Simon & Schuster Children's Publishing.

- BECOMING NAOMI LEÓN, by Pam Muñoz Ryan (Scholastic). Family, inner strength, emotional and physical journeys, and loyalty are overriding themes in this evocative, award-winning story of a Mexican American girl whose mother returns after seven years, and the ensuing conflicts that event triggers. Reading level: fifth grade.

- ESPERANZA RISING, by Pam Muñoz Ryan (Scholastic); Set in the Depression era, this is the story of a 13-year-old girl who emigrates to America from Mexico after her family loses their wealth; she learns about life, a new culture, and herself. Reading level: fifth grade.

- HARRIET THE SPY, by Louise Fitzhugh (HarperCollins). When Harriet's spy journal is revealed to her sixth-grade classmates, the trouble begins; a classic with an unforgettable heroine. See also the sequel, THE LONG SECRET. Reading level: fifth grade.

- LOVE, RUBY LAVENDER, by Deborah Wiles (Harcourt). Nine year-old Ruby and her grandmother are best buddies in this warm, entertaining novel set in Halleluia, Mississippi. When Miss Eula goes to Hawaii to visit her new grandchild, Ruby grows in her absence, with the help of their correspondence and her own delightful pluck. Reading level: fifth grade.

Courtesy Harcourt, Inc.

- BLOOMABILITY, by Sharon Creech (HarperCollins). Dinnie's experiences at an international school lead to growth and an appreciation of the value of being open to life's possibilities—or "bloomabilities," as her sidekick would say. Reading level: fifth grade.

- THE REPORT CARD, by Andrew Clements (Simon & Schuster). Despite the fact that she is a genius, Nora gets below-average grades—on purpose. A solid story by a popular author for middle-grade readers examines the issue of tests and their fallout, and is certain to stimulate animated discussion. Reading level: fifth grade.

THE REPORT CARD by Andrew Clements. Copyright © 2004. Used with permission of Simon & Schuster Books for Young Readers, an imprint of Simon & Schuster Children's Publishing.

- LOSER, by Jerry Spinelli (HarperCollins). Donald is a likeable loser with an admirable attitude in this touching story with a powerful message about how we treat those who are "different." Reading level: fifth grade.

- THE PENDERWICKS: A SUMMER TALE OF FOUR SISTERS, TWO RABBITS, AND A VERY INTERESTING BOY, by Jeanne Birdsall (Knopf); charming, entertaining, light-hearted, and satisfying tale of four sisters and their summer adventures in the Berkshires; winner of the 2005 National Book Award for Young People's Literature. Reading level: fifth grade.

- WHEN ZACHARY BEAVER CAME TO TOWN, by Kimberly Willis Holt (Holt). Toby thinks his life is pretty bad until "the fattest boy in the world" rolls into town. How their friendship develops and Toby's perspective changes earned this memorable novel the National Book Award for Young People's Literature. Reading level: fifth grade.

Courtesy of Henry Holt and Co.

- AGNES PARKER . . . GIRL IN PROGRESS, by Kathleen O'Dell (Dial). An endearing character learns about life and herself while navigating the trials of sixth grade in this upbeat, satisfying story. See also the sequel, AGNES PARKER . . . HAPPY CAMPER. Reading level: fifth grade.

- DEVIL'S BRIDGE, by Cynthia DeFelice (HarperCollins). Action and suspense make this story about a boy in a fishing derby, whose sense of fairness puts him in danger, a compelling read. Reading level: fifth grade.

- YOLONDA'S GENIUS, by Carol Fenner (McElderry). After moving from Chicago to a suburb in Michigan, African American Yolonda sets out to prove that her little brother, Andrew, is a genius, despite the fact that he cannot read. He makes beautiful music on his harmonica, and it's Yolonda's intention to bring that talent to light; Newbery Honor. Reading level: fifth grade.

YOLONDA'S GENIUS by Carol Fenner. Copyright © 1995. Used with permission of Margaret K. McElderry Books, an imprint of Simon & Schuster Children's Publishing.

- JUST AS LONG AS WE'RE TOGETHER, by Judy Blume (Orchard); an upbeat, funny, and poignant story about preteen girls' friendship, told in Blume's trademark style. Reading level: fifth grade.

- COUSINS, by Virginia Hamilton (Philomel). Family relationships are at the center of this thought-provoking novel about loss and growth. Reading level: fifth grade.

- EVERYWHERE, by Bruce Brooks (HarperCollins). A boy's grandfather (and best friend) flirts with death in this story of love, hope, and family. Reading level: fifth grade.

- THE CAT ATE MY GYMSUIT, by Paula Danziger (Penguin); a modern classic about a young teen who comes out of her shell to fight for the teacher she believes in. Reading level: fifth grade.

- SIXTH GRADE SECRETS, by Louis Sachar (Scholastic). Secrets get out of control in this sixth-grade class when Laura's secret club, Pig City, is challenged by Gabriel's Monkey Town! Reading level: fifth grade.

- GOING FOR GREAT, by Carole Brockmann (American Girl). Friendship, courage, and a music competition combine in a solid story centered on a sixth-grade girl. Reading level: fifth grade.

- THE SUMMER OF THE SWANS, by Betsy Byars (Penguin); "a day in the life" of 14-year-old Sara, who cares for her mentally handicapped brother and longs for freedom. When Charlie becomes lost, what Sara learns about herself makes for an unforgettable story; Newbery Medal. Reading level: fifth grade.

- A SONG FOR JEFFREY, by Constance M. Foland (American Girl); affecting tale of friendship between narrator Dodie and Jeffrey, who has muscular dystrophy. Reading level: fifth grade.

- HOW I BECAME A WRITER AND OGGIE LEARNED TO DRIVE, by Janet Taylor Lisle (Penguin). Adventure, writing, and even driving enter into this story about 11-year-old Archie, who pens stories to help his little brother, Oggie, and himself cope with their parents' separation and the changes it brings; when life begins to mirror fiction, the adventure begins. Reading level: fifth grade.

• THE GRADUATION OF JAKE MOON, by Barbara Park (Simon & Schuster). A moving novel about an eighth grader and his gradual acceptance of his grandfather's advancing Alzheimer's disease. Reading level: fifth grade.

THE GRADUATION OF JAKE MOON by Barbara Park, illustrated by Paul Colin. Copyright © 2000. Used with permission of Atheneum Books for Young Readers, an imprint of Simon & Schuster Children's Publishing.

• 101 WAYS TO BUG YOUR TEACHER, by Lee Wardlaw (Dial); sequel to 101 WAYS TO BUG YOUR PARENTS; a fun read with humor, insight, and believable characters; not as obnoxious as the title might suggest. Reading level: fifth grade.

- REMEMBER ME TO HAROLD SQUARE, by Paula Danziger (Penguin). Three kids get to know New York City, each other, and themselves during one memorable summer. Reading level: fifth grade.

- SWITCHAROUND, by Lois Lowry (Houghton Mifflin). NYC kids Caroline and her bro, J. P., spend the summer with their father and his new family in a small town; funny and touching. Reading level: fifth grade.

Cover from SWITCHAROUND by Lois Lowry. Jacket art © 1985 by Diane de Groat. Reprinted by permission of Houghton Mifflin Company. All rights reserved.

- THE (SHORT) STORY OF MY LIFE, by Jennifer B. Jones (Walker). Sixth-grader Michael Jordan is the shortest guy in his class, and it seems to be all he thinks about. How he comes to learn he has a place in the world is told with humor, insight, and warmth; a pleasurable read. Reading level: fifth grade.

- BABY, by Patricia MacLachlan (Bantam Doubleday Dell). The baby left in a basket on the driveway won't replace the baby they lost, but so begins this family's healing in this heartfelt tale. Reading level: fifth grade.

- THE SECRET LANGUAGE OF GIRLS, by Frances O'Roark Dowell (Atheneum). Preteens Kate and Marylin, best buds and neighbors for, like, forever, navigate new friends, boys, peer-driven meanness, and loyalty in this contemporary, worthwhile offering. Reading level: fifth grade.

THE SECRET LANGUAGE OF GIRLS by Frances O'Roark Dowell. Copyright © 2004. Used with permission of Atheneum Books for Young Readers, an imprint of Simon & Schuster Children's Publishing.

- SMOKE SCREEN, by Amy Goldman Koss (American Girl). Funny, endearing sixth grader Mitzi's life gets dizzy when she tells a lie to the boy she has a crush on. Reading level: fifth grade.

- MILLICENT MIN, GIRL GENIUS, by Lisa Yee (Scholastic). Eleven-year-old Millie finally has a friend, but when her trust falters, so does the friendship. See also STANFORD WONG FLUNKS BIG TIME, in which another character in MILLICENT MIN takes center stage. Reading level: fifth grade.

- WING NUT, by M. J. Auch (Holt). Friendship with an irascible, yet grandfatherly, neighbor, who raises purple martins, brings stability and security to 12-year-old Grady's nomadic life. Reading level: fifth grade.

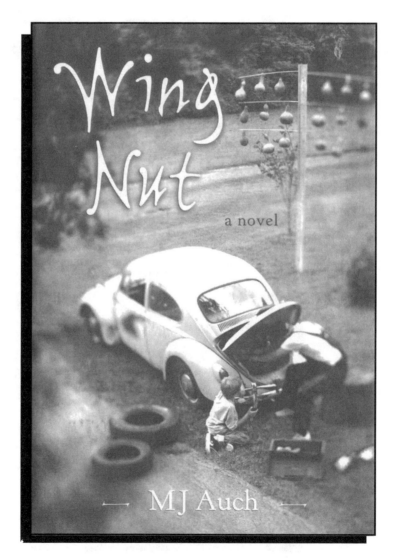

Courtesy of Henry Holt and Co.

- Matthew Martin books, by Paula Danziger (Penguin). Eleven-year-old pun master Matthew is a likeable character who steers through the ups and downs of looming adolescence; satisfying tales from a master at juxtaposing the humorous with the agonizing. See EVERYONE ELSE'S PARENTS SAID YES, MAKE LIKE A TREE AND LEAVE, and NOT FOR A BILLION GAZILLION DOLLARS. Reading level: fifth grade.

- BEEKMAN'S BIG DEAL, by Michael de Guzman (Farrar Straus Giroux). Twelve-year-old Beekman O'Day, whose life has not been rosy, is used to moving around every time his father's schemes fall through. When he finds a place he'd like to stay, Beekman works out a deal of his own with the help of a cast of offbeat but lovable neighbors. Reading level: fifth grade.

BEEKMAN'S BIG DEAL © 2004 by Michael de Guzman. Cover Art © 2004 by Joe Ciardiello. Used with the permission of Farrar Straus Giroux.

- MOLLY MCGINTY HAS A REALLY GOOD DAY, by Gary Paulsen (Random House). The self-proclaimed "old boy" writes from a girl's point of view in this story about one day in the life of a sixth grader whose wacky grandmother/caregiver comes to school. Reading level: fifth grade.

- SIXTH GRADE, by Susie Morganstern (Viking); chronicles Margot's transition to middle school; originally published in France. Reading level: fifth grade.

- WRINGER, by Jerry Spinelli (HarperCollins). Soon to be ten years old, Palmer resists the town's traditional rite of passage of wringing the necks of wounded pigeons in this controversial coming-of-age novel that is certain to spark discussions of moral issues; Newbery Honor Award. Reading level: fifth grade.

- ARE YOU THERE, GOD? IT'S ME, MARGARET, by Judy Blume (Bradbury); the modern classic story of 11-year-old Margaret and her navigation of preteen girl issues and religion. Reading level: fourth–fifth grades.

ARE YOU THERE GOD? IT'S ME MARGARET by Judy Blume. Copyright © 2001. Used with permission of Richard Jackson Books/Atheneum Books for Young Readers, an imprint of Simon & Schuster Children's Publishing.

- P.S. LONGER LETTER LATER, by Paula Danziger and Ann M. Martin (Scholastic). Seventh-grade best friends, now apart, continue their relationship through correspondence. See also SNAIL MAIL NO MORE, in which they graduate to e-mail. Reading level: fourth–fifth grades.

- ROPE BURN, by Jan Siebold (Whitman). As a result of an English assignment related to proverbs, a boy explores his feelings about his life, including his parents' divorce and a recent move. Reading level: fourth–fifth grades.

- COLDER THAN ICE, by David Patneaude (Whitman). New school, new friends, bullies, and more make for a solid story and a worthwhile read. Reading level: fourth–fifth grades.

Cover illustration by Doron Ben-Ami from COLDER THAN ICE by David Patneaude. Illustration © 2003 by Doron Ben-Ami. Reprinted by permission of Albert Whitman & Company.

- IDA B . . . AND HER PLANS TO MAXIMIZE FUN, AVOID DISASTER, AND (POSSIBLY) SAVE THE WORLD, by Katherine Hannigan (Greenwillow). When homeschooled Ida learns that her mother has cancer, her parents have decided to send her to public school, and part of the family's orchard will be sold, she takes solace in the beloved apple trees she has named, and she learns to overcome her anger at things out of her control with the help of loving parents, a wise fourth-grade teacher, and her deciduous friends; multiple award–winning debut novel. Reading level: fourth–fifth grades.

- BRIDGE TO TERABITHIA, written by Katherine Paterson and illustrated by Donna Diamond (HarperCollins). The accidental death of a friend is the catalyst in this classic novel; winner of numerous awards including the Newbery Medal. Reading level: fourth grade.

- DOING TIME ONLINE by Jan Siebold (Whitman). As a result of a mean prank, 12-year-old Mitch must spend time chatting online with a nursing home resident . What the two teach each other in a month's time is the crux of this story suitable for reluctant readers. Reading level: fourth grade.

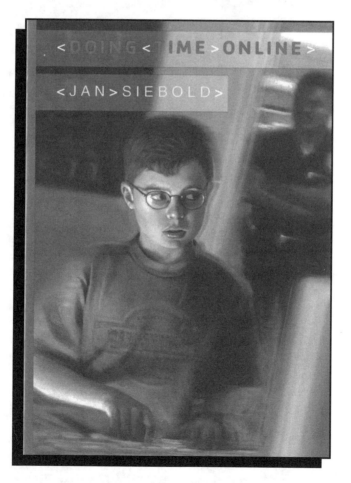

Cover illustration by Layne Johnson from DOING TIME ONLINE by Jan Siebold. Illustration © 2002 by Layne Johnson. Reprinted by permission of Albert Whitman & Company.

- Anastasia Krupnik series, written by Lois Lowry (Bantam, Doubleday, Dell); chronicles the everyday life of a spunky, adorable, independent, and resourceful character. Titles include ANASTASIA KRUPNIK, ANASTASIA AGAIN, ANASTASIA ON HER OWN, ANASTASIA'S CHOSEN CAREER, ANASTASIA HAS THE ANSWERS, ANASTASIA AT YOUR SERVICE, and ANASTASIA ABSOLUTELY. Reading level: fourth grade.

- Joey Pigza Books, by Jack Gantos (Farrar Straus Giroux); From the National Book Award finalist, JOEY PIGZA SWALLOWED THE KEY to the Newbery Honor Award winner, JOEY PIGZA LOSES CONTROL, to the final book in the trilogy, WHAT WOULD JOEY DO?, these fictional accounts of a boy plagued by ADD tug at the heart while managing at the same time to be hilarious. Joey is a boy who won't soon be forgotten. Reading level: fourth grade.

WHAT WOULD JOEY DO? © 2002 by Jack Gantos. Cover Art © 2002 by Beata Szpura. Used with the permission of Farrar Straus Giroux.

- FLYING SOLO, by Ralph Fletcher (Clarion). When both the teacher and the substitute don't show up on one memorable Friday in April, a sixth-grade class takes matters into their own hands; told from the points of view of different students in the class. Reading level: fourth grade.

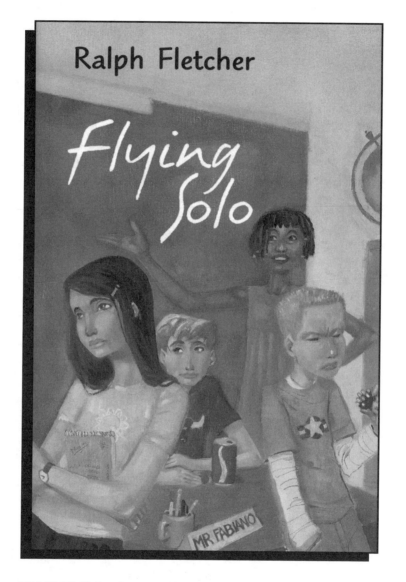

Cover from FLYING SOLO by Ralph Fletcher. Jacket illustration copyright © 1998 by Ben Caldwell. Reprinted by permission of Clarion Books, an imprint of Houghton Mifflin Company. All rights reserved.

Family

- MIRACLE'S BOYS, by Jacqueline Woodson (Putnam); poignant story of three brothers who must rely on themselves and each other as they struggle with life after the death of their parents; Coretta Scott King Award. Reading level: fifth–sixth grades.

- A DAY NO PIGS WOULD DIE, by Robert Newton Peck (Knopf); coming-of-age novel set in rural Vermont; a moving and memorable story of the relationship between a Shaker man and his son; somewhat violent. Reading level: sixth grade.

- SHAPER, by Jessie Haas (Greenwillow). Fourteen-year-old Chad has no intention of forgiving his grandfather for the part he played in the loss of his dog ,Shep, or of bonding with the new dog, Queenie. How his new neighbor, a "shaper" who trains animals, and his daughter help Chad learn about himself makes for a thoughtful read. Reading level: sixth grade.

- BELLE PRATER'S BOY, by Ruth White (Farrar Straus Giroux). Virginia in the 1950s is the setting for this story about cousins and best friends, Gypsy and Woodrow, and the losses they face together in their sixth-grade year; Newbery Honor. See also the acclaimed sequel, THE SEARCH FOR BELLE PRATER. Reading level: fifth–sixth grades.

- EACH LITTLE BIRD THAT SINGS, by Deborah Wiles (Harcourt). Ten-year-old Comfort, the daughter of the owner of a funeral home, learns about death when her dear great-great aunt Florentine dies suddenly—and about life, friendship, family, and herself with the help of a wonderfully singular cast of characters with unique names, such as Dismay (Comfort's loyal dog), Peaches Shuggars (her annoying cousin), and Declaration (her not-so-true friend); letters, lists, and recipes further enhance the storytelling. Reading level: fifth–sixth grades.

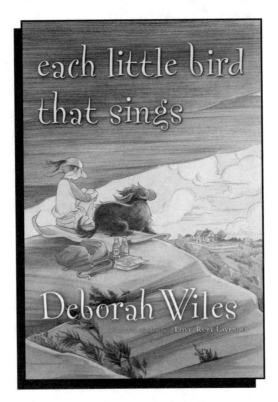

Courtesy Harcourt, Inc.

- BECOMING JOE DIMAGGIO, by Maria Testa (Candlewick). New York City in the 1930s and 1940s is the setting for this story in poems about a boy and his Italian grandfather and the dreams they hold in their hearts. Reading level: fifth–sixth grades.

- HEARTBEAT, by Sharon Creech (HarperCollins); story in poems that is simple yet deep about 12-year-old Annie, who loves to run, and her changing relationships with her friend, Max, her ailing grandfather, the new baby her mother is carrying, and her interest in art. Reading level: fifth–sixth grade.

- THE TROLLS, by Polly Horvath (Farrar Straus Giroux). Aunt Sally comes to stay while the parents are off on vacation and regales the Anderson kids with hilarious, memorable stories she swears are true; National Book Award finalist; Boston Globe-Horn Book Honor Award. Reading level: fifth–sixth grades.

- TRACKER, by Gary Paulsen (Atheneum). Hunting for deer and the meaning of life, a boy grapples with the end of his grandfather's life. Reading level: fifth–sixth grades.

- DOGSONG, by Gary Paulsen (Simon & Schuster); dog-sledding adventure/ survival story; Newbery Honor Award. Reading level: fifth–sixth grades.

- THE BORNING ROOM, by Paul Fleischman (HarperCollins); events in the life of Ohioan Georgina Caroline Lott and her family between 1851 and 1918 that revolve around the borning room, a room off the kitchen reserved for births and deaths. Reading level: fifth–sixth grades.

- A GATHERING OF DAYS: A NEW ENGLAND GIRL'S JOURNAL, 1830–32, by Joan W. Blos (Simon & Schuster). Journal entries chronicle major and everyday events in the life of a farm girl after the loss of her mother; Newbery Medal. Reading level: fifth–sixth grades.

- MY DANIEL, by Pam Conrad (HarperCollins); a grandmother's remembrance of her life with and loss of her brother and their quest for a dinosaur on their farm in Nebraska. Reading level: fifth–sixth grades.

- THE YEAR MY PARENTS RUINED MY LIFE, by Martha Freeman (Holiday House). The move from sunny, surfin' California to a small town in Pennsylvania drives the story of 12-year-old Kate's struggle to adjust; entertaining, endearing story about change, friendship, and family. Reading level: fifth–sixth grades.

- THE WATSONS GO TO BIRMINGHAM—1963, by Christopher Paul Curtis (Delacorte); debut novel that won a slew of awards, including the Newbery Honor and the Coretta Scott King Honor; at once funny and deeply moving. Ten-year-old Kenny Watson and his warm-hearted, everyday family embark on an unforgettable road trip to visit their grandmother in Birmingham—the site of the bombing of the Sixteenth Avenue Baptist Church with four children inside. Reading level: fifth grade.

- BECAUSE OF WINN-DIXIE, by Kate DiCamillo (Candlewick). Opal's mother deserted her and her preacher dad seven years ago, but it's not until a tail-wagging stray comes to stay that the healing begins; Newbery Honor. Reading level: fifth grade.

- MY LOUISIANA SKY, by Kimberly Willis Holt (Random House). Set in 1957, this is the multiple award–winning debut novel about 12-year-old Tiger Ann Parker, who is bright, athletic, and shunned by her peers because her parents are "slow"; when she is offered the chance to leave the small Southern town in which she has lived with her parents and grandmother, Tiger Ann comes to realize what she values most. Reading level: fifth grade.

- MISSING MAY, by Cynthia Rylant (Scholastic). Twelve-year-old Summer and her Uncle Ob deal with the loss of Aunt May; Newbery Medal, Boston Globe/Horn Book Award. Reading level: fifth grade.

- FROM THE LIGHTHOUSE, written by Liz Chipman (Dutton). In this story set in the late 1930s in a lighthouse on the Hudson River, Weezie, her brothers, and her father, cope with Ma's leaving and the impact this loss (and later the death of the middle sibling) has on the family over the course of a year; although sad, the story, beautifully written, offers hope and celebrates the strength of family—a unit of related individuals. Reading level: fifth grade.

- BECOMING NAOMI LEÓN, by Pam Muñoz Ryan (Scholastic). Family, inner strength, emotional and physical journeys, and loyalty are themes in this evocative, award-winning story of a Mexican American girl whose mother returns after seven years, and the ensuing conflicts that event triggers. Reading level: fifth grade.

- ESPERANZA RISING, by Pam Muñoz Ryan (Scholastic); set in the Depression era; a 13-year-old girl who emigrates from Mexico to America after her family loses their wealth learns about life, a new culture, and herself. Reading level: fifth grade.

- THE PENDERWICKS: A SUMMER TALE OF FOUR SISTERS, TWO RABBITS, AND A VERY INTERESTING BOY, by Jeanne Birdsall (Knopf); charming, entertaining, light-hearted, and satisfying tale of four sisters and their summer adventures in the Berkshires; winner of the 2005 National Book Award for Young People's Literature. Reading level: fifth grade.

- LOVE, RUBY LAVENDER, by Deborah Wiles (Harcourt). Nine year-old Ruby and her grandmother are best buddies in this warm, entertaining novel set in Halleluia, Mississippi. When Miss Eula goes to Hawaii to visit her new grandchild, Ruby grows in her absence, with the help of their correspondence and her own delightful pluck. Reading level: fifth grade.

- THE BIG HOUSE, written by Carolyn Coman and illustrated by Rob Shepperson (Front Street). This sister and brother team sticks together through mystery, comedy, bed-wetting, and a trial—of sorts. Reading level: fifth grade.

THE BIG HOUSE, by Carolyn Coman, illustrated by Rob Shepperson. Copyright © 2004. Published by Front Street, an imprint of Boyds Mills Press. Reprinted by permission.

- THE NIGHT SWIMMERS, by Betsy Byars (Delacorte); the adventures of three siblings who are left to their own devices while their dad is out performing in the evenings; winner of the American Book Award and a Boston Globe/Horn Book Honor Award. Reading level: fifth grade.

- EVERYWHERE, by Bruce Brooks (HarperCollins). A boy's grandfather (and best friend) flirts with death in this story of love, hope, and family. Reading level: fifth grade.

- COUSINS, by Virginia Hamilton (Philomel). Family relationships are at the center of this thought-provoking novel about loss and personal growth. Reading level: fifth grade.

- BELLE TEAL, by Ann M. Martin (Scholastic). Set in the rural South in the 1960s, this powerhouse of a story of a poor girl's experiences with racial hatred and social injustice also explores the themes of judging individuals rather than their appearances, the strength of family bonds, and the inevitability of change. Reading level: fifth grade.

- SWITCHAROUND, by Lois Lowry (Houghton Mifflin). NYC kids Caroline and her bro, J. P., spend the summer with their father and his new family in a small town, funny and touching. Reading level: fifth grade.

- YOLONDA'S GENIUS, by Carol Fenner (McElderry). After moving from Chicago to a suburb in Michigan, African American Yolonda sets out to prove that her little brother, Andrew, is a genius, despite the fact that he cannot read. He makes beautiful music on his harmonica, and it's Yolonda's intention to bring that talent to light; Newbery Honor. Reading level: fifth grade.

- THE GRADUATION OF JAKE MOON, by Barbara Park (Simon & Schuster). A moving novel about an eighth grader and his gradual acceptance of his grandfather's advancing Alzheimer's disease. Reading level: fifth grade.

- WING NUT, by M. J. Auch (Holt). Friendship with an irascible, yet grandfatherly neighbor, who raises purple martins, brings stability and security to 12-year-old Grady's nomadic life. Reading level: fifth grade.

- BEEKMAN'S BIG DEAL, by Michael de Guzman (Farrar Straus Giroux). Twelve-year-old Beekman O'Day, whose life has not been rosy, is used to moving around every time his father's schemes fall through. When he finds a place he'd like to stay, Beekman works out a deal of his own with the help of a cast of offbeat but lovable neighbors. Reading level: fifth grade.

- HOW I BECAME A WRITER AND OGGIE LEARNED TO DRIVE, by Janet Taylor Lisle (Penguin). Adventure, writing, and even driving enter into this story about 11-year-old Archie, who pens stories to help his little brother, Oggie, and himself cope with their parents' separation and the changes it brings; when life begins to mirror fiction, the adventure begins. Reading level: fifth grade.

- JUST AS LONG AS WE'RE TOGETHER, by Judy Blume (Orchard); upbeat, funny, and poignant story about preteen girls' friendship, told in Blume's trademark style. Reading level: fifth grade.

- BABY, by Patricia MacLachlan (Bantam Doubleday Dell). The baby left in a basket on the driveway won't replace the baby they lost, but so begins the healing in this heartfelt tale. Reading level: fifth grade.

- IDA B . . . AND HER PLANS TO MAXIMIZE FUN, AVOID DISASTER, AND (POSSIBLY) SAVE THE WORLD, by Katherine Hannigan (Greenwillow). When homeschooled Ida learns that her mother has cancer, her parents have decided to send her to public school, and part of the family's orchard will be sold, she takes solace in the beloved apple trees she has named and learns to overcome her anger at things out of her control with the help of loving parents, a wise fourth-grade teacher, and her deciduous friends; multiple award–winning debut novel. Reading level: fourth–fifth grade.

- FLY AWAY HOME, by Eve Bunting (Clarion); picture book story about a homeless man and his son, who live in an airport. Ages 6 and up.

- MY MAN BLUE, poems by Nikki Grimes and illustrated by Jerome Lagarrigue (Penguin). Poems form the story of a boy without a father and a man who has lost his son, and the friendship they forge that helps them both heal. Ages 7 and up.

Divorce

- FROM THE LIGHTHOUSE, by Liz Chipman (Dutton). In this story set during the late 1930s in a lighthouse on the Hudson River, Weezie, her brothers, and her father cope with Ma's leaving and the impact this loss (and later the death of the middle sibling) has on the family over the course of a year; although sad, the story, beautifully written, offers hope and celebrates the strength of family—a unit of related individuals. Reading level: fifth grade.

- IT'S NOT THE END OF THE WORLD, by Judy Blume (Simon & Schuster). Karen Newman deals with her parents' separation. Reading level: fifth grade.

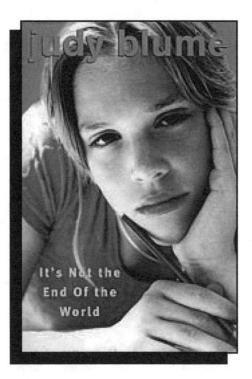

IT'S NOT THE END OF THE WORLD by Judy Blume. Copyright © 2002. Used with permission of Richard Jackson Books/Atheneum Books for Young Readers, an imprint of Simon & Schuster Children's Publishing.

- JUST AS LONG AS WE'RE TOGETHER, by Judy Blume (Orchard); upbeat, funny, and poignant story of preteen girls' friendship story, told in Blume's trademark style; one conflict in this story is the separation of the narrator's parents. Reading level: fifth grade.

- HOW I BECAME A WRITER AND OGGIE LEARNED TO DRIVE, by Janet Taylor Lisle (Penguin). Adventure, writing, and even driving enter into this story about 11-year-old Archie, who pens stories to help his little brother, Oggie, and himself cope with their parents' separation and the changes it brings; when life begins to mirror fiction, the adventure begins. Reading level: fifth grade.

- ROPE BURN, by Jan Siebold (Whitman), As a result of an English assignment related to proverbs, a boy explores his feelings about his life, including his parents' divorce and a recent move. Reading level: fourth–fifth grades.

Cover illustration by Michael Rohani from ROPE BURN by Jan Siebold. Illustration © 1998 by Michael Rohani. Reprinted by permission of Albert Whitman & Company.

Death

- A DAY NO PIGS WOULD DIE, by Robert Newton Peck (Knopf); coming-of-age novel set in rural Vermont; a moving and memorable story of the relationship between a Shaker man and his son; somewhat violent. Reading level: sixth grade.

- SHAPER, by Jessie Haas (Greenwillow). Fourteen-year-old Chad has no intention of forgiving his grandfather for the part he played in the loss of his dog, Shep, or of bonding with the new dog, Queenie. How his new neighbor, a "shaper" who trains animals, and his daughter help Chad learn about himself makes for a thoughtful read. Reading level: sixth grade.

- MIRACLE'S BOYS, by Jacqueline Woodson (Putnam); poignant story of three brothers who must rely on themselves and each other as they struggle with life after the death of their parents; Coretta Scott King Award. Reading level: fifth–sixth grades.

- BELLE PRATER'S BOY, by Ruth White (Farrar Straus Giroux). Virginia in the 1950s is the setting for this story about cousins and best friends, Gypsy and Woodrow, and the losses they face together in their sixth-grade year; Newbery Honor. See also the acclaimed sequel, THE SEARCH FOR BELLE PRATER. Reading level: fifth–sixth grades.

- EACH LITTLE BIRD THAT SINGS, by Deborah Wiles (Harcourt). Ten year-old Comfort, the daughter of the owner of a funeral home, learns about death when her dear great-great aunt Florentine dies suddenly—and about life, friendship, family, and herself, with the help of a wonderfully singular cast of characters with unique names, such as Dismay (Comfort's loyal dog), Peaches Shuggars (her annoying cousin), and Declaration (her not-so-true friend); letters, lists, and recipes further enhance the storytelling. Reading level: fifth–sixth grades.

- LOVE THAT DOG, by Sharon Creech (HarperCollins); humorous yet touching story told in poems; poetry helps Jack overcome his grief over the loss of his dog; poems from authors such as Robert Frost, William Carlos Williams, and Walter Dean Myers are woven into the telling of this wonderful story. Reading level: fifth–sixth grades.

- TRACKER, by Gary Paulsen (Atheneum). Hunting for deer and the meaning of life, a boy grapples with the end of his grandfather's life. Reading level: fifth–sixth grades.

- A SUMMER TO DIE, by Lois Lowry (Houghton Mifflin). Meg copes with her older sister's leukemia and eventual death. Reading level: fifth–sixth grades.

- A GATHERING OF DAYS: A NEW ENGLAND GIRL'S JOURNAL, 1830-32, by Joan W. Blos (Simon & Schuster). Journal entries chronicle major and everyday events in the life of a farm girl after the loss of her mother; Newbery Medal. Reading level: fifth–sixth grades.

- ON MY HONOR, by Marion Dane Bauer (Clarion). This slim novel is the heart-wrenching tale of a summer afternoon that becomes tragic; a boy wrestles with his conscience after his best friend dies a senseless death. Reading level: fifth grade.

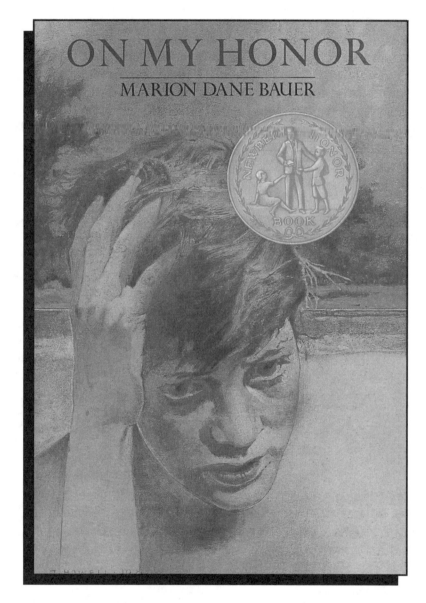

Cover from ON MY HONOR by Marion Dane Bauer. Copyright © 1986 by Marion Dane Bauer. Reprinted by permission of Houghton Mifflin Company. All rights reserved.

- MISSING MAY, by Cynthia Rylant (Scholastic). Twelve year-old Summer and her Uncle Ob deal with the loss of Aunt May; Newbery Medal, Boston Globe/Horn Book Award. Reading level: fifth grade.

- FROM THE LIGHTHOUSE, by Liz Chipman (Dutton). In this story set during the late 1930s in a lighthouse on the Hudson River, Weezie, her brothers, and her father cope with Ma's leaving and the impact this loss (and later the death of the middle sibling) has on the family over the course of a year; although sad, the story, beautifully written, offers hope and celebrates the strength of family—a unit of related individuals. Reading level: fifth grade.

- EVERYWHERE, by Bruce Brooks (HarperCollins). A boy's grandfather (and best friend) flirts with death in this story of love, hope, and family. Reading level: fifth grade.

- AUTUMN STREET, by Lois Lowry (Houghton Mifflin). Set during World War II, this is the story of Elizabeth, who befriends her grandfather's cook's son and experiences tragedy firsthand. Reading level: fifth grade.

Cover from AUTUMN STREET by Lois Lowry. Copyright © 1980 by Lois Lowry. Reprinted by permission of Houghton Mifflin Company. All rights reserved.

- COUSINS, by Virginia Hamilton (Philomel). Family relationships are at the center of this thought-provoking novel about loss and personal growth. Reading level: fifth grade.

- MY LOUISIANA SKY, by Kimberly Willis Holt (Random House); set in 1957; the multiple award–winning debut novel about 12-year-old Tiger Ann Parker, who is bright, athletic, and shunned by her peers because her parents are "slow"; when she is offered the chance to leave the small Southern town in which she has lived with her parents and grandmother, Tiger Ann comes to realize what she values most. Reading level: fifth grade.

- BRIDGE TO TERABITHIA, by Katherine Paterson (HarperCollins); centers around the death of a friend as a result of innocent but foolish kids' play; numerous awards including the Newbery Medal. Reading level: fourth grade.

- A TASTE OF BLACKBERRIES, by Doris Buchanan Smith (HarperCollins). A boy's innocent prank ends in death in this spare, heartrending story. Reading level: fourth grade.

- MICHAEL ROSEN'S SAD BOOK, written by Michael Rosen and illustrated by Quentin Blake (Candlewick); explores sadness due to loss of a loved one in simple, spare language and signature art. All ages.

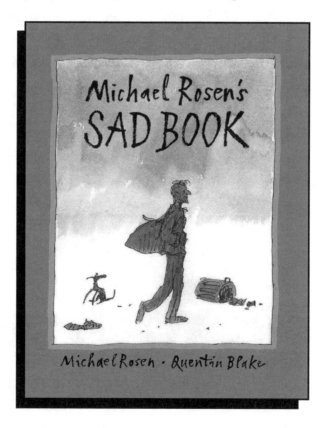

MICHAEL ROSEN'S SAD BOOK. Text Copyright © 2004 Michael Rosen. Illustrations Copyright © 2004 Quentin Blake. Candlewick Press, Inc. on behalf of Walker Books, Ltd.

Animal Stories

- SOUNDER, by William H. Armstrong (HarperCollins); the heartrending story of a sharecropper and his experiences with prejudice; a classic Newbery Medal winner. Reading level: sixth grade.

- THE INCREDIBLE JOURNEY, by Sheila Burnford (Little, Brown); classic tale of the journey of three pets in search of home and their family. Reading level: sixth grade.

- SHAPER, by Jessie Haas (Greenwillow). Fourteen-year-old Chad has no intention of forgiving his grandfather for the part he played in the loss of his dog, Shep, or of bonding with the new dog, Queenie. How his new neighbor, a "shaper" who trains animals, and his daughter help Chad learn about himself makes for a thoughtful read. Reading level: sixth grade.

- WOODSONG, by Gary Paulsen (Simon & Schuster); autobiographical account of Paulsen's experiences dog sledding and his first Iditarod, a race across Alaska's frozen wilderness. Reading level: fifth–sixth grades.

WOODSONG by Gary Paulsen, illustrated by Ruth Wright Paulsen. Copyright © 1990. Used with permission of Simon & Schuster Books for Young Readers, an imprint of Simon & Schuster Children's Publishing.

- LOVE THAT DOG, by Sharon Creech (HarperCollins); humorous yet touching story told in poems; poetry helps Jack overcome his grief over the loss of his dog; poems from authors such as Robert Frost, William Carlos Williams, and Walter Dean Myers are woven into the telling of this wonderful story. Reading level: fifth–sixth grades.

- TRACKER, by Gary Paulsen (Atheneum). Hunting for deer and the meaning of life, a boy grapples with the end of his grandfather's life. Reading level: fifth–sixth grades.

- BECAUSE OF WINN-DIXIE, by Kate DiCamillo (Candlewick). Opal's mother deserted her and her preacher dad seven years ago, but it's not until a happy, tail-wagging stray comes to stay that the healing begins; Newbery Honor. Reading level: fifth grade.

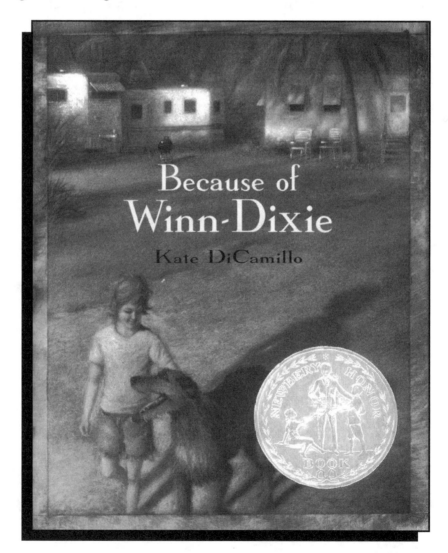

BECAUSE OF WINN-DIXIE. Copyright © 2000 Kate DiCamillo. Cover Illustration Copyright © 2000 Chris Sheban. Candlewick Press, Inc.

- DOGSONG, by Gary Paulsen (Simon & Schuster); dog-sledding adventure/survival story; Newbery Honor Award. Reading level: fifth–sixth grades.

- STEALING THUNDER, by Mary Casanova (Hyperion); well-paced, satisfying adventure about a girl who sets out to save an abused horse from its owner. Reading level: fifth–sixth grades.

- WANTED . . . MUD BLOSSOM, by Betsy Byars (Delacorte). The fifth in a series of rollicking books chronicling the travails of the Blossom family, this story spotlights Mud, the dog who is at the center of the mystery of Junior's missing hamster; an unforgettable trial scene!; an ALA Notable Children's Book and winner of the Edgar Allan Poe Award. Reading level: fifth grade.

- A DOG'S LIFE: THE AUTOBIOGRAPHY OF A STRAY, by Ann M. Martin (Scholastic). Squirrel's story of 10 years of life includes his experiences as a stray after his separation from his mom and brother, facing fierce dogs, and life with both good and bad humans; a dog lover's delight. Reading level: fifth grade.

- MISTY OF CHINCOTEAGUE, by Marguerite Henry (HarperCollins); classic horse story that has won the hearts of readers for over 50 years. See also STORMY: MISTY'S FOAL. Reading level: fifth grade.

- JULIE OF THE WOLVES by Jean Craighead George (HarperCollins); Newbery Award–winning survival story about an Eskimo girl on the run who meets up with a pack of wolves; the first in a trilogy; see also MY SIDE OF THE MOUNTAIN, a Newbery Honor Award book and the first in another trilogy by George. Reading level: upper fourth–sixth grades.

- STONE FOX, written by John Reynolds Gardiner and illustrated by Greg Hargreaves (HarperCollins); poignant story about a boy and his loyal sled dog. Reading level: fourth grade.

- SHILOH, by Phyllis Reynolds Naylor (Atheneum). A boy cares for an abused dog; life lessons and ethical issues abound; Newbery Medal; see also the sequels, SHILOH SEASON and SAVING SHILOH. Reading level: fourth grade.

- RED DOG, by Bill Wallace (Holiday House). A boy, his dog, and three nasty gold prospectors make for one memorable, fast-paced adventure. Reading level: fourth grade.

- Wild at Heart series (American Girl): tales about youngsters who volunteer at an animal clinic; created by award-winning author Laurie Halse Anderson. Reading level: fourth grade.

Mystery

- THE GHOST IN THE TOKAIDO INN, by Dorothy Hoobler and Thomas Hoobler (Philomel). Set in Japan in 1735, this gripping tale centers around the theft of a ruby and the sharp investigative work of 14-year-old Seikei, who dreams of being a samurai despite his merchant class status. An Edgar Allan Poe Award finalist, and winner of numerous other awards. Reading level: sixth grade.

- SAMMY KEYES AND THE HOTEL THIEF, by Wendelin Van Draanen (Knopf); winner of the Edgar Allan Poe Award for best children's mystery. Other titles in the series about this curious whippersnapper include SAMMY KEYES AND THE ART OF DECEPTION, SAMMY KEYES AND THE SISTERS OF MERCY, SAMMY KEYES AND THE CURSE OF MOUSTACHE MARY, and SAMMY KEYES AND THE HOLLYWOOD MUMMY. Reading level: fifth–sixth grades.

- THE CASE OF THE BAKER STREET IRREGULAR, by Robert Newman (Aladdin). Andrew seeks help from Sherlock Holmes when his guardian is kidnapped and he himself faces danger. Reading level: fifth–sixth grades.

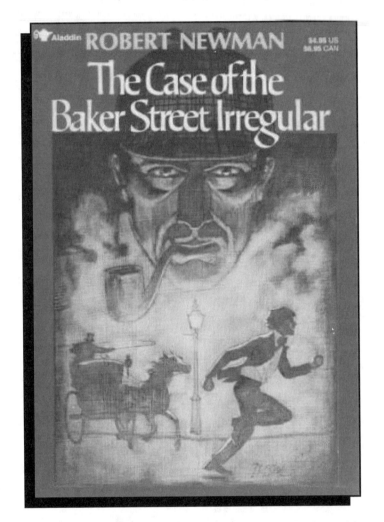

CASE OF THE BAKER STREET IRREGULAR by Robert Newman. Copyright © 1984. Used with permission of Aladdin Paperbacks, an imprint of Simon & Schuster Children's Publishing.

- HOOT, by Carl Hiaasen (Knopf); a wild and wacky hoot-of-a-mystery/ adventure that earned a Newbery Honor Award and a long stint on the New York Times Bestsellers List. The story takes place in Florida and revolves around the new kid at Trace Middle School and his eventual involvement in a campaign to save an endangered species of owls (which all starts with a quintessential bully on the school bus). This is the first novel for children written by this well-known and successful author for adults. See also FLUSH. Reading level: fifth–sixth grades.

- Shakespeare Stealer series, by Gary Blackwood (Dutton). Widge, an orphan in Elizabethan England, solves Shakespeare-related mysteries in stories that also happen to teach about the era and its main drama man. Titles include THE SHAKESPEARE STEALER, SHAKESPEARE'S SCRIBE, and SHAKESPEARE'S SPY. Reading level: fifth–sixth grades.

- KNEE-KNOCK RISE, by Natalie Babbitt (Farrar Straus Giroux). A fable about Egan, who dares to think outside the box to solve a mystery that has been tradition in mythic Instep. Reading level: fifth–sixth grades.

KNEE-KNOCK RISE © 1970 by Natalie Babbitt. Used with the permission of Farrar Straus Giroux.

- HOLES, by Louis Sachar (Farrar Straus Giroux); popular Newbery Medal book about Stanley Yelnats, who digs holes at Camp Green Lake detention center to serve out a sentence he doesn't deserve, and what he unearths about the warden, and ultimately, himself. Reading level: fifth–sixth grades.

HOLES © 1998 by Louis Sachar. Cover Art © 1998 by Vladimir Radunsky. Used with the permission of Farrar Straus Giroux.

- FROM THE MIXED-UP FILES OF MRS. BASIL E. FRANKWEILER, by E. L. Konigsburg (Simon & Schuster). Mystery and adventure await Claudia and Jamie after hours in the Metropolitan Museum of Art; classic tale that won the Newbery Medal. Reading level: fifth–sixth grades.

• BELLE PRATER'S BOY, by Ruth White (Farrar Straus Giroux). Virginia in the 1950s is the setting for this story about cousins and best friends, Gypsy and Woodrow, in their sixth-grade year and the losses they face together, one of which involves the disappearance of Woodrow's mother; Newbery Honor. See also the acclaimed sequel, THE SEARCH FOR BELLE PRATER. Reading level: fifth–sixth grades.

THE SEARCH FOR BELLE PRATER © 2005 by Ruth White. Cover Art © 2005 by Allen Garns. Used with the permission of Farrar Straus Giroux.

- THE STRANGER NEXT DOOR, by Peg Kehret (Penguin). Pete the cat can't talk, but he sure is helpful in solving mysteries with Alex! The cat's thoughts are printed in italics so readers know just what this sleuth is thinking. See also SPY CAT. Reading level: fifth–sixth grades.

- Spy Mice Series, written by Heather Vogel Frederick and illustrated by Sally Wern Comport (Simon & Schuster); sure to appeal to readers seeking books in the spy genre. THE BLACK PAW and FOR YOUR PAWS ONLY are the first two titles in the series. Reading level: fifth–sixth grades.

SPY MICE: THE BLACK PAW by Heather Vogel Frederick, illustrated by Sally Wern Comport. Copyright © 2005. Used with permission of Simon & Schuster Books for Young Readers, an imprint of Simon & Schuster Children's Publishing.

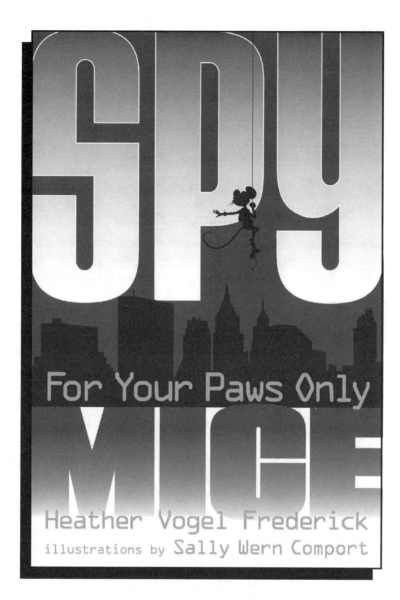

SPY MICE: FOR YOUR PAWS ONLY by Heather Vogel Frederick, illustrated by Sally Wern Comport. Copyright © 2005. Used with permission of Simon & Schuster Books for Young Readers, an imprint of Simon & Schuster Children's Publishing.

- CHASING VERMEER, written by Blue Balliett and illustrated by Brett Helquist (Scholastic Press); winner of the 2005 Edgar Allan Poe Award for best children's mystery; see the read-aloud plan found elsewhere in this resource. Reading level: fifth grade.

- WRIGHT 3, written by Blue Balliett and illustrated by Brett Helquist (Scholastic Press); sequel to CHASING VERMEER, in which the dynamic pair of sleuths, Petra and Calder, team up with Tommy, who was off-stage in CHASING VERMEER, to solve an art mystery revolving around Frank Lloyd Wright's Robie House in Chicago. Reading level: fifth grade.

- WANTED . . . MUD BLOSSOM, by Betsy Byars (Delacorte). The fifth in a series of rollicking books chronicling the travails of the Blossom family, this story spotlights Mud, the dog who is at the center of the mystery of Junior's missing hamster; an unforgettable trial scene!; an ALA Notable Children's Book and winner of the Edgar Allan Poe Award. Reading level: fifth grade.

- THE BIG HOUSE, by Carolyn Coman and illustrated by Rob Shepperson (Front Street); this sister and brother team stick together through mystery, comedy, bed-wetting, and a trial—of sorts. Reading level: fifth grade

- BUNNICULA, by Deborah Howe and James Howe (Atheneum). With millions of copies in print, it's no secret that the mystery stories starring Harold the dog and Chester the cat, residents of the Monroe house, are sure to please young readers. This first title has been in print for over 25 years. Other Bunnicula titles by James Howe include HOWLIDAY INN, RETURN TO HOWLIDAY INN, THE CELERY STALKS AT MIDNIGHT, NIGHTY-NIGHTMARE, and HOWIE MONROE AND THE DOGHOUSE OF DOOM, featuring Chester's "nephew", a wire-haired dachshund pup. Reading level: fifth grade

BUNNICULA: THE 25th ANNIVERSARY EDITION by Deborah and James Howe, illustrated by Alan Daniel. Copyright © 2004. Used with permission of Atheneum Books for Young Readers, an imprint of Simon & Schuster Children's Publishing.

Tales from the House of Bunnicula: HOWIE MONROE AND THE DOGHOUSE OF DOOM by James Howe, illustrated by Brett Helquist. Copyright © 2002. Used with permission of Atheneum Books for Young Readers, an imprint of Simon & Schuster Children's Publishing.

- THE LONG SECRET, by Louise Fitzhugh (HarperCollins); sequel to HARRIET THE SPY, in which Harriet intends to find out who is leaving mysterious notes all over the neighborhood. Reading level: fifth grade

- EAT YOUR POISON, DEAR, by James Howe (Atheneum). Is the cafeteria food poisoned? Sebastian is on the case! Other Sebastian Barth Mysteries include WHAT ERIC KNEW, STAGE FRIGHT, and DEW DROP DEAD. Reading level: fifth grade.

EAT YOUR POISON, DEAR by James Howe. Copyright © 1986. Used with permission of Atheneum Books for Young Readers, an imprint of Simon & Schuster Children's Publishing.

- Wright & Wong Mystery Series, by Laura J. Burns and Melinda Metz (Penguin/Razorbill); a mystery series starring odd couple middle-school buddies B. Orville Wright, who has Asperger's syndrome (Orville loves math and science, but emotions are beyond him), and Agatha Wong, who revels in social situations. The plot lines are current and appealing to middle graders, from a suspicious fire at school that involves a pile of fertilizer and causes quite a stink, to a popular soap opera star who just happens to be a pickpocket. Titles include THE CASE OF THE PRANK THAT STANK, THE CASE OF THE NANA-NAPPER, THE CASE OF THE TRAIL MIX-UP, and THE CASE OF THE SLIPPERY SOAP STAR. Reading level: fifth grade.

- COFFIN ON A CASE, by Eve Bunting (HarperCollins). The Coffin in the title is 12-year-old Henry, whose father runs the Coffin and Pale Detective Agency, and who finally has a case of his own to solve. Motherless himself since he was a baby, he helps a high school "babe" find her kidnapped mom; winner of the Edgar Allan Poe Award. Reading level: fourth grade.

Note: Every April, the Mystery Writers of America presents the coveted Edgar Allan Poe Awards for achievement in the mystery field. http://www.mysterynet.com/edgar-allan-poe/ For a complete listing of children's books that have won the Edgar Award, go to http://www.mysterywriters.org/. Click on "Database of All Winners and Nominees" on the lower right-hand side, then choose an Award Category (juvenile and young adult are separate categories).

Adventure

- WEASEL, by Cynthia DeFelice (Atheneum). Set in Ohio in the 1800s, this riveting adventure handles hatred of Native Americans and the morality of vengeance with great skill; a well-crafted, award-winning novel. Reading level: sixth grade.

- THE CAY, by Theodore Taylor (Delacorte); award-winning classic tale of survival on a deserted island, with themes of prejudice and friendship; set in 1942. Reading level: sixth grade.

- THE GOLDEN FLEECE AND THE HEROES WHO LIVED BEFORE ACHILLES, by Padriac Colum (Macmillan). This telling of the story of Jason and the Argonauts won a Newbery Honor. Reading level: sixth grade and up.

- TRACKER, by Gary Paulsen (Atheneum). Hunting for deer and the meaning of life, a boy grapples with the end of his grandfather's life. Reading level: fifth–sixth grades.

- DOGSONG, by Gary Paulsen (Simon & Schuster); dog-sledding adventure/survival story; Newbery Honor Award. Reading level: fifth–sixth grades.

- WOODSONG, by Gary Paulsen (Simon & Schuster) autobiographical account of Paulsen's experiences dog sledding and his first Iditarod, a race across Alaska's frozen wilderness. Reading level: fifth–sixth grades.

- STEALING THUNDER, by Mary Casanova (Hyperion); well-paced, satisfying adventure about a girl who sets out to save an abused horse from its owner. Reading level: fifth–sixth grades.

Hyperion Books for Children

- DEVIL'S BRIDGE, by Cynthia DeFelice (Atheneum). Action and suspense make this story about a boy in a fishing derby, whose sense of fairness puts him in danger, a compelling read. Reading level: fifth grade.

- THE HALF-A-MOON INN, by Paul Fleischman (HarperCollins); suspense story about Aaron, a mute, who sets out in a blizzard to locate his mother and comes upon an inn with a nefarious owner; well-crafted, with chills aplenty. Reading level: fifth grade.

- JULIE OF THE WOLVES, by Jean Craighead George (HarperCollins); Newbery Award winning survival story about an Eskimo girl on the run who meets up with a pack of wolves; the first in a trilogy; see also MY SIDE OF THE

MOUNTAIN, a Newbery Honor Award book and the first in another trilogy by George. Reading level: upper fourth–sixth grades.

- STONE FOX, written by John Reynolds Gardiner and illustrated by Greg Hargreaves (HarperCollins); poignant story about a boy and his loyal sled dog. Reading level: fourth grade.

- RED DOG, written by Bill Wallace (Holiday House). A boy, his dog, and three nasty gold prospectors make for one memorable, fast-paced adventure. Reading level: fourth grade.

Fantasy

- THE HOBBITT and The Lord of the Rings trilogy (FELLOWSHIP OF THE RING, THE TWO TOWERS, and RETURN OF THE KING), by J. R. R. Tolkien (Houghton Mifflin). Good and evil, in the guise of hobbits and wizards, duke it out in Middle Earth. Reading level: sixth grade and up.

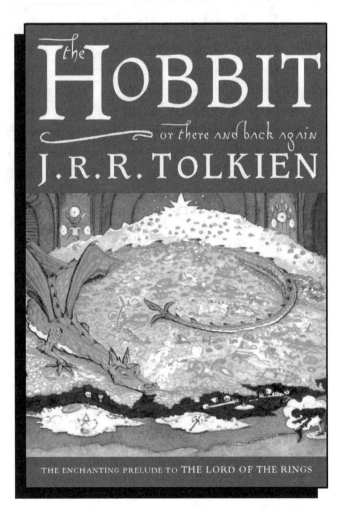

Cover from THE HOBBITT, or THERE AND BACK AGAIN by J.R.R. Tolkien. Copyright © 1966 by J.R.R. Tolkien. Reprinted by permission of Houghton Mifflin Company. All rights reserved.

- The Chronicles of Narnia, by C. S. Lewis (HarperCollins); classic fantasy series with timeless themes of good and evil, hope, faith, love, and redemption; titles include THE MAGICIAN'S NEPHEW; THE LION, THE WITCH AND THE WARDROBE; THE HORSE AND HIS BOY; PRINCE CASPIAN; THE VOYAGE OF THE DAWN TREADER; THE SILVER CHAIR; and THE LAST BATTLE. Reading level: sixth grade and up.

- A WRINKLE IN TIME (Newbery Medal), A WIND IN THE DOOR, A SWIFTLY TILTING PLANET, and MANY WATERS, by Madeleine L'Engle (Farrar Straus Giroux); a quartet that begins with the grabber line, "It was a dark and stormy night" and goes on to spin a classic fantasy that has been enchanting readers for decades. Reading level: sixth grade.

A WRINKLE IN TIME © 1979 by Madeleine L'Engle. Cover Art © 1979 by Leo and Diane Dillon. Used with the permission of Farrar Straus Giroux.

- THE GOLDEN FLEECE AND THE HEROES WHO LIVED BEFORE ACHILLES, by Padriac Colum (Macmillan). This telling of the story of Jason and the Argonauts won a Newbery Honor. Reading level: sixth grade and up.

- His Dark Materials Trilogy, by Philip Pullman (Knopf); high adventure fantasy of parallel universes; explores timeless themes with dazzling, well-crafted language and a thrilling, complex plot; somewhat controversial; titles include THE GOLDEN COMPASS, THE SUBTLE KNIFE, and THE AMBER SPYGLASS. Reading level: sixth grade and up.

- The Dark Is Rising Sequence, by Susan Cooper (Simon & Schuster); sweeping saga of good and evil; titles include OVER SEA, UNDER STONE; THE DARK IS RISING (Newbery Honor); GREENWITCH; THE GREY KING (Newbery Medal), and SILVER ON THE TREE. Reading level: sixth grade.

THE DARK IS RISING by Susan Cooper, illustrated by Alan Cober. Copyright © 1973. Used with permission of Margaret K. McElderry Books, an imprint of Simon & Schuster Children's Publishing.

THE GREY KING by Susan Cooper, illustrated by Michael Heslop. Copyright © 1975. Used with permission of Margaret K. McElderry Books, an imprint of Simon & Schuster Children's Publishing.

- TIME CAT, by Lloyd Alexander (Penguin). A talking cat with the ability to time travel takes his boy, Jason, on nine adventures back in time; just one of many outstanding titles by this author. See also the Newbery Medal winner, THE HIGH KING, and other titles in the Chronicles of Prydain series. Reading level: sixth grade.

- THE PHANTOM TOLLBOOTH, by Norton Juster (Knopf). Bored, bored Milo sets out on the journey of a lifetime in this much-beloved classic fantasy written in 1961; hilarious, ironic, playful, witty, and smart. Reading level: sixth grade.

- JAMES AND THE GIANT PEACH, written by Roald Dahl and illustrated by Lane Smith (Knopf) (another edition is illustrated by Quentin Blake [Penguin]). Adventures galore begin inside a magic peach. Reading level: sixth grade.

• HEIR APPARENT, by Vivian Vande Velde (Harcourt). Giannine passes protestors on her way into the arcade where she plays the virtual reality game of her life—literally; humorous, action-packed, and clever. Reading level: sixth grade.

Courtesy Harcourt, Inc.

• THE VARIOUS, by Steve Augarde (David Fickling/Random House). The fairy people who live in the woods on Midge's uncle's farm catch her attention and the reader's in this vivid, action-packed fantasy; first in a trilogy. Reading level: sixth grade.

• THE CRICKET IN TIMES SQUARE, written by George Selden and illustrated by Garth Williams (Farrar Straus Giroux); Newbery Honor Award classic about the adventures of a cricket, a boy, a mouse, and a cat; see also other Chester Cricket and His Friends titles, including CHESTER CRICKET'S PIGEON RIDE, CHESTER CRICKET'S NEW HOME, and HARRY KITTEN AND TUCKER MOUSE. Reading level: sixth grade.

- THE GOLDEN HOUR, by Maiya Williams (Abrams); award-winning debut novel about Rowan, who is sent with his sister, Nina, to spend the summer with his aunt in Maine after the unexpected death of their mom; time travel, hauntings, a disappearance, and more make for an entertaining read. Reading level: sixth grade.

THE GOLDEN HOUR by Maiya Williams. Reprinted with permission of Abrams Books for Young Readers (www.abramsyoungreaders.com).

- TUCK EVERLASTING, by Natalie Babbitt (Farrar Straus, Giroux); classic tale that explores the ramifications of immortality. Reading level: sixth grade.

TUCK EVERLASTING © 1975 by Natalie Babbitt.
Used with the permission of Farrar Straus Giroux.

- A HIVE FOR THE HONEYBEE, by Soinbhe Lally (Scholastic). This well-crafted allegory based on the real workings of a honeybee colony is thought-provoking yet amusing. Reading level: sixth grade.

- BLITZCAT, by Robert Westall (Macmillan). Set in Europe during World War II, this is the story of Lord Gort, the good-luck black cat in search of her master. Reading level: sixth grade.

- MRS. FRISBY AND THE RATS of NIMH, by Robert C. O'Brien (Simon & Schuster). Mrs. Frisby is a mouse with four children and a problem who turns to intelligent lab rats for help and ultimately repays their good deed; Newbery Medal. Reading level: sixth grade.

- TIME STOPS FOR NO MOUSE, by Michael Hoeye (Penguin). Hermux Tantamoq, a watchmaker/detective/mouse, is the hero in this fantasy that began as e-mail from the author to his wife. See also THE SANDS OF TIME and NO TIME LIKE SHOW TIME. Reading level: sixth grade.

- INKHEART, by Cornelia Funke (Scholastic); fantasy adventure with a story within a story, in which book characters come alive; see also the sequel, INKSPELL, and Funke's international best seller, THE THIEF LORD. Reading level: fifth–sixth grades.

- JUST ELLA, by Margaret Peterson Haddix (Simon & Schuster); a Cinderella story with a twist; the heroine is strong and wise in this version of the fairy tale. Reading level: fifth–sixth grades.

- The Sisters Grimm Series, written by Michael Buckley and illustrated by Peter Ferguson (Amulet/Abrams). two orphaned sisters go to live with Grandmother Grimm, and the mystery/magical adventure, spiced with humor, begins. THE FAIRY TALE DETECTIVES AND THE UNUSUAL SUSPECTS are the first two installments in this series. Reading level: fifth–sixth grades.

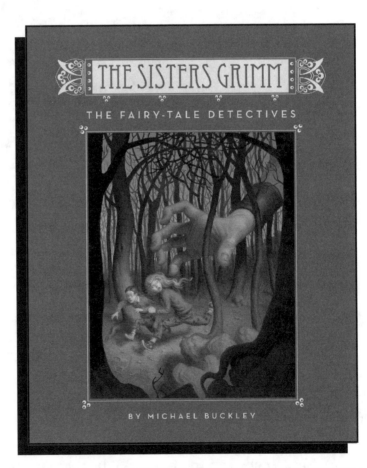

THE SISTERS GRIMM: THE FAIRY TALE DETECTIVES by Michael Buckley. Reprinted with permission of Abrams Books for Young Readers (www.abramsyoungreaders.com)

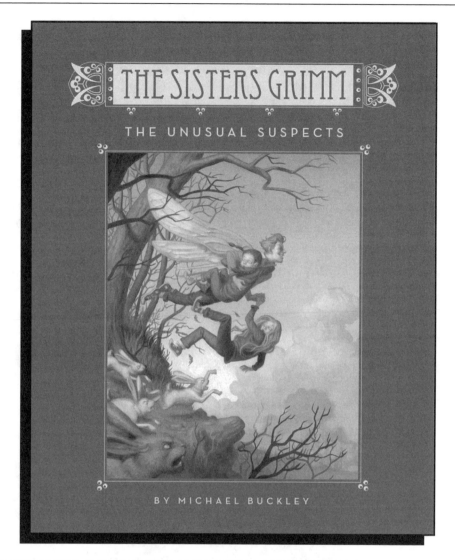

*THE SISTERS GRIMM: THE UNUSUAL SUSPECTS by Michael Buckley.
Reprinted with permission of Abrams Books for Young Readers
(www.abramsyoungreaders.com)*

- PIGS MIGHT FLY, by Dick King-Smith (Penguin). Daggie Dogfoot may be the runt of Mrs. Barleylove's litter, but he is the hero in this delightful, funny, and warm story about strength of spirit. Reading level: fifth–sixth grades.

- THE GAWGON AND THE BOY, by Lloyd Alexander (Dutton). Old Aunt Annie and 11-year-old David experience wild and memorable adventures in their year together. Reading level: fifth–sixth grades.

- THE CAT WHO WISHED TO BE A MAN, by Lloyd Alexander (Penguin). Lionel the cat gets his wish and learns the pros and cons of being human. Reading level: fifth–sixth grades.

- Harry Potter series, by J. K. Rowling (Scholastic); blockbuster instant classic that changed the way the world looked at children's books; tales of sorcery, wizardry, friendship, family, and, of course, good and evil; titles include HARRY POTTER AND THE SORCERER'S STONE, HARRY POTTER AND THE CHAMBER OF SECRETS, HARRY POTTER AND THE GOBLET OF FIRE, HARRY POTTER AND THE ORDER OF THE PHOENIX, HARRY POTTER AND THE PRISONER OF AZKABAN, and HARRY POTTER AND THE HALF-BLOOD PRINCE. Reading level: fifth grade and up.

- MANIAC MAGEE, by Jerry Spinelli (Little, Brown); a modern folk tale/tall tale that explores the search for home, racism, heroism, and strength of spirit, while also managing to be funny; Newbery Medal. Reading level: fifth grade.

- SMART DOG, by Vivian Vande Velde (Harcourt). A dog that talks escapes from a university laboratory and so begins a series of funny but thought-provoking events. Reading level: fifth grade.

Courtesy Harcourt, Inc.

- ELLA ENCHANTED, by Gail Carson Levine (HarperCollins). What was the fairy thinking, giving a gift of obedience? Ella's determination to break the curse is a memorable story indeed; Newbery Honor Award. Reading level: fifth grade.

- THE BOGGART, by Susan Cooper (Simon & Schuster); a comic ghost story about a Scottish spirit (a boggart) who ends up with a family in Toronto and yearns to go home; numerous awards. Reading level: fifth grade.

THE BOGGART by Susan Cooper. Copyright © 1993. Used with permission of Margaret K. McElderry Books, an imprint of Simon & Schuster Children's Publishing.

- UGLY, written by Donna Jo Napoli and illustrated by Lita Judge (Hyperion). An ugly duckling is helped by friends in his search for self. Reading level: fifth grade.

Hyperion Books for Children.

- THE ELF OF UNION SQUARE, by Jan Carr (Putnam). The well-known New York City park is the setting for a passel of trouble when an elf tries to undermine a renovation project. How 10-year-old Jack and Will, a reporter for the *Times,* come to the rescue, is the crux of this story. Reading level: fifth grade.

- Bruce Coville's Alien Adventures series, by Bruce Coville (Simon & Schuster). Sci-fi high-jinks entertain while offering timeless messages; titles include ALIENS ATE MY HOMEWORK, I LEFT MY SNEAKERS IN DIMENSION X, THE SEARCH FOR SNOUT, and ALIENS STOLE MY BODY. See also My Teacher Books: MY TEACHER IS AN ALIEN, MY TEACHER FRIED MY BRAINS, MY TEACHER GLOWS IN THE DARK, and MY TEACHER FLUNKED THE PLANET. Reading level: fifth grade.

- DIARY OF A FAIRY GODMOTHER, written by Esmé Raji Codell and illustrated by Drazen Kozjan (Hyperion); a terrific fractured fairy tale centering around Hunky Dory's problem of caring more about *wish*craft than she does witchcraft. Reading level: fourth–fifth grades.

Hyperion Books for Children.

- THREE GOOD DEEDS, by Vivian Vande Velde (Harcourt). Howard becomes How-Word the goose when a spell is cast on him by a witchy old lady who dislikes his behavior. How he finds three good deeds he can perform to regain his boyish figure—and what he learns in the process—is the crux of this humorous tale. Reading level: fourth–fifth grades.

Courtesy Harcourt, Inc.

- Indian in the Cupboard Books, by Lynne Reid Banks (Doubleday); series of four novels that have won the hearts of young fantasy readers: THE INDIAN IN THE CUPBOARD, THE RETURN OF THE INDIAN, THE SECRET OF THE INDIAN, THE MYSTERY OF THE CUPBOARD, and THE KEY TO THE INDIAN. Reading level: fourth grade and up.

- Magic Shop Books, written by Bruce Coville (Harcourt); middle grade fantasy chock full of humor and universal truths; includes THE MONSTER'S RING, THE SKULL OF TRUTH, JENNIFER MURDLEY'S TOAD, and JEREMY THATCHER, DRAGON HATCHER. Reading level: fourth grade and up.

Courtesy Harcourt, Inc.

- THE DRAGON OF LONELY ISLAND, by Rebecca Rupp (Candlewick); light fantasy in which a three-headed dragon meets and imparts wisdom to three siblings on summer vacation. See also THE RETURN OF THE DRAGON. Reading level: fourth grade.

- SIDEWAYS STORIES FROM WAYSIDE SCHOOL, by Louis Sachar (HarperCollins); hilarious, interrelated short stories about one very weird and wacky school. See also related titles, including WAYSIDE SCHOOL GETS A LITTLE STRANGER, WAYSIDE SCHOOL IS FALLING DOWN, and SIDEWAYS ARITHMETIC FROM WAYSIDE SCHOOL (Scholastic). Reading level: fourth grade.

Shorties: Fiction and Nonfiction Short Story Collections

When the timing isn't right for beginning a new book, such as just before a school break or the last day of the week, consider reaching for a short story for your read-aloud session. The collections listed here offer a variety of genres, from historical to humorous, from mystery to musings, from fiction to factual. Penned by some of the best authors writing for children today, these pieces are meant to be read in one sitting. Short stories are also great choices to initiate author studies or to introduce children to a new author. Encourage listeners who love the story to look for longer works by that author. You might even want to have a few books penned by an author available for loan following the reading of one of his or her short stories.

- FRIENDS: STORIES ABOUT NEW FRIENDS, OLD FRIENDS, AND UNEXPEDTEDLY TRUE FRIENDS, edited by Ann M. Martin and David Levithan (Scholastic); stories by Pam Muñoz Ryan, Meg Cabot, Rachel Cohn, Virginia Euwer Wolff, and others. All proceeds from this book go to Lisa Libraries (www.lisalibraries.org), a nonprofit organization serving needy children through the donation of children's books.

- THE HERO'S TRAIL: A GUIDE FOR A HEROIC LIFE, by T. A. Barron (Philomel); short profiles of heroic young people in themed chapters; quotations; reflections of the author.

- HEADING OUT: THE START OF SOME SPLENDID CAREERS, edited by Gloria Kamen (Bloomsbury); excerpts from autobiographies and reflections written by those with careers in writing, the arts, business, politics, science, and medicine, who overcame obstacles to reach their dreams; contributors include Dan Rather, Sidney Poitier, Pablo Casals, Nelson Mandela, Lance Armstrong, Isaac Asimov, and Katherine Paterson.

- LIVES OF THE WRITERS: COMEDIES, TRAGEDIES (AND WHAT THE NEIGHBORS THOUGHT), written by Kathleen Krull and illustrated by Kathryn Hewitt (Harcourt). Brief, humorous sketches offer the "inside scoop" on 20 literary giants, from William Shakespeare and Miguel de Cervantes to Emily Dickinson and Langston Hughes. Did you know that Robert Louis Stevenson agreed with his wife's opinion that he was beautiful, and that he never passed a mirror without checking himself out; that E. B. White once sold roach powder; or that Carl Sandburg was jailed at the age of 14 for swimming in the nude? Forget *People* magazine. Encourage kids to pick up this book instead! See also other titles in the series, including LIVES OF THE MUSICIANS: GOOD TIMES, BAD TIMES (AND WHAT THE NEIGHBORS THOUGHT); LIVES OF THE ARTISTS: MASTERPIECES, MESSES (AND WHAT THE NEIGHBORS THOUGHT); and LIVES OF THE PRESIDENTS: FAME, SHAME (AND WHAT THE NEIGHBORS THOUGHT).

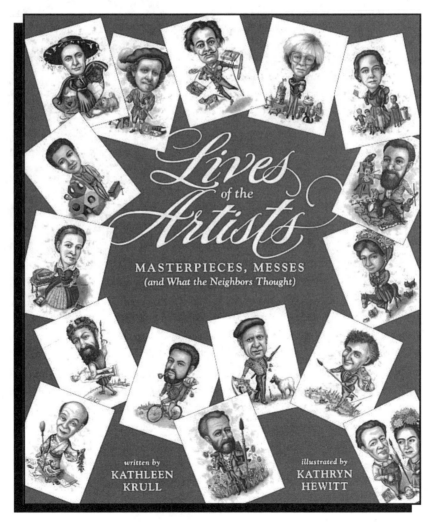

Courtesy Harcourt, Inc.

• THE SKY'S THE LIMIT: STORIES OF DISCOVERY BY WOMEN AND GIRLS, written by Catherine Thimmesh and illustrated by Melissa Sweet (Houghton Mifflin); stories about smart, curious females who wondered, studied, uncovered, and discovered.

Cover from THE SKY'S THE LIMIT: Stories of Discovery by Women and Girls by Catherine Thimmesh, illustrated by Melissa Sweet. Jacket art © 2002 by Melissa Sweet. Reprinted by permission of Houghton Mifflin Company. All rights reserved.

- SHELTER DOGS: AMAZING STORIES OF ADOPTED STRAYS, written by Peg Kehret with photographs by Greg Farrar (Whitman); true stories with related facts of interest following each account.

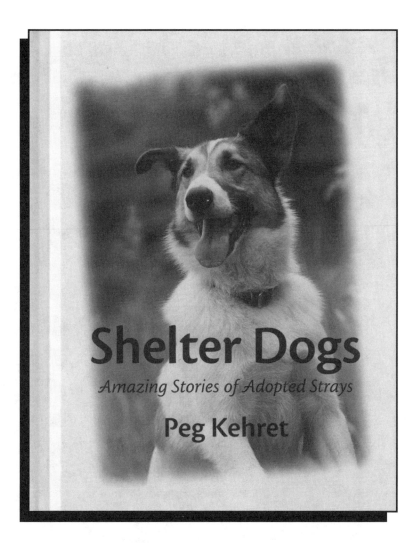

Cover photograph by Greg Farrar from SHELTER DOGS: AMAZING STORIES OF ADOPTED STRAYS by Peg Kehret. Photographs © 1999 by Greg Farrar. Reprinted by permission of Albert Whitman & Company.

- GUYS WRITE FOR GUYS READ, edited by Jon Scieszka (Viking); short stories, poems, pearls of wisdom, and illustrations created by greats in the field of children's literature and chosen by readers on the Guys Read Web site; contributors include Walter Dean Myers, Jack Gantos, Bruce Hale, James Howe, Dav Pilkey, Richard Peck, and Lloyd Alexander. Royalties support www.guysread.com.

• SING A SONG OF TUNA FISH: HARD-TO-SWALLOW STORIES FROM FIFTH GRADE, written by Esmé Raji Codell and illustrated by LeUyen Pham (Hyperion); a handful of true stories from the year Codell was in fifth grade.

Hyperion Books for Children

• IT'S TERRIFIC TO BE TEN (Scholastic); a collection of stories by Barbara Park, Lois Lowry, Katherine Paterson, Christopher Paul Curtis, Elizabeth Levy, and others about the first year of being in the double digits.

- HEADS OR TAILS: STORIES FROM SIXTH GRADE, by Jack Gantos (Farrar Straus Giroux); eight stories by one of the funniest award-winning authors writing for middle graders today.

HEADS OR TAILS: STORIES FROM SIXTH GRADE © 1994 by Jack Gantos. Cover Art © 2005 by Neal Layton. Used with the permission of Farrar Straus Giroux.

- TRIPPING OVER THE LUNCH LADY AND OTHER SCHOOL STORIES, edited by Nancy E. Mercado (Dial); a collection of stories by Avi, Sarah Weeks, Angela Johnson, and others.

- FIG PUDDING, by Ralph Fletcher (Clarion). Chapters narrated by the oldest kid in a family of eight are interrelated stand-alone stories that chronicle humorous, warm-hearted family travails from one Christmas to the next.

Cover from FIG PUDDING by Ralph Fletcher. Jacket illustration © 1995 by Arthur Howard. Reprinted by permission of Clarion Books, an imprint of Houghton Mifflin Company. All rights reserved.

- STORIES FROM WAYSIDE SCHOOL, by Louis Sachar (HarperCollins); hilarious, interrelated stories about one very weird and wacky school; see also related titles, including SIDEWAYS ARITHMETIC FROM WAYSIDE SCHOOL (Scholastic).

- THE LIBRARY CARD, by Jerry Spinelli (Scholastic); four stories in which a mysterious library card plays a pivotal role in the characters' lives.

- THE POND GOD AND OTHER STORIES, written by Samuel Jay Keyser and illustrated by Robert Shetterly (Front Street); one-page fables in verse about gods with some very human qualities.

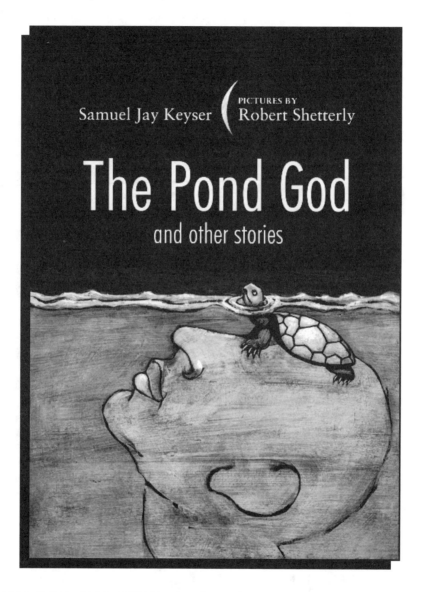

THE POND GOD AND OTHER STORIES, by Samuel Jay Keyser, illustrated by Robert Shetterly. Copyright © 2003. Published by Front Street, an imprint of Boyds Mills Press. Reprinted by permission.

- MIKHAIL BARYSHNIKOV'S STORIES FROM MY CHILDHOOD, edited and compiled by Joan Borsten and Oleg Vidov (Abrams); fairy tales, including "The Snow Queen", "Cinderella", and "Pinocchio and the Golden Key."

- NEWFANGLED FAIRY TALES: CLASSIC STORIES WITH A TWIST, edited by Bruce Lansky (Meadowbrook); a collection of original fairy tales written by well-known and well-loved authors.

- THE RUMPELSTILTSKIN PROBLEM, by Vivian Vande Velde (Scholastic); see the read-aloud plan found elsewhere in this resource.

- GIRLS TO THE RESCUE: TALES OF CLEVER, COURAGEOUS GIRLS FROM AROUND THE WORLD, edited by Bruce Lansky (Meadowbrook); a set of books that feature collections of fairy tales, folk tales, and modern short stories from across the globe in which the heroes are girls.

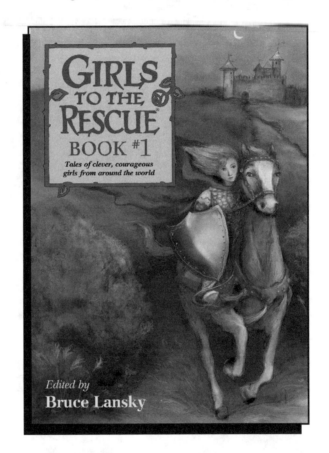

GIRLS TO THE RESCUE #1 © 1995. (www.meadowbrookpress.com)

- THE LADY OR THE TIGER AND OTHER STORIES, by Frank Stockton (Tor); fantasy and adventure by an American storyteller of the 1800s.

- NO ROOM IN THE INN AND OTHER STORIES FROM A MIDNIGHT CLEAR, by Katherine Paterson (Penguin); four stories by the well-known and well-loved author.

- A NEWBERY CHRISTMAS, selected by Martin H. Greenberg and Charles G. Waugh (Delacorte); 14 holiday stories by Newbery Award–winning authors, including Beverly Cleary, Madeleine L'Engle, Nancy Willard, and Katherine Paterson.

Glossy Grabbers: Magazines of Interest to Preteens

One of the most effective ways to encourage reading is to find appealing and current print material on a topic of interest and at a suitable reading level for youngsters. Match a kid to a magazine targeting his or her interests, and you've made it to first base. Add bright photos, short and snappy sidebars, and topic headings that aid in comprehension by identifying the main idea, and you've rounded to third. Get children to pick up a magazine on their own, and you're home free. Pretty good deal for the cost of a subscription that brings fresh material to the mailbox every month or so, wouldn't you say?

Listed here in alphabetical order are magazines of interest to children in the middle grades. Before subscribing, send for a trial issue or peruse a magazine of interest in your local bookstore or library to decide if it meets your needs .

Note: Reader interests, reading levels, and needs vary; choose accordingly.

- **American Cheerleader Junior**—articles of interest related to the sport of cheerleading; 23rd Floor, 110 William Street, New York, NY 10038

- **American Girl**—reinforces self-esteem, self-confidence, and curiosity in girls; crafts, book reviews, stories, and more; Pleasant Company Publications, 8400 Fairway Place, Middleton, WI 53562

- **Boys' Life**—published by the Boy Scouts of America; a variety of articles and stories especially for boys; Boy Scouts of America, PO Box 152079, 1325 West Walnut Hill Lane, Irving, TX 75015-2079

- **Boys' Quest**—theme-related topics of interest to boys; PO Box 227, Bluffton, OH 45717-0227

- **Calliope**—theme-related history, biography, and historical fiction; Cobblestone Publishing, Suite C, 30 Grove Street, Peterborough, NH 03458

- **Children's Digest**—emphasizes a healthy lifestyle; short stories, articles, activities, and poetry; Children's Better Health Institute, 1100 Waterway Boulevard, Indianapolis, IN 46202

- **Cobblestone**—articles, stories, and activities focusing on American history; Cobblestone Publishing, Suite C, 30 Grove Street, Peterborough, NH 03458

- **Cousteau Kids**—explores all areas of science that relate to global waters; The Cousteau Society, 710 Settlers Landing Road, Hampton, VA 23669-4035

- **Cricket**—folk tales, adventures, fantasy, articles, poems, craft activities; Cricket Magazine Group, PO Box 300, 315 5th Street, Peru, IL 61354

- **Crinkles**—articles, activities, puzzles, and crafts that will foster interest in people, places, things, and events; 3401 Stockwell Street, Lincoln, NE 68506

- **Faces**—through monthly themes, explores people, culture, and places around the world; Cobblestone Publishing Company, Suite C, 30 Grove Street, Peterborough, NH 03458

- **Fun For Kidz**—themed issues offer activities, stories, how-to articles, jokes, and puzzles; PO Box 227, Bluffton, OH 45817-0227

- **Girls' Life**—fashion, beauty, friends, family, reviews, proflles, and more; 4517 Harford Road, Baltimore, MD 21214

- **Highlights for Children**—a mainstay in the children's magazine market; articles, stories, poetry, art, and activities; 803 Church Street, Honesdale, PA 18431

- **Hopscotch**—fun, wholesome pieces that focus on letting kids be kids; PO Box 164, Bluffton, OH 45817-0164

- **Horsepower**—for young horse lovers; PO Box 670, Aurora, ON L4G 4J9 Canada

- **International Gymnast**—info on competitions, nutrition, fitness, training, and techniques; PO Box 721020, Norman, OK 73070

- **Kids Discover**—themed issues on the subject of nature, environment, archaeology, geography, ecology, travel, and more; 12th Floor, 149 5th Avenue, New York, NY 10010-6801

- **The Kids Hall of Fame News**—spotlights achievements of youth; 3 Ibsen Court, Dix Hills, NY 11746

- **Mr. Marquis' Museletter**—publishes work by young writers and artists; Box 29556, Maple-Ridge, BC V2X 2V0 Canada

- **Muse**—published in conjunction with *Smithsonian Magazine*; intellectual articles suitable for children on topics including nature, pets, science, computers, history, math, and the arts; Carus Publishing, Suite 1450, 140 S. Dearborn Street, Chicago, IL 60603

- **National Geographic Kids**—articles on science, current events, world cultures, and entertainment; National Geographic Society, 1145 17th Street NW, Washington, DC 20036-4688

- **New Moon**—bills itself as a magazine "for girls and their dreams"; Suite 200, 34 East Superior Street, Duluth, MN 55802

- **Read**—Weekly Reader publication with a variety of articles, plays, short stories, and language games; Weekly reader, 200 First Stamford Place, Stamford, CT 06912

- **Science Weekly**—classroom magazine devoted to stimulating an interest in the sciences; Suite 202, 2141 Industrial Parkway, Silver Springs, MD 20904

- **Skating**—especially for members of the US Figure Skating Association; United States Figure Skating Association, 20 First Street, Colorado Springs, CO 80906

- **Skipping Stones**—ecological awareness and cultural diversity; PO Box 3939, Eugene, OR 97403-0939

- **Sports Illustrated for Kids**—covers the world of sports; Time & Life Building, 1271 Avenue of the Americas, New York, NY 10020

- **Stone Soup**—stories, poems, reviews, and art created by young people; PO Box 83, Santa Cruz, CA 95063

- **Swimming World** and **Junior Swimmer**—focus on competitive swimming; Suite 200, 90 Bell Rock Plaza, Sedona, AZ 86351

- **U Magazine**—free to dependents of USAA members (military); articles and activities that promote responsible and healthy citizenship; United States Automobile Association, 9800 Fredericksburg Road, San Antonio, TX 78288-0264

- **Winner**—preventive drug education and lifestyles skills; 55 West Oak Ridge Drive, Hagerstown, MD 21740

- **Young Rider**—for young equestrians; PO Box 8237, Lexington, KY 40533

Authors on the World Wide Web: Sites of Particular Interest to Fifth and Sixth Grade Readers

- **Betty G. Birney**, author of a handful of books for children; visit her writing house, learn about her dog, her books, and her TV writing on her Web site at www.bettyblrney.com/.

- **Judy Blume**, extensive Web site of the beloved author highlights her numerous books for preteen and teen girls, at www.judybume.com.

- **Louise Borden**, author of a number of picture book biographies and historical perspectives suitable for children in the middle and upper elementary grades; http://www.louiseborden.com/index2.html.

- **Liz Chipman**, visit the Web site of this teacher/author to read her tips for writers and to browse her suggested list of useful resources as well as information about her historical novel, FROM THE LIGHTHOUSE; www.lizchipman.com.

- **Esmé Raji Codell**, teacher, librarian, author; visit her extensive "Www.onderful world of children's literature" at www.planetesme.com.

- **Bruce Coville,** author of dozens of funny books for children, including I WAS A SIXTH GRADE ALIEN, the Magic Shop series, and The Unicorn Chronicles series, as well as a handful of handsomely illustrated Shakespeare retellings; www.brucecoville.com.

- **Sharon Creech**, author of numerous award-winning novels just right for fifth and sixth graders, including WALK TWO MOONS, which won the Newbery Award; www.sharoncreech.com.

- **Christopher Paul Curtis**, author of BUD, NOT BUDDY (Newbery Award) and THE WATSONS GO TO BIRMINGHAM—1963 (Newbery Honor), among other memorable books; tribute site at http://christopherpaulcurtis.smartwriters.com/; see also publisher's page at http://www.randomhouse.com/features/christopherpaulcurtis/.

- **Karen Cushman**, author of the Newbery Award winner THE MIDWIFE'S APPRENTICE; the Newbery Honor book CATHERINE, CALLED BIRDY; and other highly entertaining historical fiction titles; tribute Web site at http://www.karencushman.com/.

- **Kalli Dakos**, a teacher, an author, and a poet, offers writing ideas, lesson plans, and more on her Web site at http://www.kallidakos.com/.

- **Cynthia DeFelice**, author of riveting historical fiction, ghost stories, and contemporary fiction; www.cynthiadefelice.com.

- **Louise Fitzhugh**, author of the beloved HARRIET THE SPY and THE LONG SECRET; tribute Web site at http://www.purple-socks.com/.

- **Anna Grossnickle Hines**, author of many books for young children and poetry collections illustrated with quilts; her Web site offers links to other children's authors, advice, articles, and information on quilting; http://www.aghines.com.

- **Kathleen Krull**, author of a number of insightful, zesty biographies for children; www.kathleenkrull.com.

- **Lois Lowry**, award-winning, beloved author of numerous books in a variety of genres for young readers ranging in age from eight to young adult; www.loislowry.com.

- **Katherine Paterson**, award-winning author of outstanding books for children, especially those in the middle and upper elementary grades; http://www.terabithia.com/.

- **Donna Jo Napoli**, award-winning author of several memorable books spanning all grade levels and a variety of genres; www.donnajonapoli.com.

- **Linda Sue Park**, author of award-winning historical and contemporary fiction for the elementary grades, including PROJECT MULBERRY, and the Newbery Award winner, A SINGLE SHARD; an extensive and inviting site at www.lspark.com.

- **Richard Peck**, award-winning, beloved author of humorous, multilayered historical fiction for middle graders and up, including A LONG WAY FROM CHICAGO, A YEAR DOWN YONDER, and THE TEACHER'S FUNERAL: A COMEDY IN THREE PARTS; information about Peck and his books can be found on these Web sites: www.carolhurst.com/authors/rpeck.html; http://www.randomhouse.com/author/results.pperl?authorid=23514; http://www.tallmania.com/peck.html; http://richardpeck.smartwriters.com/index.2ts.

- **Susan Goldman Rubin**, author of biographies and historical perspectives for young children; http://www.susangoldmanrubin.com/index2.html.

- www.guysread.com, created by **Jon Scieszka** to "help boys find stuff they like to read"; leveled recommendations and links.

- **Cynthia Leitich Smith**, author whose Web site is cited as a "Great Web Site for Kids" by the American Library Association; also offers extensive resources for teachers; www.cynthialeitichsmith.com.

- **R. L. (Robert Lawrence) Stine**, author of Goosebumps, Fear Street Nights, and other horror genre series; an interview is at http://www.teenink.com/Past/2001/June/Interviews/RLStine.html

- **Greg Tang**, author of a number of creative books about math; www. gregtang.com.

- **Vivian Vande Velde**, award-winning author of dozens of books for kids, many of them suitable for children in the middle and upper elementary grades; an interesting and useful feature of her Web site is the explanations of how she got the idea for each of her popular books; www.vivianvandevelde.com.

- **Carole Boston Weatherford**, award-winning poet and author of numerous books; in addition to information on her books, her Web site offers teaching ideas, online resources, and related links at www.caroleweatherford.com.

- **Jacqueline Woodson**, award-winning author of books about the African American experience, from picture books (THE OTHER SIDE) to middle grade (MIRACLE'S BOYS; LOCOMOTION; MAIZON AT BLUE HILL) to young adult literature; www.jacquelinewoodson.com.

- **Jane Yolen**, the prolific, award-winning author of over 200 books for children ranging in age from the very young to young adult, offers an extensive site for teachers, children, and others interested in children's literature at www.janeyolen.com

- **Tracie Vaughn Zimmer**, author of SKETCHES FROM A SPY TREE; lessons, links, and more; www.tracievaughnzimmer.com

For a list of "Great Web Sites for Kids: Author and Illustrators" generated by the American Library Association (ALA) and the American Library Services for Children (ALSC), go to http://www. ala.org/gwstemplate.cfm?section=greatwebsites&template=/cfapps/gws/displaysection.cfm&sec=16.

Note: Although Web sites can be valuable resources that provide a wealth of information, the author cannot guarantee the accuracy of their information or their safety for children. Use the Internet wisely.

Reading-Related Resources for Teachers and Librarians

RESOURCE BOOKS

These informative, accessible guides are user-friendly, helpful time-savers for today's busy teachers and librarians. Keep them handy and readily available on your professional shelf. The more use these books get, the better it is for everyone, from teachers and administrators to parents, and all the kids in between.

- **Reconsidering Read-Aloud**, by Mary Lee Hahn (Stenhouse)

- **Reading Aloud and Beyond: Fostering the Intellectual Life with Older Readers**, by Frank Serafini and Cyndi Giorgis (Heinemann) (see especially Chapters 1 and 2, and the appendixes)

- **The New Read-Aloud Handbook**, by Jim Trelease (Penguin Books)

- **100 Best Books for Children**, by Anita Silvey (Houghton Mifflin)

- **Hey! Listen to This: Stories to Read-Aloud**, by Jim Trelease (Penguin Books)

- **Let's Read About . . . Finding Books They'll Love to Read**, by Bernice Cullinan (Scholastic)

- **Pass the Poetry, Please! 3rd edition**, by Lee Bennett Hopkins (HarperCollins)

- **Read It in the Classroom!: Organizing an Interactive Language Arts Program, Grades 4–9**, by Linda Hart-Hewins and Jan Wells (Pembroke)

- **Winning Authors: Profiles of the Newbery Medalists**, by Kathleen Long Bostrom (Libraries Unlimited)

- **The Essential Guide to Children's Books and Their Creators**, edited by Anita Silvey (Houghton Mifflin)

- **The Allure of Authors: Author Studies in the Elementary Classroom**, by Carol Brennan Jenkins (Heinemann)

- **The Undergraduate's Companion to Children's Writers and Their Web Sites**, by Jen Stevens (Libraries Unlimited)

- **Writing Essentials: Raising Expectations and Results While Simplifying Teaching**, by Regie Routman (Heinemann) (see especially Chapter 6 on the reading/writing connection)

- **Writing About Reading: From Book Talk to Literary Essays, Grades 3-8**, by Janet Angelillo (Heinemann) (see especially Chapter 2)

- **The Power of Reading: Insights from the Research, 2nd edition**, by Stephen D. Krashen (Heinemann/Libraries Unlimited)

- **The Art of Teaching Reading**, by Lucy McCormick Calkins (Longman)

- **Read Any Good Math Lately? Children's Books for Mathematical Learning, K–6**, by David J. Whitin and Sandra Wilde (Heinemann)

Dual-purpose reference books, written for parents but great for use by teachers and librarians working with parents:

- **How to Get Your Child to Love Reading: For Ravenous and Reluctant Readers Alike,** by Esmé Raji Codell (Algonquin Books)

- **Reading Magic: Why Reading Aloud to Our Children Will Change Their Lives Forever**, by Mem Fox (Harcourt)

Courtesy Harcourt, Inc.

- **Great Books About Things Kids Love**, by Kathleen Odean (Ballantine)

- **Raising a Reader: A Mother's Tale of Desperation and Delight**, by Jennie Nash (St. Martin's Press)

PERIODICALS

These publications provide timely information about recently released books, spotlight authors and illustrators, announce awards, and explore other subjects of interest related to the field of children's literature.

The Horn Book Magazine—Published every other month, this magazine, founded in 1924, is chock full of reviews, editorials, and features reflecting a deep passion for and commitment to enduring quality in books for children and young adults. Address: 56 Roland St., Suite 200, Boston, MA 02129; Telephone: 800-325-1170; Fax: 617-628-0882; Internet: magazine@hbook.com.

Booklist—Published twice monthly September through June and monthly in July and August by the American Library Association, this is a highly regarded source of reviews on all literature. Address: Kable Fulfillment Services, Agency Processing Team, 308 E. Hitt St., Mount Morris, IL 61054; Telephone: 888-350-0949; Fax: 815-734-1252; E-mail: blnk@kable.com.

Book Links—Published six times per year by the American Library Association, this resource connects children's books, K–8, to curricula in science, social studies, and language arts. Included in each issue are suggestions for novels to teach, author interviews, reviews, and thematic bibliographies. Address: PO Box 615, Mt. Morris, IL 61054-7566; Telephone: 888-350-0950; Fax: 815-734-1252; E-mail: blnk@kable.com.

School Library Journal—Founded in 1954, and currently in both print and online formats, this resource serves librarians in school and public libraries. It boasts more book reviews than any other resource of its kind. Address: PO Box 16178, North Hollywood, CA 91615-6178; Telephone: 800-595-1066; Fax: 818-487-4566; E-mail: slj@reedbusiness.com.

Curriculum Connections—This useful guide, published seasonally by *School Library Journal*, highlights worthwhile instructional and supplemental resources —print, multimedia, and on the Web—for all grade levels.

Kirkus Review—Founded in 1933, this resource is currently available in print and online editions. Specialists review 5,000 titles per year in a number of categories, of which children's books is one. Telephone: 646-654-5865; Fax: 646-654-5518; E-mail: mhazzard@vnubuspubs.com.

The Reading Teacher—Published eight times per year by the International Reading Association, this magazine targets elementary school teachers. Address: 800 Barksdale Rd., PO Box 8139, Newark, DE 19714-8139; Telephone: 800-336-7323; Internet: www.reading.org.

Children's Book Council—This nonprofit organization is the official sponsor of National Children's Book Week and Young People's Poetry Week. "Dedicated to encouraging literacy and the use and enjoyment of children's books," the CBC distributes a variety of materials about books, reading, and related media. Their catalog offers posters, friezes, streamers, bookmarks, postcards, and a variety of other products for sale. Address: 568 Broadway, New York, NY 10012; Telephone: 212-966-1990; Fax: 212-966-2073. Credit card orders for materials: 800-999-2160 or e-mail: catalogs@cbcbooks.org.

WEB SITES

Want to learn more about children's literature from the computer screen? Here is a list of professional Web sites that deliver a wealth of information on books for children. A list of publisher Web sites follows it.

- **www.ala.org**—American Library Association Web site; click on "Awards and Scholarships" and then "Book/Media Awards" or go to http://www.ala.org/Template.cfm?Section=bookmediaawards for a complete listing of the awards sponsored by the ALA, including the Newbery Award.

- **www.ala.org/gwstemplate.cfm?section=greatwebsites&template=/cfapps/gws/displaysection.cfm&sec=16**—American Library Association's "Great Web Sites for Kids" link to authors' and illustrators' Web sites.

- **www.slj.com/articles/articles/articlesindex.asp**—*School Library Journal* link; offer reviews, articles, "Best Books of the Week" and more.

- **www.readingrainbow.org**—Web site of the Emmy Award–winning PBS children's literacy series, *Reading Rainbow*, includes a complete list of the books covered on its episodes since the program's inception, as well as free classroom resources.

- **www.acs.ucalgary.ca/~dkbrown/**—Visit "The Children's Literature Web Guide" for an in-depth look at various aspects of books for children and young adults, developed by David K. Brown, Director of Doucette Library of Teaching Resources at the University of Calgary, Alberta, Canada

- **www.reading.org**—International Reading Association Web site. Products, services, and professional information are clearly available. Subscribers can also access IRA journals. Go to http://www.reading.org/resources/tools/choices_childrens.html for downloadable Children's Choices lists, favorite books chosen by children; Young Adults' Choices; and Teachers' Choices, an annotated list of books that coordinate well with curriculum.

- **www.readwritethink.org**—A partnership of the International Reading Association (IRA), the National Council of Teachers of English (NCTE), and the MCI Foundation, as part of the MarcoPolo project (see below). The ReadWriteThink Web site focuses on practices and resources related to reading and language arts instruction. Provided on the site are reading and English language arts lessons, standards, and student materials. The calendar feature located in the Highlights section on the home page offers timely classroom activities and online resources related to literacy and books.

- **www.ncte.org**—Web site of the National Council of Teachers of English; see "Teaching Resource Collections" on the home page for detailed information on poetry, reading and writing on the Web, and more.

- **www.trelease-on-reading.com**—Web site of Jim Trelease, author of *The Read-Aloud Handbook* (Penguin Books). Be sure to visit the "Treasury of Read-Alouds" at http://www.trelease-on-reading.com/rah_treasury.html.

- **www.cbcbooks.org**—Web site of the Children's Book Council, a nonprofit trade association of children's book publishers and packagers, the purpose of which is to promote reading in children. Consult their reading lists for outstanding book choices. For information, tips, and activities for Children's Book Week, celebrated annually in November, go to http://www. cbcbooks.org/cbw/. For information on Young People's Poetry Week, held annually in the spring, go to http://www.cbcbooks.org/yppw/. For book lists, go to www.cbcbooks.org/readinglists.

- **http://falcon.jmu.edu/~ramseyil/biochildhome.htm**—Internet School Library Media Center's Index to Children's and Young Adults' Authors and Illustrators' Internet sites.

- **www.education.wisc.edu/ccbc/books**—Web site of the Cooperative Children's Book Center; part of the University of Wisconsin-Madison (UW) School of Education; lists of recommended titles.

- **http://www.underdown.org/childrens-book-awards.htm**—Lists recipients of a wide spectrum of children's book awards.

- **www.rifreadingplanet.org**—An interactive site for adults and children provided by Reading Is Fundamental (RIF), considered to be the nation's oldest and largest nonprofit children's literacy organization. Be sure to visit the "Book Zone," where you can browse book lists, learn about authors and illustrators and submit questions to them, and review children's books.

- **http://marcopolo.worldcom.com**—Provides high-quality, standards-based Internet content for teachers and students, and offers professional development to K–12 teachers. The site features material in seven areas in conjunction with the following providers:

  - ArtsEdge, provided by the Kennedy Center; http://artsedge.kennedy-center. org

  - EconEdLink, provided by the National Council on Economic Education; www.econedlink.org/

  - EDSITEment, provided by the National Endowment for the Humanities; http://edsitement.neh.gov/

  - Illuminations, provided by the National Council of Teachers of Mathematics; http://illuminations.nctm.org/

- ReadWriteThink; see information found elsewhere on this page.

- ScienceNetLinks, provided by the American Association for the Advancement of Science; www.sciencenetlinks.com/

- Xpeditions, provided by the National Geographic Society; www.nationalgeographic.com/xpeditions/

- Also available through this site is the MarcoGram, a free themed monthly e-mail newsletter for educators that features warm-up activities for class discussions based on the theme, and links to related lessons. Subscribe at www.marcopolo-education.org/mg/subscribe.aspx. Archived MarcoGram material can be accessed at www.marcopolo-education.org/teacher/marcograms.aspx.

- **www.nationalbook.org/nba.html**—In mid-November the National Book Awards, the Oscars of the book world, are announced. Check this Web site for winners, which include the category "Young People's Literature".

- **www.bankstreet.edu/bookcom/**—Web site of the Children's Book Committee at Bank Street College of Education; reading lists, links, publications, and information on their three annual awards: The Josette Frank Award (fiction), the Flora Stieglitz Straus Award (nonfiction), and the Claudia Lewis Award (poetry).

- **www.icdlbooks.org**—International Children's Digital Library; a project of the University of Maryland; its purpose is to "select, collect, digitize, and organize children's materials in their original languages and to create appropriate technologies for access and use by children 3-13 years old."

- **www.minnesotahumanities.org**—Provides support to those working to improve literacy of both children and their parents. Includes free reading guides for children's books, ways to involve dads, and bilingual initiatives.

- **www.bookhive.org/books/**—On this Web site of the Public Library of Charlotte and Mecklenburg County, North Carolina, reviews of books are handily listed according to author, title, illustrator, age level, genre, and number of pages.

- **www.kidsource.com/NICHCY/literature.html**—A bibliography of children's books on or about various disabilities.

- **www.SimonSaysTEACH.com**—Powered by Simon& Schuster Children's Books, this site, launched in May 2005, offers teachers and librarians "tools to meet all your educational needs." Included are monthly themes; award announcements; parents' night kits; reading group guides; and special sections for parents who homeschool, guidance counselors, and administrators.

- **www.randomhouse.com/teachers/authors/results.pperl?authorid=10018**—Teachers @ Random Web site offers resources for teachers, including information on authors and illustrators, teacher's guides, and planning calendar suggestions.

- **www.randomhouse.com/teachers/librarians/**—Librarians @ Random Web site offers news on latest award announcements, suggestions for booktalks, and suggestions for activities on timely topics.

Online Bookstores

- www.amazon.com mega bookstore

- www.bn.com Barnes & Noble online

- www.bookcloseouts.com Great deals; click on Children's, and then refine your search by choosing a subject, age range, author's name, series name, format, or price. Be sure to peruse award winners and "scratch & dent" inventory.

Publishers

To order directly from publishers, visit their Web sites for information. Note that some of the larger publishers with a number of imprints have links from the main Web address, while at other publishing companies, imprints act independently of one another. At some publishing houses, marketing departments are shared among imprints, while at others they operate independently.

- **Harry N. Abrams, Inc.**: www.abramsbooks.com

- **American Girl:** www.americangirl.com

- **Atheneum**. *See* Simon & Schuster

- **Bloomsbury Children's Books:** www.bloomsburyusa.com

- **Boyds Mills Press**: www.boydsmillspress.com

Imprints: Wordsong (Poetry); Calkins Creek Books (U.S. history; fiction and nonfiction)

- **Broadman & Holman:** www.broadmanholman.com

- **Candlewick Press:** www.candlewick.com

- **Clarion:** www.houghtonmifflinbooks.com

- **Crown**. *See* Random House

- **Dial Books for Young Readers**. *See* Penguin Group

- **Dutton Children's Books.** *See* Penguin Group

- **Farrar Straus Giroux:** www.fsgkidsbooks.com

- **Free Spirit Publishing:** www.freespirit.com

- **Front Street Books:** www.frontstreetbooks.com (an imprint of Boyds Mills Press)

- **Greenwillow.** *See* HarperCollins

- **Grosset & Dunlap.** *See* Penguin Group

- **Harcourt Children's Book Division:** www.harcourtbooks.com

- **HarperCollins Children's Books:** www.harperchildrens.com

Imprints: Joanna Cotler Books, Greenwillow

- **Henry Holt and Company:** www.henryholt.com

- **Holiday House:** www.holidayhouse.com

- **Holt:** www.henryholtchildrensbooks.com

- **Houghton Mifflin:** www.houghtonmifflinbooks.com

- **Hyperion Books for Children:** www.hyperionchildrensbooks.com (an imprint of Disney Children's Book Group)

- **Ideals Publications:** www.idealspublications.com

- **Kids Can Press:** www.kidscanpress.com

- **Knopf Delacorte Dell Young Readers Group.** *See* Random House

- **Lee and Low:** www.leeandlow.com

- **Little, Brown & Company:** www.littlebrown.com

- **Margaret K. McElderry Books.** *See* Simon & Schuster

- **Meadowbrook Press:** www.meadowbrookpress.com

- **Millbrook Press:** www.millbrookpress.com

- **Orchard Books.** *See* Scholastic

- **Penguin Group USA:** http://us.penguingroup.com/static/html/aboutus/imprints-youngreaders.html

Imprints: Dial Books for Young Readers, Dutton Children's Books, G.P. Putnam's Sons, Grosset & Dunlap, Philomel, Putnam, Puffin, Penguin, Viking

- **Philomel.** *See* Penguin Group

- **Random House:** www.randomhouse.com/kids/

Imprints: Knopf Delacorte Dell Young Readers Group, Random House Children's Books, Golden Books for Young Readers, Crown

- **Scholastic:** www.scholastic.com

Imprints: Scholastic Press, Orchard Books, Arthur A. Levine Books

- **Simon & Schuster Children's Publishing:** www.simonsayskids.com

Imprints: Aladdin, Atheneum, Margaret K. McElderry Books, Simon & Schuster Books for Young Readers

- **Tricycle Press:** http://www.tenspeedpress.com/catalog/tricycle/index.php3

- **Albert Whitman & Company**: www.albertwhitman.com

- **Williamson Books:** www.idealspublications.com/index.asp?PageAction= VIEWCATS&Category=35

Children's Book Awards

Numerous awards honor children's books. Knowing about these awards and where you can find information about recent winners allows you to have at your fingertips reliable sources for the best of the best in the field of children's literature. *The Horn Book* announces recent award winners in the back of each issue in a section entitled "The Hunt Breakfast" (Web site at www.hbook.com). Other useful Web sites to visit for listings of prestigious national and international children's book awards are www.ala.org and www.childrenslit.com.

The **Newbery Award** is the benchmark for books intended for mid- and upper-elementary grade readers (see Parent Pull-Out Pages for more information on this prestigious award and a partial list of winners). For picture books, look for news of the **Caldecott Award** winners. Both awards are presented annually by the American Library Association, and winners are listed on its Web site, www.ala.org. The award that recognizes outstanding books written for young adult readers is the **Michael L. Printz Award**, also listed on the ALA Web site.

Following is a list of other notable awards presented in the United States of particular interest to those working with students in the upper elementary grades.

IRA Children's Choice Award—Each year thousands of students from across the country choose their favorite books from a list of recently published titles. Votes are tabulated, and books are grouped according to reading levels. The lists are distributed by the International Reading Association (IRA) in conjunction with the Children's Book Council. They appear in the October issue of the IRA journal, *The Reading Teacher*. (**Teachers' Choice Awards**—a list of 30 books rated by teams of teachers, librarians, and reading specialists—are announced in the November issue of *Reading Teacher*.) Copies can be obtained for $1.00, accompanied by a self-addressed. 9-by-12-inch envelope, from IRA, 800 Barksdale Rd., PO Box 8139, Newark, DE 19714-8139, or lists can be downloaded as PDF files from the IRA Web site at www.reading.org.

The Golden Kite Award—This annual award, established in 1973, is announced in late spring. It is presented to a member of the Society of Children's Book Writers and Illustrators for excellence in the field of children's books in each of four categories: fiction, nonfiction, picture book, text and picture book illustration. Web site: www.scbwi.org.

Boston Globe-Horn Book Award—Awarded annually in the fall for excellence in literature for children and young adults in the categories of Outstanding Fiction or Poetry, Outstanding Nonfiction, and Outstanding Illustration. Winners are listed in *The Horn Book* in January. Web site: www.hbook.com.

American Booksellers BookSense Book of the Year Award—Presented each year to the children's book voted by members as the title they most enjoy recommending to customers; formerly the ABBY award. Web site: www.bookweb. org/news/awards/.

Coretta Scott King Awards—Given annually in honor of Martin Luther King Jr. and Coretta Scott King to African American authors and illustrators whose books for children provide inspiration and educate. Go to www.ala.org for more information.

Pura Belpré Medal—Recognizes outstanding children's literature and illustration that celebrate the Latino/a cultural experience, created by Latino/Latina writers and illustrators; given biennially. Go to www.ala.org for more information.

The Children's Book Committee at Bank Street College of Education gives three annual awards: **The Josette Frank Award** (fiction), the **Flora Stieglitz Straus Award** (nonfiction), and the **Claudia Lewis Award** (poetry). Go to http://www.bankstreet.edu/bookcom/ for reading lists, links, publications, and information on the award winners.

Parents' Choice Awards—Awarded to books as well as a variety of other media products that "meet and exceed standards set by educators, scientists, performing artists, librarians, parents, and . . . kids." Award levels include Classic, Gold, Silver, Recommended, Approved, and Fun Stuff. Go to www.parents-choice.org for complete lists.

The Charlotte Zolotow Award—Named for the well-known picture book author and awarded annually for outstanding text in a picture book. Go to www.soemadison.wisc.edu/ccbc/zolotow.htm for more information.

Laura Ingalls Wilder Award—Presented every two years by the Association for Library Services to Children (ALSC) to an author or illustrator whose books, published in the United States, have made a lasting contribution to the field over a period of years. Go to www.ala.org for more information.

Christopher Awards—Founded in 1945 and "committed to the Judeo-Christian tradition of service to God and humanity," the Christopher Awards honor books, films, TV programs, and people who "affirm the highest values of the human spirit." Information and a list of winners can be found on the Web site at www.christophers.org.

Jane Addams Book Award—Awarded by the Women's International League of Peace and Freedom and the Jane Addams Peace Association to a children's book that promotes peace, social justice, world community, and equality of the sexes and all races. Go to www.janeaddamspeace.org for more information.

Scott O'Dell Award for Historical Fiction—This honor was established by the author to encourage the writing of historical fiction for young readers. It is awarded to a book of historical fiction written for children or young adults, published in English in the United States, and set in the Americas. Web site: www.scottodell.com.

Robert F. Sibert Informational Book Award—Awarded annually to the author of the best informational book for children, this distinction is named in honor of the long-time head of Bound to Stay Bound Books. Go to www.ala.org for more information.

Orbis Pictus Award for Outstanding Nonfiction for Children—Awarded annually by the National Council of Teachers of English (NCTE) for excellence in this genre. The award is named in honor of Johannes Amos Comenius, whose work, Orbis Pictus—*The World in Pictures*, published in 1657, is recognized as the first book written expressly for children. For more information, visit www.ncte.org/elem/awards/orbispictus/.

Jefferson Cup—Awarded annually since 1983 by the Virginia Library Association's Children's and Young Adult Round Table to a biography, historical fiction, or American history book written for children. For more information go to www.co.fairfax.va.us/library/reading/ya/jeffcup.htm.

Washington Post—Children's Book Guild Nonfiction Award—Established in 1977, this award honors an author of children's nonfiction for his or her body of work.

Outstanding Science Trade Books for Students K–12—Originally known as Outstanding Science Trade Books for Children; books are selected by a review panel of the National Science Teachers Association (NSTA) in coordination with the Children's Book Council (CBC). Web site: www.nsta.org/ostbc.

Notable Books for a Global Society (NBGS)—The Committee of the International Reading Association's Reading and Children's Literature Special Interest Group annually selects 25 works written for children in grades K–12 that are notable for enhancing an understanding of cultural differences across the globe. Go to www.csulb.edu/org/childrens-lit or review the fall issue of *The Dragon Lode*, which includes teaching ideas and titles of related books.

Batchelder Award—Awarded to an American publisher for the most outstanding children's book originally published in a foreign language in a foreign country and then translated into English and published in the United States. Go to www.ala.org for more information.

Lee Bennett Hopkins Poetry Award—Founded by this American poet in 1993 to promote poetry, the award is presented annually to an American poet or anthologist for the most outstanding new book of children's poetry published in the previous calendar year. Web site: www.pabook.libraries.psu.edu/hopkinsaward.html

Lee Bennett Hopkins Promising Poet Award—Given every three years by the International Reading Association to a promising new poet who writes for children and young adults, and who has published no more than two books of children's poetry. Go to http://www.reading.org/association/awards/childrens_hopkins.html for a list of winners.

National Council of Teachers of English (NCTE) Award for Poetry for Children
—Established in 1977 to honor a living American poet for his or her body of work for children ages three to thirteen. The award is given every three years. For more information and a list of previous winners, go to http://www.ncte. org/elem/awards/poetry/.

Many states also give awards, such as the **Texas Bluebonnet Award** (see www.txla.org/groups/tba), Minnesota's **Maud Hart Lovelace Book Award** (see www. isd77.k12.mn.us/lovelace/lovelace.html), New York's **Charlotte Award** (www.nysreading. org/awards), and Wyoming's **Indian Paintbrush Book Award** (www.ccpls.org/html/ indianp.html). Go to www.carr.lib.md.us/read/stateawardsbks.htm for a list of state awards and their Web sites.

International awards worth noting are the **Hans Christian Andersen Award** (www.ibby.org/seiten/04_andersen.htm), considered to be the most prestigious award in children's literature in the world. Bestowed every two years by the International Board on Books for Young People (IBBY), it honors an author whose work has made a significant contribution internationally to children's literature.

Three British awards are the **Carnegie Medal,** which recognizes an outstanding children's book written in English and first published in the United Kingdom; the **Kate Greenaway Medal,** which parallels the Caldecott Award (go to www.carnegiegreenaway. org.uk); and the **Nestle Children's Book Prize** (formerly the **Smarties Book Prize**), awarded annually to the best books published in the United Kingdom for children under 11 years of age. The Nestle Prizes are awarded in three categories (ages five and under, ages six to eight, and ages nine to eleven), with bronze, silver, and gold distinctions in each age group (www.booktrusted.com/nestle).

The **Canadian Library Association Book of the Year for Children Award** honors a children's book of literary distinction written by a Canadian, while the **Amelia Frances Howard-Gibbon Medal** is awarded to an outstanding illustrated book published in Canada and written by an author who resides in or is a native of Canada. Web sites: www.cla.ca/awards/boyc.htm and www.cla.ca/awards/afhg.htm respectively.

The **Australian Children's Books of the Year Awards**, bestowed annually by the Children's Book Council of Australia, recognize the Book of the Year for Older Readers, Book of the Year for Younger Readers, Book of the Year for Early Childhood, Picture Book of the Year, and Eve Pownall Award for Information Books. Winners must be books written by Australians or residents of Australia. Go to http://www.cbc.org.au/awards1.htm for more information.

Parent Pull-Out Pages

There is more treasure in books than in all the pirate's loot on Treasure Island . . .
and best of all, you can enjoy these riches every day of your life.—Walt Disney

Raising Readers

Tips and Techniques for Parents

by Judy Bradbury

HOW DO YOU SPELL SCHOOL SUCCESS?
R-E-A-D A-L-O-U-D T-O Y-O-U-R C-H-I-L-D

Isn't a preteen too old to be read to?

No way!!

Reading aloud to your child is the single most important thing you can do to improve his or her attitude toward reading. Try these strategies, and you'll find that even you are looking forward to the next chapter of the book you're reading to your child. *What's going to happen next?* you wonder. A love of reading—that's what. Can you spell **s-u-c-c-e-s-s**?

1. Choose books together. Read aloud (every day!) stories that appeal to both you and your child. Find books that'll have you giggling or shivering together. If a story makes you want to keep reading even when you're missing something desperately intriguing on TV, it's a winner. If you love a book, you'll convey that to your child. If, on the other hand, you aren't interested, you'll give that away, too.

2. Skim a book before choosing it. Consider content and length. Review each chapter before reading it aloud. By becoming familiar with the plot, you'll be more apt to read with expression. When a character is frightened, shake! When the forest is creepy and spooky, whisper. Narrow your eyes, raise your eyebrows; show fear, happiness, or surprise in your voice;. And when some-thing silly happens, enjoy those laughs! Draw your child into the story with the first sentence and make the last line memorable. You'll find your child begging you not to stop reading at a chapter's end and reaching for that book the next day. Good, good, good. Because, remember our mantra: **Read every day**.

3. Choose a cozy, quiet spot to read aloud to your child. Cuddle up, cover up, lie head-to-head beneath the reading lamp—do whatever will make your daily read-aloud time special. Your child will cherish this time together.

Reading aloud is one of the best gifts you can give to your child. It's free, it's easy, it expands your child's horizons, and it introduces one of life's most satisfying pleasures: the wonders awaiting us between the covers of a book.

Children's Book Corner: A READ-ALOUD Resource with Tips, Techniques, and Plans for Teachers, Librarians, and Parents, by Judy Bradbury. Westport, CT: Libraries Unlimited, 2006

Raising Readers

Tips and Techniques for Parents

by Judy Bradbury

PARENT POWER: YOU CAN MAKE A DIFFERENCE!

It's never too late to raise a reader. Just because your preteen has never been crazy about reading doesn't mean you have to give up on books. Here are a few things you can do to nudge away apathy about the printed page. Because, as we all know,

BOOKS + READING = SUCCESS IN SCHOOL AND LIFE.

- Read aloud to your child every day. Even if you only have 15 minutes, read something to your child. Every day.

- Take weekly trips to the library and browse for books and magazines of interest. They're free, there are plenty to choose from, and librarians are nice people.

- Listen to audio books in the car. Talk about them. Then bring home other books by the authors your child likes.

- Be sure your child sees you reading and writing. (Actions speak loudly.)

- Read billboards and discuss word choice and placement, and other aspects of the message.

- Subscribe to a magazine about something your child is interested in.

- Designate a shelf for your child's favorite books. You need one, too.

- Be sure to grant *at least* equal time for reading as there is for TV.

- Praise school accomplishments. This builds self-confidence, self-esteem, a desire to succeed in school, and a zest for learning.

You can do it; you can, you can!

You're a great parent; you are, you are!

Children's Book Corner: A READ-ALOUD Resource with Tips, Techniques, and Plans for Teachers, Librarians, and Parents, by Judy Bradbury. Westport, CT: Libraries Unlimited, 2006

Raising Readers

Tips and Techniques for Parents

by Judy Bradbury

TURN OFF THE TV*:
TOSS THE REMOTE AND SURF A BOOK INSTEAD

The average elementary student watches over 25 hours of television a week. That's a lot of tube time. Cut that time in half and read a book instead, and you'll be attending your child's college graduation because:

READING BREEDS SCHOOL SUCCESS.

Television, if overused:

- Can cause a short attention span.

- Reduces creative thinking and problem solving.

- Lowers physical activity (making it hard to turn the pages of a book).

So, here's the deal:

- View television wisely. Connect TV to reading by watching programs related to books and reading books related to TV shows or movies that interest your child. Show interest in what your child reads; discuss books and magazine articles.

- Play board games. There's reading, thinking, talking, memory, strategy, and family FUN involved!

- Plan a menu. Make something from a new recipe. You bake and cook, your child reads, measures, talks, thinks, plans, and learns to cook.

- Read, read, read. And read some more. Read together, you to your child, your child to you, side by side to yourselves. Just read.

- And then start planning your child's college graduation party.

*And the computer and electronic games, too!

Children's Book Corner: A READ-ALOUD Resource with Tips, Techniques, and Plans for Teachers, Librarians, and Parents, by Judy Bradbury. Westport, CT: Libraries Unlimited, 2006

Raising Readers

Tips and Techniques for Parents
by Judy Bradbury

**FIFTH GRADE ALERT:
AUTHORS KNOWN TO SNAG KIDS' INTEREST**

Tuck this list in your pocket when you go shopping for a gift for a fifth grader.

Betsy Byars (realistic fiction)

Sharon Creech (realistic fiction)

Christopher Paul Curtis (humorous historical fiction)

Roald Dahl (zany fantasy)

Paula Danziger (realistic fiction)

Jean Fritz (nonfiction)

Patricia Reilly Giff (historical and realistic fiction)

Polly Horvath (humorous, insightful, realistic fiction)

Dick King-Smith (fantasy)

Lois Lowry (realistic fiction)

Linda Sue Park (historical and realistic fiction)

Katherine Paterson (realistic fiction)

Louis Sachar (humorous fiction; fantasy)

Jerry Spinelli (realistic fiction)

Kathleen Krull (biography)

Note: Authors often write books for a variety of age levels; choose accordingly.

Children's Book Corner: A READ-ALOUD Resource with Tips, Techniques, and Plans for Teachers, Librarians, and Parents, by Judy Bradbury. Westport, CT: Libraries Unlimited, 2006

Raising Readers

Tips and Techniques for Parents

by Judy Bradbury

SIXTH GRADE ALERT:
AUTHORS KNOWN TO SNAG KIDS' INTEREST

Here's a handy list of authors who make readers of sixth graders who aren't and who satisfy sixth graders who are.

Lloyd Alexander (fantasy)

Joan Bauer (contemporary fiction; especially of interest to girls)

Judy Blume (contemporary fiction; especially of interest to girls)

Bruce Coville (humorous science fiction/fantasy)

Karen Cushman (historical fiction)

Cynthia DeFelice (suspense and adventure)

Paul Fleischmann (historical fiction and poetry)

Sid Fleischmann (humorous historical fiction)

Russell Freedman (nonfiction)

Karen Hesse (historical fiction, novels in verse)

Gary Paulsen (adventure, survival; especially of interest to boys)

Richard Peck (historical fiction)

Robert Newton Peck (historical fiction)

Vivian Vande Velde (fantasy)

Jacqueline Woodson (realistic and historical fiction)

Note: Authors often write books for a variety of age levels; choose accordingly.

Children's Book Corner: A READ-ALOUD Resource with Tips, Techniques, and Plans for Teachers, Librarians, and Parents, by Judy Bradbury. Westport, CT: Libraries Unlimited, 2006

Raising Readers

Tips and Techniques for Parents
by Judy Bradbury

BOOKS PRETEEN BOYS FLIP (OFF THE TV) FOR

These stories grip the reader's interest and never let go. Crammed with action, adventure, suspense, or humor—or all of these—boys (especially) love 'em.

DEVIL'S BRIDGE and WEASEL, by Cynthia DeFelice (action and adventure)

WOOD SONG and DOGSONG, by Gary Paulsen (survival/wilderness tales)

GUYS WRITE FOR GUYS READ, selected by Jon Scieszka (short stories)

BUD, NOT BUDDY and THE WATSONS GO TO BIRMINGHAM—1963, by Christopher Paul Curtis (humorous historical fiction)

LOSER and MANIAC MAGEE, by Jerry Spinelli (riveting contemporary fiction; fable)

THERE'S A BOY IN THE GIRLS' BATHROOM and SIDEWAYS STORIES FROM WAYSIDE SCHOOL, by Louis Sachar (funny, zany stuff)

MIRACLE'S BOYS and LOCOMOTION, by Jacqueline Woodson (realistic fiction about African American boys)

THE BOY WHO SAVED BASEBALL, by John H. Ritter (memorable!)

See also books written by Andrew Clements, Walter Dean Myers, David Macaulay, Russell Freedman, Lemony Snicket, Bruce Coville, James Howe, and Roald Dahl.

For lists of books for boys recommended by boys and the popular, award-winning author Jon Scieszka, visit www.guysread.com.

Note: Web sites can provide a wealth of information, but the author cannot guarantee the accuracy of their information or their safety for children. Use them wisely.

Note: Authors often write books for a variety of age levels; choose accordingly.

Children's Book Corner: A READ-ALOUD Resource with Tips, Techniques, and Plans for Teachers, Librarians, and Parents, by Judy Bradbury. Westport, CT: Libraries Unlimited, 2006

Raising Readers

Tips and Techniques for Parents

by Judy Bradbury

BOOKS PRETEEN GIRLS FLIP (OFF THE PHONE RINGER) FOR

Books about girlfriends, cool friends, true friends, who sits where in the cafeteria on any given day and why, life's embarrassing moments, and girls figuring out who they are and where they fit, will appeal to preteen girls like cheese on a burger and sparkly lip gloss. And these books will stay with them longer, too.

YANKEE GIRL, by Mary Ann Rodman: This story, set in the 1960s, is based on the author's experiences with school integration in Mississippi.

CATHERINE, CALLED BIRDY, by Karen Cushman: Set in the Middle Ages, this is the diary of a spunky girl who made her own choices in a time when it just wasn't done!

FEVER 1793, by Laurie Halse Anderson: Mattie grows up as she tries to escape the yellow fever epidemic enveloping Philadelphia in 1793.

ANNE OF GREEN GABLES, by L. M. Montgomery: Classic tale of the unforgettable red-headed orphan who comes to Prince William Island.

MY LOUISIANA SKY, by Kimberly Willis Holt: Tiger Ann Parker—bright, athletic, and shunned by her peers because her parents are "slow"—comes to realize what she values most.

THE WISH, by Gail Carson Levine: Wilma is a smart eighth grader whose wish to be popular is granted.

STEALING THUNDER, by Mary Casanova: A girl sets out to save an abused horse from its owner.

BECOMING NAOMI LEÓN, by Pam Muñoz Ryan: Portrays the emotional and physical journeys of a Mexican American girl whose mother returns after seven years, and the ensuing conflicts that event triggers.

Note: Interests, maturity, and reading levels vary among children; choose accordingly.

Children's Book Corner: A READ-ALOUD Resource with Tips, Techniques, and Plans for Teachers, Librarians, and Parents, by Judy Bradbury. Westport, CT: Libraries Unlimited, 2006

Raising Readers

Tips and Techniques for Parents

by Judy Bradbury

MASTERFUL MYSTERIES . . . *NOT* FOR THE CLUELESS!

One of the great things about selecting books for fifth and sixth graders is the variety of entertaining, meaty mysteries suitable for maturing readers. From classics, such as the Nancy Drew and Hardy Boys series (which have been repackaged and widely expanded over the past decade) to novels by new stars whose story-spinning talents rival Agatha Christie's, you'll find plenty of suspenseful, twisty tales that will light the fire for those children who think reading is boring and fuel the fire for voluminous readers.

- CHASING VERMEER, written by Blue Balliett and illustrated by Brett Helquist; three letters, countless unexplainable coincidences, and the theft of a painting, adding up to one absorbing mystery; winner of the 2005 Edgar Allan Poe Award for best children's mystery. See also the sequel, WRIGHT 3.

- SAMMY KEYES AND THE HOTEL THIEF by Wendelin Van Draanen; winner of the Edgar Allan Poe Award for best children's mystery; other titles in the series centering around one very curious investi-kid include SAMMY KEYES AND THE ART OF DECEPTION, SAMMY KEYES AND THE SISTERS OF MERCY, SAMMY KEYES AND THE CURSE OF MOUSTACHE MARY, and SAMMY KEYES AND THE HOLLYWOOD MUMMY.

- HOOT by Carl Hiaasen; a wild and wacky mystery/adventure that takes place in Florida and revolves around the new kid at school and his involvement in a campaign to save an endangered species of owls; Newbery Honor Award winner and New York Times Bestseller. See also FLUSH.

- WANTED . . . MUD BLOSSOM by Betsy Byars; fifth in a series of rollicking stories about the Blossom family; spotlights Mud, the dog, at the center of the mystery of Junior's missing hamster; unforgettable trial scene!

See also BUNNICULA (and related titles) and the Sebastian Barth Mysteries by James Howe, THE STRANGER NEXT DOOR and SPY CAT by Peg Kehret; and just about any title by Mary Downing Hahn.

Note: Authors often write books for a variety of age levels; choose accordingly.

Children's Book Corner: A READ-ALOUD Resource with Tips, Techniques, and Plans for Teachers, Librarians, and Parents, by Judy Bradbury. Westport, CT: Libraries Unlimited, 2006

Raising Readers

Tips and Techniques for Parents

by Judy Bradbury

FABULOUS FAMILIES

The families that populate the pages of these books are memorable. Feel-real characters, humor, warmth, and love inevitably extend to the lucky reader who joins these families on the printed page.

THE NOT-JUST-ANYBODY FAMILY, by Betsy Byars (see also THE BLOSSOMS MEET THE VULTURE LADY, THE BLOSSOMS AND THE GREEN PHANTOM, WANTED . . . MUD BLOSSOM, and A BLOSSOM PROMISE)

WALK TWO MOONS, by Sharon Creech

Little House on the Prairie series, by Laura Ingalls Wilder

YOLONDA'S GENIUS, by Carol Fenner

THE WATSONS GO TO BIRMINGHAM—1963, by Christopher Paul Curtis

ANASTASIA KRUPNIK, first in a series by Lois Lowry

FIG PUDDING, by Ralph Fletcher

ESPERANZA RISING, by Pam Muñoz Ryan

AL CAPONE DOES MY SHIRTS, by Gennifer Choldenko

SWITCHAROUND, by Lois Lowry

SURVIVING THE APPLEWHITES, by Stephanie S. Tolan

EACH LITTLE BIRD THAT SINGS, by Deborah Wiles

MIRACLE'S BOYS, by Jacqueline Woodson

Note: Authors often write books for a variety of age levels; choose accordingly.

Children's Book Corner: A READ-ALOUD Resource with Tips, Techniques, and Plans for Teachers, Librarians, and Parents, by Judy Bradbury. Westport, CT: Libraries Unlimited, 2006

Raising Readers

Tips and Techniques for Parents

by Judy Bradbury

FANTASTIC FANTASY: OUT-OF-THE-ORDINARY STORIES

One of the most phenomenal things that has happened in the book world in the last decade is Harry Potter. He flipped the switch on interest in children's books. And it's a mega-watt halogen light kind of attention. Kids are reading books—hefty books—and eagerly anticipating the arrival of new titles by authors they have come to know and love. Kids talk about books and characters on the bus, at birthday parties, and in the cafeteria. Whether you like Harry and his adventures or not, there's no denying that books have magically come onto the radar screen for millions of children, in large part due to an author who sat in a coffee shop to keep warm while she wrote her mythical stories.

Listed here are other fantasies that mesmerize young readers.

THE LION, THE WITCH AND THE WARDROBE (and other titles in the Chronicles of Narnia series), by C. S. Lewis

A WRINKLE IN TIME (and other titles), by Madeleine L'Engle

The Dark Is Rising series, by Susan Cooper

INKHEART and INKSPELL, by Cornelia Funke

His Dark Materials Trilogy, by Philip Pullman

TIME CAT (and other outstanding titles), by Lloyd Alexander

THE PHANTOM TOLLBOOTH, by Norton Juster

THE CRICKET IN TIMES SQUARE, by George Selden

MRS. FRISBY AND THE RATS OF NIMH, by Robert C. O'Brien

PIGS MIGHT FLY (and other outstanding titles), by Dick King-Smith

Note: Interests, maturity, and reading levels vary among children; choose accordingly.

Children's Book Corner: A READ-ALOUD Resource with Tips, Techniques, and Plans for Teachers, Librarians, and Parents, by Judy Bradbury. Westport, CT: Libraries Unlimited, 2006

Raising Readers

Tips and Techniques for Parents

by Judy Bradbury

NO LONGER BORING:
TODAY'S NONFICTION PUTS AN END TO THE
SNOOZER-LOSER LABEL

In the last 10 years or so, nonfiction for children has prettied up. Gone are the dry, intimidating fact books illustrated with black-and-white photos that I'm betting you remember reading as a child. Yawn no more. Today's nonfiction is enthralling, engaging, colorful, and hip. It wows young readers who have curious minds, and challenges the child who is indifferent. Give a youngster a book by one of these authors . . . and watch for sparks!

Susan Campbell Bartoletti

Louise Borden

Russell Freedman

James Cross Giblin

Jan Greenberg

Jim Haskins

Barbara Kerley

Kathleen Krull

David Macaulay

Jim Murphy

Susan Goldman Rubin

Children's Book Corner: A READ-ALOUD Resource with Tips, Techniques, and Plans for Teachers, Librarians, and Parents, by Judy Bradbury. Westport, CT: Libraries Unlimited, 2006

Raising Readers

Tips and Techniques for Parents

by Judy Bradbury

THE NEWBERY MEDAL:
THE "BIG ENCHILADA" IN CHILDREN'S BOOK AWARDS

One of the most prestigious awards in the children's book world is the Newbery Medal, given annually by the American Library Association to the most outstanding American children's book published in the previous year. Listed below are selected winners especially of interest to fifth- and sixth-grade readers.

KIRA-KIRA, by Cynthia Kadohata

THE TALE OF DESPEREAUX, written by Kate DiCamillo

A SINGLE SHARD, by Linda Sue Park

A YEAR DOWN YONDER, by Richard Peck

BUD, NOT BUDDY, by Christopher Paul Curtis

HOLES, by Louis Sachar

OUT OF THE DUST, by Karen Hesse

THE MIDWIFE'S APPRENTICE, by Karen Cushman

WALK TWO MOONS, by Sharon Creech

SHILOH, by Phyllis Reynolds Naylor

MANIAC MAGEE, by Jerry Spinelli

NUMBER THE STARS, by Lois Lowry

JOYFUL NOISE: POEMS FOR TWO VOICES, by Paul Fleischman

LINCOLN: A PHOTOBIOGRAPHY, by Russell Freedman

Note: Interests, maturity, and reading levels vary among children; choose accordingly.

Children's Book Corner: A READ-ALOUD Resource with Tips, Techniques, and Plans for Teachers, Librarians, and Parents, by Judy Bradbury. Westport, CT: Libraries Unlimited, 2006

Raising Readers

Tips and Techniques for Parents

by Judy Bradbury

PAPERBACK SERIES FICTION: BOOKS THAT WHET THE READING APPETITE

There's nothing wrong with reading series fiction. These tuck-in-your-back-pocket books are friendly, inexpensive, and widely available. Bright and appealing, they often make readers out of those who never saw a use for books. Series fiction taps into an interest, hobby, or fascination—whether it's horses, babysitting, mysteries, time travel, or outer space—and feeds those interests with numerous, tasty installments. Featuring familiar elements—whether it's the main character, the format or style, or the setting—series fiction makes kids feel friendly toward the printed page, and that's a very good thing. Lots of titles = lots of reading = improved reading skills. Series fiction is seriously nothing to sniff at.

Listed here are the names of just a few popular series suited to fifth and sixth graders. Pick one and let the noshing begin. Nutritious, delicious, award-winning books are only a nibble away. Bon appetit!

- Hardy Boys Mysteries; Frank and Joe are on the case!
- Nancy Drew Mysteries; classic girls' mystery stories
- Herculeah Jones Mystery; laudable series penned by Betsy Byars
- Wishbone; mystery and adventure with a classical twist, featuring a doggone great detective!
- History Mysteries; historical fiction mysteries
- Roman Mysteries, by Caroline Lawrence; fast-paced adventures in ancient Roman times
- Dear America; historical fiction written as girls' diaries
- My Name Is America; ordinary boys become heroes; historical fiction
- The Wolfbay Wings, by Bruce Brooks; hockey series
- Winning Season, by Rich Wallace; sports series
- Thoroughbred, created by Joanna Campbell; riding and horse racing
- The Saddle Club, by Bonnie Bryant; horseback riding drama
- Hoofbeats, by Kathleen Duey; historical fiction horse stories
- Sweet Valley Twins, created by Francine Pascal; girl-friendly fiction
- A Series of Unfortunate Events, by Lemony Snicket; orphans' misadventures
- Animorphs, by K.A. Applegate; kids "morph" into animals

Note: Interests, maturity, and reading levels vary among children; choose accordingly.

Children's Book Corner: A READ-ALOUD Resource with Tips, Techniques, and Plans for Teachers, Librarians, and Parents, by Judy Bradbury. Westport, CT: Libraries Unlimited, 2006

Raising Readers

Tips and Techniques for Parents

by Judy Bradbury

GLOSSY GRABBERS: MAGAZINES PARTICULARLY OF INTEREST TO FIFTH AND SIXTH GRADERS

One of the most effective ways to encourage your child to read is to find current material on a topic of interest and at an appropriate level. Match a child to a magazine targeting his or her interests, and you've made it to first base. Add bright photos and topic headings that help identify the main ideas, and you've rounded to third. Get your child to pick up a magazine on his or her own, and you're home free. Pretty good deal for the cost of a subscription that brings fresh material to the mailbox every month or so, wouldn't you say?

Listed here in alphabetical order are magazines of interest to fifth and sixth graders. Before subscribing, send for a trial issue or flip through a magazine of interest in the bookstore or your public or school library to decide if it's right for your child.

- *American Cheerleader Junior*, articles of interest related to the sport of cheerleading

- *American Girl*; reinforces self-esteem, self-confidence, and curiosity in girls; crafts, book reviews, stories, and more

- *Boys' Life*; published by the Boy Scouts of America; a variety of articles and stories especially for boys

- Boys' *Quest*; theme-related topics of interest to boys

- *Calliope*; theme-related history, biography, and historical fiction

- *Children's Digest*; emphasizes a healthy lifestyle; short stories, articles, activities, and poetry

- *Cobblestone*; articles, stories, and activities focusing on American history

- *Cousteau Kids*; explores all areas of science that relate to global waters

- *Cricket;* folktales, adventures, fantasy, articles, poems, craft activities

- *Faces*; through monthly themes, explores people, culture, and places around the world

Children's Book Corner: A READ-ALOUD Resource with Tips, Techniques, and Plans for Teachers, Librarians, and Parents, by Judy Bradbury. Westport, CT: Libraries Unlimited, 2006

- *Fun For Kidz*; themed issues offer activities, stories, how-to articles, jokes, and puzzles

- *Girls' Life*; fashion, beauty, friends, family, reviews, profiles, and more especially for girls

- *Highlights for Children*; a mainstay in the children's magazine market; articles, stories, poetry, art, and activities

- *Hopscotch*; fun, wholesome pieces that focus on letting kids be kids

- *Horsepower*; for young horse lovers

- *International Gymnast*; competitions, nutrition, fitness, training, and techniques

- *Kids Discover*; themed issues on nature, environment, archaeology, geography, ecology, travel, and more

- *The Kids Hall of Fame News*; spotlights achievements of youth

- *Mr. Marquis' Museletter*; publishes work by young writers and artists

- *Muse*; published in conjunction with *Smithsonian Magazine*; intellectual articles suitable for children on topics including nature, pets, science, computers, history, math, and the arts

- National Geographic Kids; articles on science, current events, world cultures, and entertainment

- *New Moon*; bills itself as a magazine "for girls and their dreams"

- *Read*; Weekly Reader publication with a variety of articles, plays, short stories, and language games

- *Science Weekly*; classroom magazine devoted to stimulating an interest in the sciences

- *Skating*; especially for members of the U.S. Figure Skating Association

- *Skipping Stones*; ecological awareness and cultural diversity

- *Sports Illustrated for Kids*; covers the world of sports

- *Stone Soup*; stories, poems, reviews, and art created by young people

- *Swimming World, Junior Swimmer*; focus on competitive swimming

- *U Magazine*; free to dependents of USAA members (military); articles and activities promote responsible and healthy citizenship

- *Winner*; preventive drug education and lifestyles skills are offered

- *Young Rider*; for young equestrians

Note: Interests and reading levels vary among children; choose accordingly.

Children's Book Corner: A READ-ALOUD Resource with Tips, Techniques, and Plans for Teachers, Librarians, and Parents, by Judy Bradbury. Westport, CT: Libraries Unlimited, 2006

Raising Readers

Tips and Techniques for Parents

by Judy Bradbury

TANTALIZING TIDBITS:
FIRST CHAPTERS SURE TO JUMP-START INDEPENDENT READING

The books listed below contain outstanding first chapters that are sure to tickle the fancy and rouse the interest of the most jaded anti-bookster in jeans and a T-shirt. Consider occasionally reading the first chapter of a great book aloud to your child. Then leave the book lying near the electronic games, the sports equipment, or the refrigerator. Reading the first chapter of a book you know your child will love is perfect before a road trip, a school break, or when that book report is due in a few weeks.

THE WATSONS GO TO BIRMINGHAM—1963, by Christopher Paul Curtis

BY THE GREAT HORN SPOON!, by Sid Fleischman

THE BOY WHO SAVED BASEBALL, by John H. Ritter

AL CAPONE DOES MY SHIRTS, by Gennifer Choldenko

FRINDLE, by Andrew Clements

STEALING THUNDER, by Mary Casanova

A DAY NO PIGS WOULD DIE, by Robert Newton Peck

CATHERINE, CALLED BIRDY, by Karen Cushman

ELLA ENCHANTED, by Gail Carson Levine

GIRLS TO THE RESCUE: TALES OF CLEVER, COURAGEOUS GIRLS FROM AROUND THE WORLD, edited by Bruce Lansky

OUT OF THE DUST, by Karen Hesse

BOY: TALES OF CHILDHOOD, by Roald Dahl

Note: Interests, maturity, and reading levels vary among children; choose accordingly.

Children's Book Corner: A READ-ALOUD Resource with Tips, Techniques, and Plans for Teachers, Librarians, and Parents, by Judy Bradbury. Westport, CT: Libraries Unlimited, 2006

Raising Readers

Tips and Techniques for Parents

by Judy Bradbury

READ THE BOOK FIRST

Popcorn, soda, a comfy seat.

Put your feet up . . . .

and read the book first!

Many popular movies for children are based on fantastic books. Often the book is better. An author can draw the reader into the mind of a character much more easily than can a screenwriter, for whom "Action! Adventure! Drama!" are the name of the game. The inner struggles, the journey a character has taken to get where he or she is at the opening credits, are often left on the cutting room floor.

So treat your child to a read-aloud of the book *before* you see the movie. Afterward, talk about what was different, what you liked better in the book or the film, and what was left out or added.

Time together, a comfy seat, conversation with your child, popcorn.

Put your feet up . . .

and read the book first!

SELECTED FILMS BASED ON GREAT CHILDREN'S BOOKS

Holes

Because of Winn-Dixie

The Lion, the Witch and the Wardrobe

Ella Enchanted

Finding Buck McHenry

Stuart Little

Note: Interests and maturity vary among children; choose accordingly.

Children's Book Corner: A READ-ALOUD Resource with Tips, Techniques, and Plans for Teachers, Librarians, and Parents, by Judy Bradbury. Westport, CT: Libraries Unlimited, 2006

Raising Readers

Tips and Techniques for Parents

by Judy Bradbury

READING RESOURCES: ESPECIALLY FOR PARENTS

The books and Web sites listed here offer friendly tips, simple strategies, and excellent advice for parents who want to encourage their children to read.

Note: Although Web sites can be valuable resources that provide a wealth of information, the author cannot guarantee the accuracy of their information or their safety for children. Use the Internet wisely.

www.reading.org/resources/tools/choices.html—International Reading Association's Children's Choices lists books kids choose as their favorites; grouped according to reading level; tips for reading aloud are also offered.

www.readingrockets.org—A service of public television, this site offers "accurate, accessible information on how to teach kids to read and help those who struggle."

www.readingrainbow.org—Web site of the Emmy Award–winning PBS children's literacy series, Reading Rainbow; includes a complete listing of the books covered on its episodes since the program's inception.

www.trelease-on-reading.com—Web site of Jim Trelease (*The Read-Aloud Handbook*); be sure to visit the "Treasury of Read-Alouds."

www.kidsource.com/NICHCY/literature.html—Offers a bibliography of children's books about various disabilities.

How to Get Your Child to Love Reading: For Ravenous and Reluctant Readers Alike, by Esmé Raji Codell (Algonquin Books)

Reading Magic: Why Reading Aloud to Our Children Will Change Their Lives Forever, by Mem Fox (Harcourt)

Great Books About Things Kids Love, by Kathleen Odean; Ballantine

Raising a Reader: A Mother's Tale of Desperation and Delight, by Jennie Nash (St. Martin's Press)

Online bookstore: **www.bookcloseouts.com**—Features many deals; click on Children's, then refine your search by choosing a subject, age range, author's name, series name, format, or price. Be sure to check out award winners and "scratch & dent" inventory.

Children's Book Corner: A READ-ALOUD Resource with Tips, Techniques, and Plans for Teachers, Librarians, and Parents, by Judy Bradbury. Westport, CT: Libraries Unlimited, 2006

Raising Readers

Tips and Techniques for Parents

by Judy Bradbury

**RELAX WITH A BOOK:
SUMMER READING RECOMMENDATIONS FOR FIFTH
AND SIXTH GRADERS**

The books on this list are lemonade-sipping, hammock-swinging, beach-lugging beauties. Grab those sunglasses, find a spot in the shade, and wile away the day reading about other kids, other times, big adventures, and crafty solutions. Ahh, the joys of summer.

EACH LITTLE BIRD THAT SINGS, by Deborah Wiles

ESPERANZA RISING, by Pam Muñoz Ryan

THE PENDERWICKS: A SUMMER TALE OF FOUR SISTERS, TWO RABBITS, AND A VERY INTERESTING BOY, by Jeanne Birdsall

SWITCHAROUND, by Lois Lowry

YOLONDA'S GENIUS, by Carol Fenner

THE GRADUATION OF JAKE MOON, by Barbara Park

IDA B . . . AND HER PLANS TO MAXIMIZE FUN, AVOID DISASTER, AND (POSSIBLY) SAVE THE WORLD, by Katherine Hannigan

BELLE PRATER'S BOY, by Ruth White

LOVE THAT DOG, by Sharon Creech

THE CASE OF THE BAKER STREET IRREGULAR, by Robert Newman

FROM THE MIXED-UP FILES OF MRS. BASIL E. FRANKWEILER, by E. L. Konigsburg

LILY'S CROSSING, by Patricia Reilly Giff

Note: Interests, maturity, and reading levels vary among children; choose accordingly.

Children's Book Corner: A READ-ALOUD Resource with Tips, Techniques, and Plans for Teachers, Librarians, and Parents, by Judy Bradbury. Westport, CT: Libraries Unlimited, 2006

Book Notes

Books, books, books!—Elizabeth Barrett Browning

An Annotated Listing of Recommended Read-Aloud Titles Suitable for Grades 5 and 6 Organized According to Content Area Themes

To assist teachers, librarians, and parents in finding just the right book to connect with curriculum, address a concern, or celebrate a season or holiday, the books listed here are categorized and cross-referenced according to subject(s) and briefly described. Subject, title, author, and illustrator indexes are located at the back of this resource to further aid in locating related titles

ENGLISH LANGUAGE ARTS

- THE MAKING OF A WRITER, by Joan Lowery Nixon (Random House). This memoir by one of the most beloved mystery writers for preteens and teens includes sage advice for young writers along with anecdotes about events in Nixon's life that shaped her as a writer.

- SEEING THE BLUE BETWEEN: ADVICE AND INSPIRATION FOR YOUNG POETS, compiled by Paul B. Janeczko (Candlewick); poetry and advice from 32 poets, including Lee Bennett Hopkins, Jack Prelutsky, Nikki Grimes, J. Patrick Lewis, and Douglas Florian.

For the titles of additional guides for young poets, refer to the Tips and Techniques for Teachers and Librarians section of this resource.

- LIVES OF THE WRITERS: COMEDIES, TRAGEDIES (AND WHAT THE NEIGHBORS THOUGHT), written by Kathleen Krull and illustrated by Kathryn Hewitt (Harcourt); brief, humorous sketches offering the "inside scoop" on 20 literary giants, from William Shakespeare and Miguel De Cervantes to Emily Dickinson and Langston Hughes. Did you know that Robert Louis Stevenson agreed with his wife's opinion that he was beautiful, and that he never passed a mirror without checking himself out; that E. B. White once sold roach powder; or that Carl Sandburg was jailed at the age of 14 for swimming in the nude?

- THE PERFECT WIZARD: HANS CHRISTIAN ANDERSEN, written by Jane Yolen and illustrated by Dennis Nolan (Dutton); biography of the youth of this famous writer of fairy tales; see the read-aloud plan elsewhere in this resource.

- THE ABRACADABRA KID: A WRITER'S LIFE, by Sid Fleischman (Greenwillow); autobiography of this reluctant reader who turned out to be a magician, as well as a successful screenwriter and award-winning children's author.

- LUCY MAUD MONTGOMERY: A WRITER'S LIFE, by Elizabeth MacLeod (Kids Can Press); biography of the woman who wrote ANNE OF GREEN GABLES; includes photos, appealing illustrations, and quotations from Montgomery and those who knew her.

LUCY MAUD MONTGOMERY: A WRITER'S LIFE by Elizabeth MacLeod. Published by Kids Can Press. Reprinted by permission.

- WALT WHITMAN: WORDS FOR AMERICA, written by Barbara Kerley and illustrated by Brian Selznick (Scholastic). This magnificent award-winning picture book is a masterpiece, with impressive back material, including the complete text of the poem, "Leaves of Grass" from which lines are excerpted throughout the book. It is most memorable for its exploration of how the Civil War shaped Whitman's life and writing.

- THE BOY ON FAIRFIELD STREET: HOW TED GEISEL GREW UP TO BECOME DR. SEUSS, written by Kathleen Krull and illustrated by Steve Johnson and Lou Fancher (Random House); details the childhood of this legendary children's author and illustrator; see the read-aloud plan in *Children's Book Corner, Grades 3–4.*

- SEQUOYAH: THE CHEROKEE MAN WHO GAVE HIS PEOPLE WRITING, by James Rumford (Houghton Mifflin); a Sibert Honor Book written in verse about the man who brought reading and writing to his people in the early 1800s by creating a writing system,.

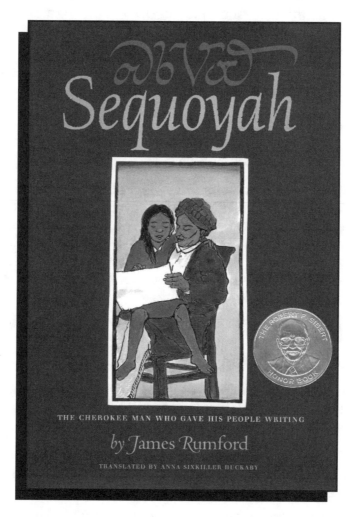

Cover from SEQUOYAH: The Cherokee Man Who Gave His People Writing by James Rumford. Jacket art copyright © 2004 by James Rumford. Reprinted by permission of Houghton Mifflin Company. All rights reserved.

- THANK YOU, SARAH! THE WOMAN WHO SAVED THANKSGIVING, written by Laurie Halse Anderson and illustrated by Matt Faulkner (Simon & Schuster); a most incredible picture book written by an inspired award-winning author, with art by an illustrator who knows what makes a picture book stand out; biography, history, power-of-the-pen message.

- HARRIET BEECHER STOWE AND THE BEECHER PREACHERS, by Jean Fritz (Penguin); a Notable Trade Book in the Language Arts biography of the author of UNCLE TOM'S CABIN by the well-known and popular children's author; part of the Unforgettable Americans series.

- LANGSTON'S TRAIN RIDE, written by Robert Burleigh and illustrated by Leonard Jenkins (Orchard); tells about the inspiration for Hughes's famous poem, "The Negro Speaks of Rivers" and how this led Hughes to a life of writing.

- LOUISA MAY & MR. THOREAU'S FLUTE, written by Julie Dunlap and Marybeth Lorbiecki and illustrated by Mary Azarian (Dial); the story of the friendship between Louisa May Alcott and Henry David Thoreau and how it inspired Alcott's writing.

- AMERICAN BOY: THE ADVENTURES OF MARK TWAIN, by Don Brown (Houghton Mifflin); picture book about Samuel Clemens's boyhood.

- BILL PEET. AN AUTOBIOGRAPHY, by Bill Peet (Houghton Mifflin); Caldecott Honor Book about this author/illustrator's life, filled with his illustrations; amusing, absorbing, informative.

- AUTHOR TALK, compiled and edited by Leonard S. Marcus (Simon & Schuster); 15 interviews with some of the best-loved children's book authors, who answer many of those often-asked questions; includes childhood and workspace photos and bibliographies of selected works. Authors include Judy Blume, Lee Bennett Hopkins, James Howe, Ann M. Martin, Gary Paulsen, and Jon Scieszka. See the index for books written by these authors that are featured in this resource.

- THE MYSTERIES OF HARRIS BURDICK, by Chris Van Allsburg (Houghton Mifflin). Illustrations that were left mysteriously at a publisher's office offer wonderful story-starters.

- IN A PICKLE AND OTHER FUNNY IDIOMS, written by Marvin Terban and illustrated by Giulio Maestro (Clarion). Idioms are explained and illustrated with comical drawings.

- MAD AS A WET HEN AND OTHER FUNNY IDIOMS, written by Marvin Terban and illustrated by Giulio Maestro (Clarion); more idioms explained and illustrated.

- IT FIGURES! FUN FIGURES OF SPEECH, written by Marvin Terban and illustrated by Giulio Maestro (Clarion). Figures of speech are defined and explained with plenty of helpful examples; illustrated with comical drawings.

- KITES SAIL HIGH: A BOOK ABOUT VERBS, by Ruth Heller (Grosset & Dunlap). Brightly illustrated verse makes learning parts of speech palatable; see the read-aloud plan in *Children's Book Corner, Grades 3–4*.

- Related titles:

    – A CACHE OF JEWELS AND OTHER COLLECTIVE NOUNS

    – MERRY-GO-ROUND A BOOK ABOUT NOUNS

    – MANY LUSCIOUS LOLLIPOPS: A BOOK ABOUT ADJECTIVES

    – UP, UP AND AWAY: A BOOK ABOUT ADVERBS

- ALL MINE: A BOOK ABOUT PRONOUNS

- FANTASTIC! WOW! AND UNREAL!: A BOOK ABOUT INTERJECTIONS AND CONJUNCTIONS

- BEHIND THE MASK: A BOOK ABOUT PREPOSITIONS

• WRITING SMARTS: A GIRL'S GUIDE TO WRITING GREAT POETRY, STORIES, SCHOOL REPORTS, AND MORE!, written by Kerry Madden and illustrated by Tracy McGuinness (American Girl). Topics include finding your voice, developing characters, choosing words, using your senses, and writing research papers; includes handy lists of commonly misspelled words, punctuation rules, and topic suggestions; simple, light, inviting approach.

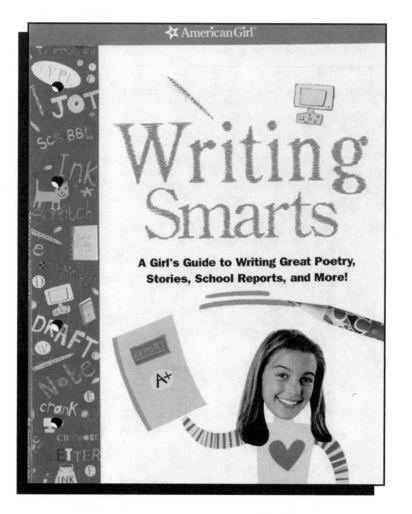

Reprinted with permission of Pleasant Company Publications from WRITING SMARTS © copyright 2002 American Girl, LLC.

• READ A RHYME, WRITE A RHYME, selected by Jack Prelutsky and illustrated by Meilo So (Knopf). Poems on 10 themes certain to delight children are paired with "poemstarts" (opening lines of poems that children are encouraged to finish) and plenty of creative Prelutsky-esque suggestions.

- FUNNY YOU SHOULD ASK: HOW TO MAKE UP JOKES AND RIDDLES WITH WORDPLAY, written by Marvin Terban and illustrated by John O'Brien (Clarion); advice and examples illustrated with comical drawings.

- WONDERFUL WORDS: POEMS ABOUT READING, WRITING, SPEAKING, AND LISTENING, selected by Lee Bennett Hopkins and illustrated by Karen Barbour (Simon & Schuster); a celebration of words, wonderful words, in poems by Emily Dickinson, Nikki Grimes, Lee Bennett Hopkins, and other poets. Don't miss "How to Say a Long, Hard Word" by David McCord, "The Word Builder" by Ann Whitford Paul, or "The Period" by Richard Armour, which is aptly the last poem in the collection.

- IN THE LAND OF WORDS: NEW AND SELECTED POEMS, written by Eloise Greenfield and illustrated by Jan Spivey Gilchrist (HarperCollins). Written and illustrated by Coretta Scott King Award winners, this book of poetry celebrating words includes "In The Land of Words", "Nathaniel's Rap", "Books", and 18 other poems.

- MY SPIN ON LIFE DIARY (American Girl); middle grade diary with spinner on front helps writer choose topic; girl-friendly illustrations within.

Reprinted with permission of Pleasant Company Publications from MY SPIN ON LIFE DIARY © copyright 2005 American Girl, LLC.

- DEAR MR. HENSHAW, written by Beverly Cleary and illustrated by Paul O. Zelinsky (HarperCollins); novel about a boy navigating his parents' divorce with the help of the letters, real and imaginary, that he writes to an author; Newbery Medal.

- HARRIET THE SPY, by Louise Fitzhugh (HarperCollins). When Harriet's spy journal is revealed to her sixth-grade classmates, the trouble begins; a classic with an unforgettable heroine. See also the sequel, THE LONG SECRET.

- CATHERINE, CALLED BIRDY, by Karen Cushman (HarperCollins). Set in the Middle Ages, this is the diary of a spunky 14-year-old girl who is determined to make her own choices in a time when that just wasn't done!; Newbery Honor.

- PEDRO'S JOURNAL: A VOYAGE WITH CHRISTOPHER COLUMBUS, written by Pam Conrad and illustrated by Peter Koeppen (Boyds Mills Press); fictional journal of a cabin boy traveling with Columbus.

- LETTERS FROM RIFKA, by Karen Hesse (Penguin); the story of 12-year-old Rifka, whose plan to flee Russia for America with her family is squashed when she is refused passage because of illness, and the ensuing events that ultimately lead to her reunion with her family; told in letters to a relative; National Jewish Book Award.

- BULL RUN, by Paul Fleischman (HarperCollins). Sixty deeply affecting narratives written as journal entries offer the points of view of 16 people from all walks of life on the first battle of the Civil War, war in general, and life in the mid-1800s.

- THE LETTER HOME, by Timothy Decker (Front Street); letter from the front lines of World War I; see the read-aloud plan elsewhere in this resource.

- ROPE BURN by Jan Siebold (Whitman); novel in which a boy, as a result of an English assignment about proverbs, a boy explores his feelings about his parents' divorce, a recent move, and other issues.

- LOVE THAT DOG, by Sharon Creech (HarperCollins); humorous yet touching story told in poems about how poetry helps Jack overcome his grief over the loss of his dog; poems from authors such as Robert Frost, William Carlos Williams, and Walter Dean Myers are woven into the plot of this wonderful story.

- STARRING SALLY J. FREEDMAN AS HERSELF, by Judy Blume (Bradbury). Set in 1947 in the immediate post–World War II era, this is the story of a girl who manages life, from an absent father and an ill brother, to a new home, with the help of a vivid and therapeutic imagination.

- P.S. LONGER LETTER LATER, by Paula Danziger and Ann M. Martin (Scholastic). Seventh-grade best friends, now apart, continue their relationship through correspondence. See also SNAIL MAIL NO MORE.

- LOVE, RUBY LAVENDER, by Deborah Wiles (Harcourt). Nine year-old Ruby and her grandmother are best buddies in this warm, entertaining novel set in Halleluia, Mississippi. When Miss Eula goes to Hawaii to visit her new grandchild, Ruby grows in her absence, with the help of their correspondence and her own delightful pluck.

- EACH LITTLE BIRD THAT SINGS, by Deborah Wiles (Harcourt). Ten year-old Comfort, the daughter of the owner of a funeral home, learns about death when her dear great-great aunt Florentine, dies suddenly—and about life, friendship, family, and herself, with the help of a wonderfully singular cast of characters with unique names, such as Dismay (Comfort's loyal dog), Peaches Shuggars (her annoying cousin), and Declaration (her not-so-true friend); letters, lists, and recipes further enhance the storytelling.

- HOW I BECAME A WRITER AND OGGIE LEARNED TO DRIVE, by Janet Taylor Lisle (Penguin). Adventure, writing, and even driving enter into this story about 11-year-old Archie, who pens stories to help his little brother, Oggie, and himself cope with their parents' separation and the changes it brings.

- KITTY AND MR. KIPLING: NEIGHBORS IN VERMONT, written by Lenore Blegvad and illustrated by Erik Blegvad (McElderry); historical novel based on fact about the friendship between a young girl and the famous author in the late 1800s.

THE ARTS

- WINGS OF AN ARTIST: CHILDREN'S BOOK ILLUSTRATORS TALK ABOUT THEIR ART (Abrams). Twenty-three illustrators recall, in both words and visual images, how art influenced them as children. Included are insights from Graeme Base, William Joyce, Jean and Mou-Sien Tseng, and Susan Jeffers. A guide can be found at the end of the book that offers suggestions for activities to do with children.

- TALKING WITH ARTISTS, complied and edited by Pat Cummings (Bradbury); a reference book for children in which children's book illustrators answer questions about where they get ideas, what their work day is like, and how they make their pictures. Artists highlighted include Chris Van Allsburg, Tom Feelings, David Wiesner, Lane Smith, Leo and Diane Dillon, and Lisa Campbell Ernst. See the index for books illustrated by these artists that are featured in this volume of the Children's Book Corner series.

- LIVES OF THE MUSICIANS: GOOD TIMES, BAD TIMES (AND WHAT THE NEIGHBORS THOUGHT), written by Kathleen Krull and illustrated by Kathryn Hewitt (Harcourt). Brief yet informative sketches also entertain the reader with information on what the musicians were *really* like; includes bios on 19 musicians from different countries, eras, and musical styles, from Vivaldi and Beethoven to Stravinsky and Guthrie.

- LIVES OF THE ARTISTS: MASTERPIECES, MESSES (AND WHAT THE NEIGHBORS THOUGHT), written by Kathleen Krull and illustrated by Kathryn Hewitt (Harcourt). Brief, humorous, human sketches offer the "inside scoop" on luminaries in the realm of the art world, from Michelangelo and Rembrandt to Dali and Warhol.

- SEEN ART?, written by Jon Scieszka and illustrated by Lane Smith (Viking); a tour of the Metropolitan Museum of Art (MOMA) in New York City by way of a boy looking for his friend, Art; Scieszka-Smith humor; brief descriptions of the art masterpieces that are featured in the story can be found at the back of the book.

- PAINT ME A POEM: POEMS INSPIRED BY MASTERPIECES OF ART, by Justine Rowden (Wordsong/Boyds Mills); 14 poems and the art that inspired them snappily presented with varying typefaces and word configurations.

- THE FANTASTIC JOURNEY OF PIETER BRUEGEL, by Anders C. Shafer (Dutton); imagined diary entries of the famous sixteenth-century painter of landscapes, biblical stories, and peasant life, during his two-year trek from Antwerp, across the Alps, to Rome. Little is known about this painter who left about 60 drawings and 40 paintings, most of them completed in the 15 years following his journey to Rome. Some of the works are reproduced in the back of the book.

- ROMARE BEARDEN: COLLAGE OF MEMORIES, by Jan Greenberg (Abrams). Using Bearden's collage art, the award-winning Greenberg brings to life the story of this African American artist whose interpretation of art was "putting something over something else."

ROMARE BEARDEN: COLLAGE OF MEMORIES by Jan Greenberg.
Reprinted with permission of Abrams Books for Young Readers
(www.abramsyoungreaders.com).

- DEGAS AND THE DANCE: THE PAINTER AND THE PETITS RATS, PERFECTING THEIR ART, by Susan Goldman Rubin (Abrams). This biography of Degas, illustrated by his paintings of young ballerinas, focuses on his realization that creating and perfecting art takes dedication, hard work, and perseverance.

DEGAS AND THE DANCE: THE PAINTER AND THE PETIT RATS, PERFECTING THEIR ART by Susan Goldman Rubin. Reprinted with permission of Abrams Books for Young Readers (www.abramsyoungreaders.com).

- THE YELLOW HOUSE: VINCENT VAN GOGH AND PAUL GAUGUIN SIDE BY SIDE, written by Susan Goldman Rubin and illustrated by Jos. A. Smith (Abrams); story about the period of time when Vincent Van Gogh and Paul Gauguin shared a house, ideas, and heated discussions in the south of France.

- SEURAT AND LA GRANDE JATTE, by Robert Burleigh (Abrams); an in-depth look at a famous painting; see the read-aloud plan in *Children's Book Corner, Grades 3–4*.

- TALLCHIEF: AMERICA'S PRIMA BALLERINA, written by Maria Tallchief with Rosemary Wells and illustrated by Gary Kelley (Penguin); picture book autobiography for older children.

- THE WORLD OF THEATER (Editions Gallimard Jeunesse; Scholastic). Lift-the-flaps, gatefolds, detachable sections, and more give this basic book about the history of theater and its workings dramatic appeal.

- ACTION JACKSON, written by Jan Greenberg and Sandra Jordan and illustrated by Robert Andrew Parker (Roaring Brook Press); a Robert F. Sibert Honor Book about Jackson Pollock.

- THE POT THAT JUAN BUILT, written by Nancy Andrews-Goebel and illustrated by David Diaz (Lee & Low Books); about Mexico's "premier potter," Juan Quezada.

- THE DINOSAURS OF WATERHOUSE HAWKINS, written by Barbara Kerley and illustrated by Brian Selznick (Scholastic); a Caldecott Honor book highlighting the life of the artist and sculptor, who in the mid-1800s showed the world what a dinosaur looked like. See the read-aloud plan in *Children's Book Corner, Grades 1–2*.

- BILL PEET: AN AUTOBIOGRAPHY, by Bill Peet (Houghton Mifflin); Caldecott Honor Book about this author/illustrator's life filled with his illustrations; amusing, absorbing, informative.

- STEVEN SPIELBERG: CRAZY FOR MOVIES, by Susan Goldman Rubin (Abrams); includes photos and family interviews that recall Spielberg's boyhood as well as his accomplishments as an adult.

- Smart About Art series (Grosset & Dunlap); titles by various authors, including VINCENT VAN GOGH: SUNFLOWERS AND SWIRLY STARS; PABLO PICASSO: BREAKING ALL THE RULES; CLAUDE MONET: SUNSHINE AND WATERLILIES; EDGAR DEGAS: PAINTINGS THAT DANCE; FRIDA KAHLO: THE ARTIST WHO PAINTED HERSELF, and HENRI MATISSE: DRAWING WITH SCISSORS.

MATH

- MATH POTATOES, written by Greg Tang and illustrated by Harry Briggs (Scholastic); see the read-aloud plan elsewhere in this resource.

- THE BEST OF TIMES: MATH STRATEGIES THAT MULTIPLY, written by Greg Tang and illustrated by Harry Briggs (Scholastic). There's more to multiplication than memorizing the tables, and this terrific book offers sensible strategies in a bright and engaging package.

- POLAR BEAR MATH: LEARNING ABOUT FRACTIONS FROM KLONDIKE AND SNOW, by Ann Whitehead Nagda and Cindy Bickel (Holt); visually appealing presentation with clear examples of application.

- TIGER MATH: LEARNING TO GRAPH FROM A BABY TIGER, by Ann Whitehead Nagda and Cindy Bickel (Holt); photographs and clear how-to explanations.

- MATH APPEAL: MIND-STRETCHING MATH RIDDLES, written by Greg Tang and illustrated by Harry Briggs (Scholastic); poems riddled with tips for making math easy and fun! Patterns, symmetry, and problem-solving skills are introduced.

- THE GRAPES OF MATH: MIND-STRETCHING MATH RIDDLES, written by Greg Tang and illustrated by Harry Briggs (Scholastic). Math problems with effective problem-solving techniques presented in a hip package. Answers are listed in the back of the book.

- SIDEWAYS ARITHMETIC FROM WAYSIDE SCHOOL, by Louis Sachar (Scholastic). In this wacky school, kids do math in memorable ways! See also MORE SIDEWAYS ARITHMETIC FROM WAYSIDE SCHOOL.

- MATH SMARTS, written by Lynette Long, Ph.D. and illustrated by Tracy McGuinness (American Girl); practical math applications; tips, and test-taking strategies; especially of interest to girls.

SCIENCE

- 53½ THINGS THAT CHANGED THE WORLD AND SOME THAT DIDN'T, written by Steve Parker and designed and illustrated by David West (Millbrook). From the toilet to fusion power, inventions are explained with the help of detailed illustrations.

- SKYSCRAPERS! SUPER STRUCTURES TO DESIGN & BUILD, by Carol A. Johmann (Williamson). Design and build a skyscraper from frame to hi-rise! The explanation and clear directions are here.

- TRANSFORMED: HOW EVERYDAY THINGS ARE MADE, by Bill Slavin (Kids Can Press). Full-page spreads explain in step-by-step format and kid-centered illustrations how common items, such as soap, aluminum foil, milk, soccer balls, and rayon, are made; great reference book to have on hand to read aloud from when a question is asked or to pique interest in things around us and how they are designed or produced.

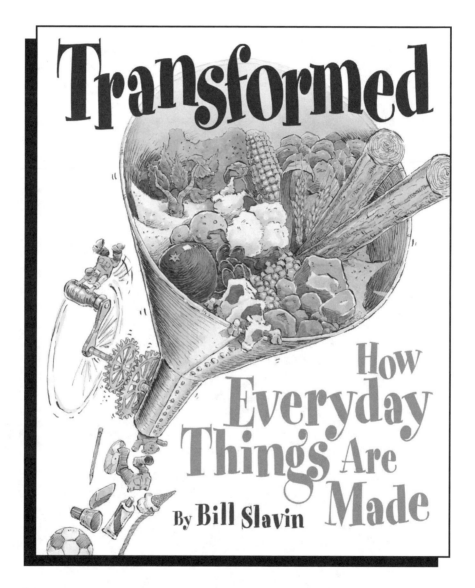

TRANSFORMED: HOW EVERYDAY THINGS ARE MADE by Bill Slavin.
Published by Kids Can Press. Reprinted by permission.

- BRIDGES! AMAZING STRUCTURES TO DESIGN, BUILD & TEST, written by Carol A. Johmann and Elizabeth J. Rieth (Willamson); how-to instructions and experiments blended with science and history; 2000 Parents' Choice Recommended.

• THE MOST BEAUTIFUL ROOF IN THE WORLD: EXPLORING THE RAINFOREST CANOPY, written by Kathryn Lasky with photographs by Christopher G. Knight (Harcourt). Follow along as scientist Meg Lowman climbs high above the rainforest floor and sleeps in a tent on a platform above a deadly viper—it's all in a day's work collecting valuable information about this mysterious ecosystem; spectacular photographs.

Courtesy Harcourt, Inc.

• THE RACE TO SAVE THE LORD GOD BIRD, by Phillip Hoose (Farrar Straus Giroux). extinction, conservation, and protection of birds are examined through the story of the ivory-billed woodpecker and the crusade to save it that spanned a century.

THE RACE TO SAVE THE LORD GOD BIRD © 2004 by Phillip Hoose.
Used with the permission of Farrar Straus Giroux.

• ENCYCLOPEDIA PREHISTORICA: DINOSAURS, by Robert Sabuda and Matthew Reinhart (Candlewick); see the read-aloud plan elsewhere in this resource.

- VOLCANOES: JOURNEYS TO THE CRATER'S EDGE, written by Helene Montardre, photographs by Philippe Bourseiller, adapted by Robert Burleigh, and drawings by David Giraudon (Abrams); amazing photography of these natural occurrences; explanations are made accessible to children by Burleigh.

VOLCANOES: JOURNEYS TO THE CRATER'S EDGE by Helene Montardre. Reprinted with permission of Abrams Books for Young Readers (www.abramsyoungreaders.com).

- MUMMIES: THE NEWEST, COOLEST & CREEPIEST FROM AROUND THE WORLD, by Shelley Tanaka with archaeological consultation by Paul Bahn (Abrams); vivid photography and clear descriptions of ancient as well as recent mummies and new discoveries made about them as a result of advances in science.

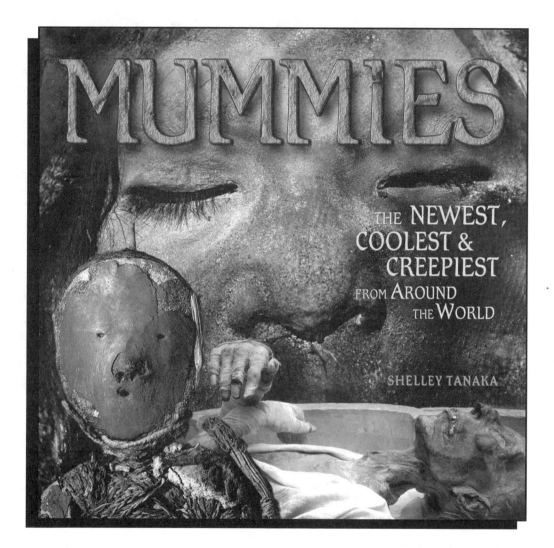

MUMMIES: THE NEWEST, COOLEST & CREEPIEST FROM AROUND THE WORLD by Shelley Tanaka. Reprinted with permission of Abrams Books for Young Readers (www.abramsyoungreaders.com).

- WHEN I HEARD THE LEARN'D ASTRONOMER, written by Walt Whitman and illustrated by Loren Long (Simon & Schuster); see the read-aloud plan elsewhere in this resource.

- THE MAN WHO MADE TIME TRAVEL, written by Kathryn Lasky and illustrated by Kevin Hawkes (Farrar Straus Giroux); detailed explanation of how the "ordinary man," John Harrison, successfully created a timepiece to accurately measure longitude in the 1700s.

THE MAN WHO MADE TIME TRAVEL © 2003 by Kathryn Lasky; illustrated by Kevin Hawkes. Used with the permission of Farrar Straus Giroux.

- LEONARDO DA VINCI, written by Kathleen Krull and illustrated by Boris Kulikov (Viking); first in the Giants of Science chapter book series, authored by this well-respected, kid-friendly biographer; tells about daVinci's insatiable curiosity and fierce determination. The series intends to show scientists as human, with brilliance as well as failings, and how they were a product of the world in which they lived.

- LEONARDO DA VINCI, by Robert Byrd (Dutton); award-winning biography of Leonardo da Vinci; see the read-aloud plan in *Children's Book Corner, Grades 3–4.*

- STARRY MESSENGER: GALILEO GALILEI, by Peter Sis (Farrar Straus Giroux); biography with absorbing illustrations; see the read-aloud plan in *Children's Book Corner, Grades 3–4.*

- ISAAC NEWTON, written by Kathleen Krull and illustrated by Boris Kulikov (Viking); second title in the Giants of Science series; you knew about the gravity thing, and maybe you knew he invented calculus, but did you know Newton was "secretive, vindictive, withdrawn, [and] obsessive" as well as brilliant?

- TREE OF LIFE, by Peter Sis (Farrar Straus Giroux); biography of naturalist and geologist Charles Darwin; see the read-aloud plan in *Children's Book Corner, Grades 3–4.*

- WIND AND WEATHER (Editions Gallimard Jeunesse; Scholastic); overlays, gatefolds, and more explain weather.

- THE SKY'S THE LIMIT: STORIES OF DISCOVERY BY WOMEN AND GIRLS, written by Catherine Thimmesh and illustrated by Melissa Sweet (Houghton Mifflin); stories about smart, curious females who wondered, studied, uncovered, and discovered.

- WESTLANDIA, written by Paul Fleischman and illustrated by Kevin Hawkes (Candlewick). A boy starts his own civilization in his backyard; ecology, environment; Parents' Choice Honor.

- SCIENCE VERSE, written by Jon Scieszka and illustrated by Lane Smith (Penguin); hilarious poems about various science-related subjects; see the read-aloud plan in *Children's Book Corner, Grades 3–4.*

- PROJECT MULBERRY, by Linda Sue Park (Clarion). Although this is a novel, it is filled with facts about silkworms.

- THE PRINCE OF THE POND, written by Donna Jo Napoli and illustrated by Judith Byron Schachner (Dutton). Although this is a fantasy, it is filled with facts about toads, pond life, and green frogs in particular.

SOCIAL STUDIES

World History

- THE RIDDLE OF THE ROSETTA STONE: KEYS TO ANCIENT EGYPT, by James Cross Giblin (HarperCollins). The discovery of the Rosetta Stone meant hieroglyphics demystified; in-depth look at the subject.

• HOW THE AMAZON QUEEN FOUGHT THE PRINCE OF EGYPT, by Tamara Bower (Atheneum); tale of war and eventual love between an Amazon queen and an Egyptian prince, told with engaging illustrations and clear depictions of hieroglyphics; based on an actual Egyptian scroll; extensive backmatter.

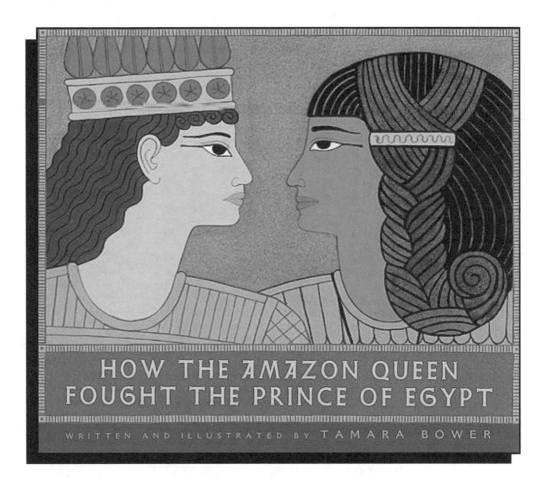

HOW THE AMAZON QUEEN FOUGHT THE PRINCE OF EGYPT by Tamara Bower. Copyright © 2005. Used with permission of Atheneum Books for Young Readers, an imprint of Simon & Schuster Children's Publishing.

• SECRETS OF THE SPHINX, written by James Cross Giblin and illustrated by Bagram Ibatoulline (Scholastic); history of the marvel told by a master of nonfiction.

• STOWAWAY, written by Karen Hesse and illustrated by Robert Andrew Parker (McElderry). This fictional account of a boy's experiences in the mid-1700s, aboard James Cook's ship bound for an unknown continent, is based on Hesse's research of the journey south of the equator of Nicholas Young, an 11-year-old boy who really was a stowaway on Cook's extraordinary voyage.

• THE ATLAS OF ANCIENT EGYPT, by Delia Pemberton, with artwork and photographs from the British Museum (Abrams); stunning photographs accompany clear, accessible text.

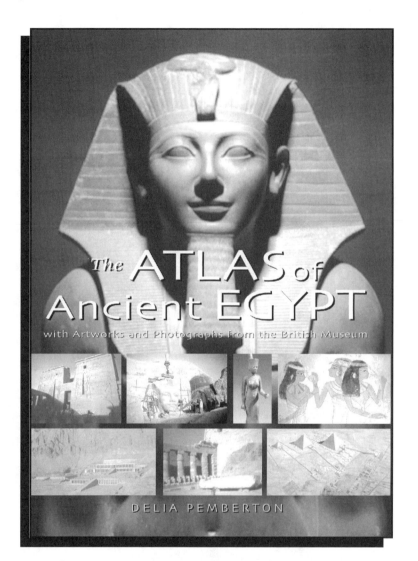

THE ATLAS OF ANCIENT EGYPT by Delia Pemberton.
Reprinted with permission of Abrams Books for Young Readers
(www.abramsyoungreaders.com).

• THE LETTER HOME, by Timothy Decker (Front Street); letter from the front lines of World War I; see the read-aloud plan elsewhere in this resource.

• THE FLAG WITH FIFTY-SIX STARS: A GIFT FROM THE SURVIVORS OF MAUTHAUSEN, written by Susan Goldman Rubin and illustrated by Bill Farnsworth (Holiday House); true account of a heartrending episode during World War II; see the read-aloud plan elsewhere in this resource.

• TALKING DRUMS: A SELECTION OF POEMS FROM AFRICA SOUTH OF THE SAHARA, edited by Veronique Tadjo (Bloomsbury); traces African history; arranged in chapters from the "Animal Kingdom and "People" to "Pride and Defiance". Poems such as "Friendship" speak universally on common themes.

American History

• A TIME FOR FREEDOM: WHAT HAPPENED WHEN IN AMERICA, by Lynne Cheney (Simon & Schuster); a reference book that chronologically lists simple, short explanations of key events in American history; with photographs.

A TIME FOR FREEDOM: WHAT HAPPENED WHEN IN AMERICA by Lynne Cheney. Copyright © 2005. Used with permission of Simon & Schuster, Inc. Jacket illustration: America's Greatest Wealth Is Her Healthy Children by N. C. Wyeth, oil on canvas, 34" x 24", 1925. From the collection of the School Department of the Town of Needham, MA. Reproduced with permission.

- A KIDS' GUIDE TO AMERICA'S BILL OF RIGHTS: CURFEWS, CENSORSHIP, AND THE 100 POUND GIANT, by Kathleen Krull and illustrated by Anna DiVito (Avon). Three chapters on the First Amendment, a chapter on each of the next nine, a chapter on the remaining seventeen amendments, and a final chapter entitled "When the Bill of Rights Goes Wrong," make for interesting, informative reading in this book written by a master at explanation who also has a great sense of humor. For those of you who are wondering (and who isn't?) the 100-pound giant is James Madison, "father" of the Bill of Rights. Perfect to read aloud one chapter at a time.

- AMERICAN MOMENTS: SCENES FROM AMERICAN HISTORY, written by Robert Burleigh and illustrated by Bruce Strachan (Holt); a wonderful compendium of 18 single-page, present tense accounts of key events in American history that offer introductions to various periods and events in American history; includes the Declaration of Independence, Lewis and Clark's expedition, Susan B. Anthony and Rosa Parks demanding their rights, Neil Armstrong on the moon, and remembering 9/11. Brief endnotes give further information on each event; illustrated with sculpted clay figures painted in oils.

- SEQUOYAH: THE CHEROKEE MAN WHO GAVE HIS PEOPLE WRITING, by James Rumford (Houghton Mifflin); a Sibert Honor Book written in verse about the man who brought reading and writing to his people in the early 1800s by creating a writing system,.

- POCAHONTAS AND THE STRANGERS, by Clyde Robert Bulla (HarperCollins); a Best Books for Children biography of the Indian princess who helped the early settlers.

- THE DOUBLE LIFE OF POCAHONTAS, by Jean Fritz (Penguin); multiple award–winning title by an author who brings life to history.

- IN A SACRED MANNER I LIVE: NATIVE AMERICAN WISDOM, edited by Neil Philip (Clarion); an anthology of speeches, poems, songs, stories, and photographs that reflect the beliefs, values, and struggles of Native Americans throughout history.

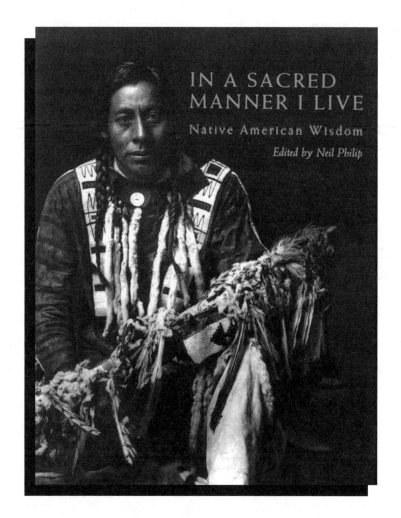

Cover from IN A SACRED MANNER I LIVE: Native American Wisdom, edited by Neil Philip. Copyright © 1997 by The Albion Press Ltd. Reprinted by permission of Clarion Books, an imprint of Houghton Mifflin Company. All rights reserved.

- THE SALEM WITCH TRIALS: AN UNSOLVED MYSTERY FROM HISTORY, written by Jane Yolen and Heidi Elisabet Yolen Stemple and illustrated by Roger Roth (Simon & Schuster); one in a series of illustrated, fact-based story books that explore popular theories on intriguing moments in history. See also ROANOKE: THE LOST COLONY: AN UNSOLVED MYSTERY FROM HISTORY.

• INDIAN CHIEFS, by Russell Freedman (Holiday House); chronicles the "decline of the American Indian" as exploration in America in the 1800s expanded into areas already inhabited by Native Americans. Six Indian leaders tell their stories, including Sitting Bull and Red Cloud.

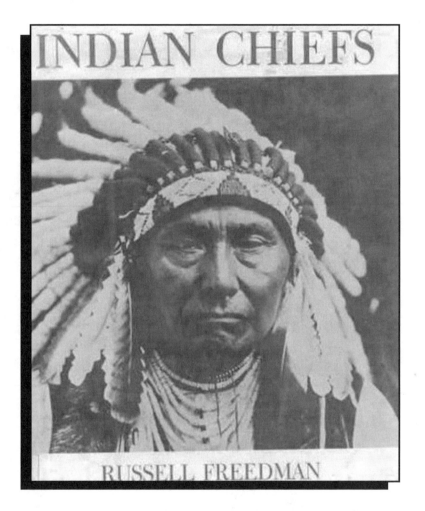

INDIAN CHIEFS by Russell Freedman. Published by Holiday House.
Reprinted by permission.

- TELL ALL THE CHILDREN OUR STORY: MEMORIES AND MEMENTOS OF BEING YOUNG AND BLACK IN AMERICA, by Tonya Bolden (Abrams); a history of the black experience, with emphasis on being young and black in America, from the 1600s through 1999.

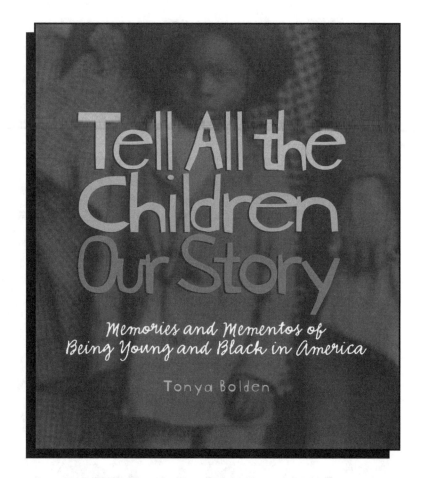

TELL ALL THE CHILDREN OUR STORY: MEMORIES AND MOMENTOS OF BEING YOUNG AND BLACK IN AMERICA by Tonya Bolden. Reprinted with permission of Abrams Books for Young Readers (www.abramsyoungreaders.com).

- TAKE THE LEAD, GEORGE WASHINGTON, written by Judith St. George and illustrated by Daniel Powers (Philomel); the second in a series of picture storybooks, written by the author of SO YOU WANT TO BE PRESIDENT? and SO YOU WANT TO BE AN INVENTOR? (see *Children's Book Corner, Grades 1–2*) that describe momentous events in the young lives of American presidents that led them to become the men they were.

- FIGHT FOR FREEDOM: THE AMERICAN REVOLUTIONARY WAR, by Benson Bobrick (Atheneum). One-page summaries with boxed "Quick Facts" opposite full-page illustrations in black and white, sepia tones, and color chronicle key events of the American Revolution.

- YORK'S ADVENTURES WITH LEWIS AND CLARK: AN AFRICAN-AMERICAN'S PART IN THE GREAT EXPEDITION, by Rhoda Blumberg (HarperCollins). Written by a Newbery Honor Book author, this historically accurate account chronicles the important contributions made by Clark's slave on the expedition to explore the western lands of what is now the United States.

- THE INCREDIBLE JOURNEY OF LEWIS & CLARK, by Rhoda Blumberg (Lothrop, Lee & Shepard). This account is an excellent, even-handed and readable introduction to this great piece of American history; winner of the Golden Kite Award.

- THE LEWIS & CLARK EXPEDITION: JOIN THE CORPS OF DISCOVERY TO EXPLORE UNCHARTED TERRITORY, written by Carol A. Johmann and illustrated by Michael Kline (Ideals); includes myriad hands-on activities, such as building a model keelboat and learning to dead reckon; 2003 Parents' Choice Silver Honor Award.

- WESTWARD HO! ELEVEN EXPLORERS OF THE WEST, by Charlotte Foltz Jones (Holiday House); biographies with black-and-white illustrations of surveyors, military men, navigators, and others whose explorations charted the course of North American westward expansion; notes, time line, and useful index are at the back of the book.

WESTWARD HO! ELEVEN EXPLORERS OF THE WEST by Charlotte Foltz Jones. Published by Holiday House. Reprinted by permission.

- APPLES TO OREGON, BEING THE (SLIGHTLY) TRUE NARRATIVE OF HOW A BRAVE PIONEER FATHER BROUGHT APPLES, PEACHES, PEARS, PLUMS, GRAPES, AND CHERRIES (AND CHILDREN) ACROSS THE PLAINS, written by Deborah Hopkinson and illustrated by Nancy Carpenter (Atheneum); spirited tall tale "loosely based on the life of a real fruiting pioneer."

- SHOW WAY, written by Jacqueline Woodson and illustrated by Hudson Talbott (Putnam); a magnificently illustrated, lyrical tale about a family whose ancestors made show ways—quilts that helped slaves make their way to freedom.

- GOOD BROTHER, BAD BROTHER: THE STORY OF EDWIN BOOTH AND JOHN WILKES BOOTH, by James Cross Giblin (Clarion); biographies of two brothers, alike and different in many ways, and the impact they had on American history, the theater, and each other's lives.

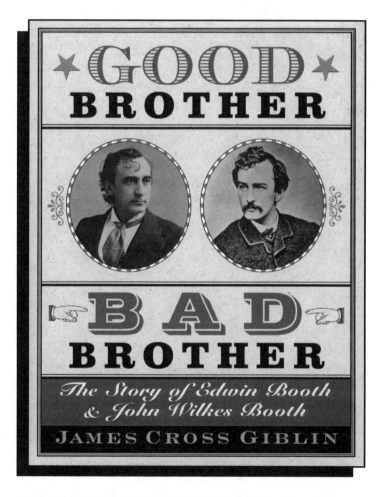

Cover from GOOD BROTHER, BAD BROTHER: The Story of Edwin Booth and John Wilkes Booth by James Cross Giblin. Copyright © 2005 by James Cross Giblin. Reprinted by permission of Clarion Books, an imprint of Houghton Mifflin Company. All rights reserved.

- HARRIET BEECHER STOWE AND THE BEECHER PREACHERS, by Jean Fritz (Penguin); a Notable Trade Book in the Language Arts biography of the author of UNCLE TOM'S CABIN by the well-known and popular children's author; part of the Unforgettable Americans series.

- GOING WEST! JOURNEY ON A WAGON TRAIN TO SETTLE A FRONTIER written by Carol A. Johmann and illustrated by Michael Kline (Williamson); history, story, and craft activities; Ben Franklin Silver Award.

- THE BOYS' WAR: CONFEDERATE AND UNION SOLDIERS TALK ABOUT THE CIVIL WAR, by Jim Murphy (Houghton Mifflin). Based on actual diaries and letters, this book explores why boys joined the war, how they lived as soldiers, and what they wore in battle.

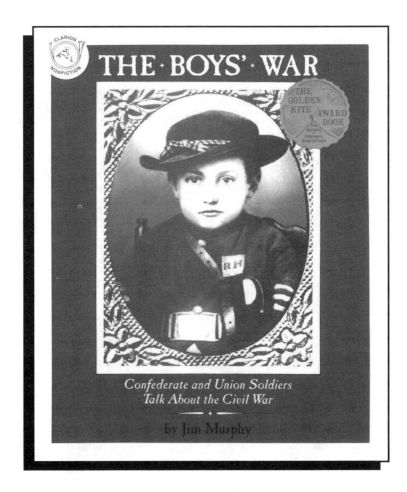

Cover from THE BOYS' WAR by Jim Murphy. Copyright © 1990 by Jim Murphy. Reprinted by permission of Clarion Books, an imprint of Houghton Mifflin Company. All rights reserved.

- BULL RUN, by Paul Fleischman (HarperCollins). Sixty deeply affecting narratives written as journal entries offer the points of view of 16 people from all walks of life on the first battle of the Civil War, war in general, and life in the mid-1800s.

- WALT WHITMAN: WORDS FOR AMERICA, written by Barbara Kerley and illustrated by Brian Selznick (Scholastic). This magnificent, award-winning picture book is a masterpiece, with impressive back material, including the complete text of the poem, "Leaves of Grass" from which lines are excerpted throughout the book. It is most memorable for its exploration of how the Civil War shaped Whitman's life and his writing.

- INTO THE AIR: THE STORY OF THE WRIGHT BROTHERS' FIRST FLIGHT, written by Robert Burleigh and illustrated by Bill Wylie (Harcourt). Graphic-style art accompanies this simple, somewhat fictionalized account of the Wright brothers' amazing accomplishment in a volume that will beckon the reluctant reader.

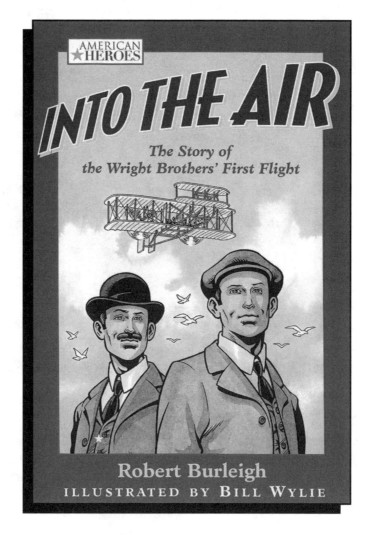

Courtesy Harcourt, Inc.

- DOWN CUT SHIN CREEK: THE PACK HORSE LIBRARIANS OF KENTUCKY, written by Kathi Appelt and Jeanne Cannella Schmitzer (HarperCollins); accounts of librarians on horseback who served patrons in eastern Kentucky during the Great Depression.

- HARVESTING HOPE: THE STORY OF CESAR CHAVEZ, written by Kathleen Krull and illustrated by Yuyi Morales (Harcourt); see the read-aloud plan elsewhere in this resource.

- OUR ELEANOR: A SCRAPBOOK LOOK AT ELEANOR ROOSEVELT'S REMARKABLE LIFE, by Candace Fleming (Atheneum). The format of this book makes it a good addition to the many books already published about this great woman; readable, accessible, filled with photos, this biography will engage young readers.

OUR ELEANOR: A SCRAPBOOK LOOK AT ELEANOR ROOSEVELT'S REMARKABLE LIFE by Candace Fleming. Copyright © 2005. Used with permission of Atheneum Books for Young Readers, an imprint of Simon & Schuster Children's Publishing.

- RED LEGS: A DRUMMER BOY OF THE CIVIL WAR, by Ted Lewin (HarperCollins). Spare text and rich illustrations tell the story of a Civil War battle; based on true accounts of the life of Stephen Benjamin Bartow, who fought in the 14th Regiment, Company E, dubbed the Red-Legged Devils "because of the color of their uniform and their tough fighting spirit."

- IMMIGRANT KIDS, by Russell Freedman (Penguin); chronicles the life of immigrant children from Europe around the beginning of the twentieth century.

- SHUTTING OUT THE SKY: LIFE IN THE TENEMENTS OF NEW YORK 1880-1924, by Deborah Hopkinson (Orchard); chronicles the assimilation of five immigrants who came to America from Europe in chapters focusing on work, education, housing, and language.

- THE FLAG WITH FIFTY-SIX STARS: A GIFT FROM THE SURVIVORS OF MAUTHAUSEN, written by Susan Goldman Rubin and illustrated by Bill Farnsworth (Holiday House); true account of a heartrending episode during World War II; see the read-aloud plan elsewhere in this resource.

- THE LETTER HOME, by Timothy Decker (Front Street); letter from the front lines of World War I; see the read-aloud plan elsewhere in this resource.

- FREEDOM ON THE MENU: THE GREENSBORO SIT-INS, written by Carole Boston Weatherford and illustrated by Jerome Lagarrigue (Dial); fictionalized story about this historic event; see the read-aloud plan elsewhere in this resource.

- A DREAM OF FREEDOM: THE CIVIL RIGHTS MOVEMENT FROM 1954 TO 1968, by Diane McWhorter (Scholastic); clear, concise chronicle of the events described by the Pulitzer Prize–winning author (who was in sixth grade in Birmingham, Alabama in 1963) as the "crossroads of history."

- ROSA PARKS: MY STORY, by Rosa Parks with Jim Haskins (Penguin); the autobiography of the woman who refused to give up her seat on a bus to a white man, an act that led to the end of segregation on buses.

- THE WHITE HOUSE: AN ILLUSTRATED HISTORY, by Catherine O'Neill Grace (Scholastic); photographs, behind-the-scenes look at day-to-day details, interviews with staff, and a "tour" of one of our nation's enduring symbols of freedom; with an introduction by Laura Bush.

- LIVES OF THE PRESIDENTS: FAME, SHAME (AND WHAT THE NEIGHBORS THOUGHT), written by Kathleen Krull and illustrated by Kathryn Hewitt (Harcourt). Brief, factual, yet humorous sketches provide insight into the human side of these historical figures. Find out who had "feet bigger than his ego", who barked like a seal, and who had a messy closet.

- NEW YORK IS ENGLISH, CHATTANOOGA IS CREEK, by Chris Raschka (Atheneum); see the read-aloud plan elsewhere in this resource.

- MY AMERICA: A POETRY ATLAS OF THE UNITED STATES, selected by Lee Bennett Hopkins and illustrated by Stephen Alcorn (Simon & Schuster). Outstanding illustrations accompany the work of well-known poets and worthy newcomers.

- LIVES: POEMS ABOUT FAMOUS AMERICANS, selected by Lee Bennett Hopkins and illustrated by Leslie Staub (HarperCollins). Sixteen men and women, from Paul Revere to Rosa Parks, are honored in poems and full-page art; includes biographical information on each subject at the back of the book.

- WE THE PEOPLE, written by Bobbi Katz and illustrated by Nina Crews (Greenwillow); Sixty-five first-person poems portray five centuries of American life; the poet conducted in-depth research to find and fuel the voices of her subjects—both real and imagined. Quotations and a time line augment the presentation.

- A POEM OF HER OWN: VOICES OF AMERICAN WOMEN YESTERDAY AND TODAY, edited by Catherine Clinton and illustrated by Stephen Alcorn (Abrams); Classic and contemporary poems reflect on the history and strength of American women. Brief biographies of the poets are at the back of the book.

Social/Culture

- MEDIA MADNESS: AN INSIDER'S GUIDE TO MEDIA, written by Dominic Ali and illustrated by Michael Cho (Kids Can Press); graphically illustrated volume that will appeal to youngsters; explores who creates media messages, why, how messages are tailored to a target audience, the values and lifestyles that media portray, how messages are read, and what might be important to know about the messages we get from the media.

MEDIA MADNESS: AN INSIDER'S GUIDE TO MEDIA by Dominic Ali, illustrated by Michael Cho. Published by Kids Can Press. Reprinted by permission.

- FLY AWAY HOME, written by Eve Bunting and illustrated by Ronald Himler (Clarion); picture book story of a homeless man and his son, who live in an airport.

• PANDA: A GUIDE HORSE FOR ANN, by Rosanna Hansen with photographs by Neil Soderstrom (Boyds Mills); true story of a miniature horse trained as a guide animal; describes the relationship between Panda and the human it serves.

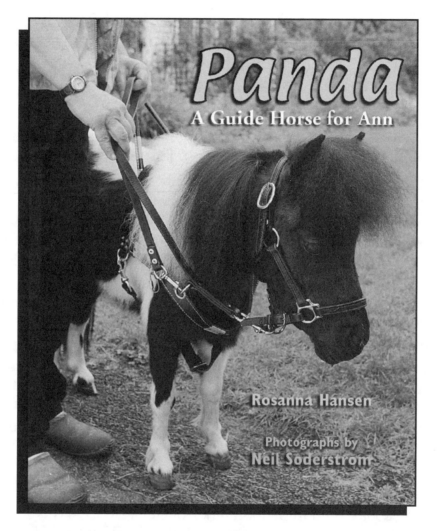

PANDA: A GUIDE HORSE FOR ANN, by Rosanna Hansen, photographs by Neil Soderstrom. Copyright © 2005. Published by Boyds Mills Press. Reprinted by permission.

• GOOD LUCK GOLD AND OTHER POEMS, by Janet S. Wong (McElderry); reflections on the ups and downs of growing up Asian American.

• NOT A COPPER PENNY IN ME HOUSE: POEMS FROM THE CARIBBEAN, written by Monica Gunning and illustrated by Frané Lessac (Boyds Mills Press); lyrical portrayal of a girl's life in the Caribbean.

BIOGRAPHY

- LEONARDO DA VINCI, written by Kathleen Krull and illustrated by Boris Kulikov (Viking); first in the Giants of Science chapter book series authored by the well-respected, kid-friendly biographer; tells about daVinci's insatiable curiosity and fierce determination. The series intends to show scientists as humans, with brilliance as well as failings, and how they were a product of the world in which they lived.

- LEONARDO DA VINCI, by Robert Byrd (Dutton); award-winning biography of Leonardo da Vinci; see the read-aloud plan in *Children's Book Corner, Grades 3–4.*

- STARRY MESSENGER: GALILEO GALILEI, by Peter Sis (Farrar Straus Giroux); biography with absorbing illustrations; see the read-aloud plan in *Children's Book Corner, Grades 3–4.*

- ISAAC NEWTON, written by Kathleen Krull and illustrated by Boris Kulikov (Viking); second title in the Giants of Science series; you knew about the gravity thing, and maybe you knew he invented calculus, but did you know Newton was "secretive, vindictive, withdrawn, [and] obsessive" as well as brilliant?

- TREE OF LIFE, by Peter Sis (Farrar Straus Giroux); biography of naturalist and geologist Charles Darwin; see the read-aloud plan in *Children's Book Corner, Grades 3–4.*

- POCAHONTAS AND THE STRANGERS, by Clyde Robert Bulla (HarperCollins); a Best Books for Children biography of the Indian princess who helped the early settlers.

- THE DOUBLE LIFE OF POCAHONTAS, by Jean Fritz (Penguin); multiple award–winning biography.

- TAKE THE LEAD, GEORGE WASHINGTON, written by Judith St. George and illustrated by Daniel Powers (Philomel); the second in a series of picture storybooks, written by the author of SO YOU WANT TO BE PRESIDENT? and SO YOU WANT TO BE AN INVENTOR? (see *Children's Book Corner, Grades 1–2*) that describe momentous events in the young lives of American presidents that led them to become the men they were.

- THE PERFECT WIZARD: HANS CHRISTIAN ANDERSEN, written by Jane Yolen and illustrated by Dennis Nolan (Dutton); biography of the youth of this famous Danish writer of fairy tales; see the read-aloud plan elsewhere in this resource.

- CARL SANDBURG: ADVENTURES OF A POET, written by Penelope Niven with poems and prose by Carl Sandburg and illustrated by Marc Nadel (Harcourt); biographical sketches on one side of the page spread face pieces of Sandburg's writing that serve to illustrate the key points in Sandburg's life. From "Vagabond" to "Pen Pal" to "Dreamer," readers trace the life of this American icon. A time line of Sandburg's life and illustration notes make for insightful backmatter.

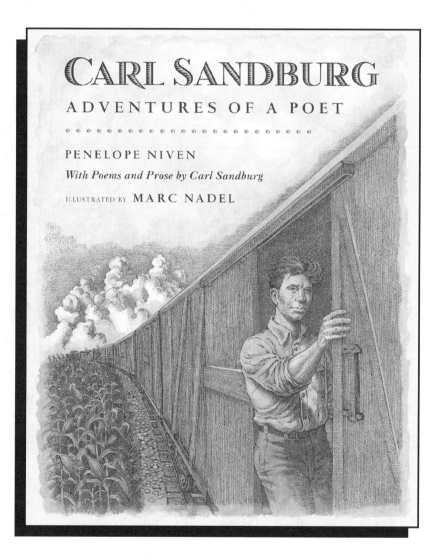

Courtesy Harcourt, Inc.

- WALT WHITMAN: WORDS FOR AMERICA, written by Barbara Kerley and illustrated by Brian Selznick (Scholastic). This magnificent, award-winning picture book is a masterpiece, with impressive back material, including the complete text of the poem, "Leaves of Grass" from which lines are excerpted throughout the book. It is most memorable for its exploration of how the Civil War shaped Whitman's life and his writing.

- LINCOLN: A PHOTOBIOGRAPHY, by Russell Freedman (Clarion); concise, clear, and well-organized; Newbery Medal.

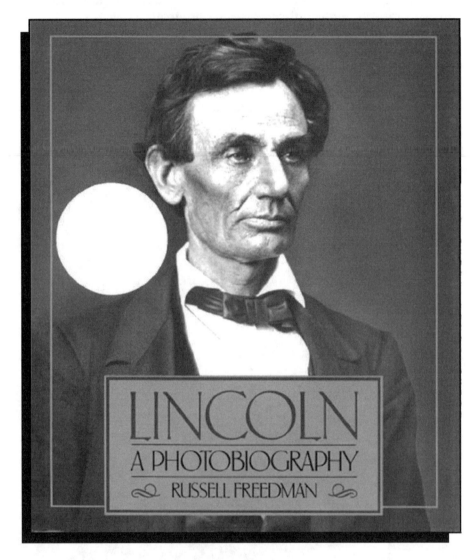

Cover from LINCOLN: A PHOTOBIOGRAPHY by Russell Freedman. Jacket © 1987 by Houghton Mifflin Company. Reprinted by permission of Clarion Books, an imprint of Houghton Mifflin Company. All rights reserved.

- HARRIET BEECHER STOWE AND THE BEECHER PREACHERS, by Jean Fritz (Penguin); a Notable Trade Book in the Language Arts biography of the author of UNCLE TOM'S CABIN by the well-known and popular children's author; part of the Unforgettable Americans series.

- GOOD BROTHER, BAD BROTHER: THE STORY OF EDWIN BOOTH AND JOHN WILKES BOOTH, by James Cross Giblin (Clarion); biographies of two brothers, alike and different in many ways, and the impact they had on American history, the theater, and each other's lives.

- LOUISA MAY & MR. THOREAU'S FLUTE written by Julie Dunlap and Marybeth Lorbiecki and illustrated by Mary Azarian (Dial); the story of the friendship between Louisa May Alcott and Henry David Thoreau, and how it inspired Alcott's writing.

- LUCY MAUD MONTGOMERY: A WRITER'S LIFE, by Elizabeth MacLeod (Kids Can Press); straightforward pictorial biography of the woman who wrote ANNE OF GREEN GABLES; includes photos, appealing illustrations, and quotations from Montgomery and those who knew her.

- YOU WANT WOMEN TO VOTE, LIZZIE STANTON?, written by Jean Fritz and illustrated by DyAnne DiSalvo-Ryan (Penguin); a title in the Unforgettable Americans series penned by the well-known children's biographer; lively and accessible.

- THANK YOU, SARAH! THE WOMAN WHO SAVED THANKSGIVING, written by Laurie Halse Anderson and illustrated by Matt Faulkner (Simon & Schuster); a most incredible picture book, written by an inspired award-winning author, with art by an illustrator who knows what makes a picture book stand out; biography, history, power-of-the-pen message.

- FLY HIGH! THE STORY OF BESSIE COLEMAN, written by Louise Borden and Mary Kay Kroeger and illustrated by Teresa Flavin (McElderry); IRA Teachers' Choice Book about the African American pilot and role model, for whom the sky was the limit.

- OUR ELEANOR: A SCRAPBOOK LOOK AT ELEANOR ROOSEVELT'S REMARKABLE LIFE, by Candace Fleming (Atheneum). The format of this books makes it a good addition to the many books already published about this great woman; readable, accessible, filled with photos, this biography will engage young readers.

- THE JOURNEY THAT SAVED CURIOUS GEORGE: THE TRUE WARTIME ESCAPE OF MARGRET AND H.A. REY, written by Louise Borden and illustrated by Allan Drummond (Houghton Mifflin); see the read-aloud plan elsewhere in this resource.

- LIVES OF EXTRAORDINARY WOMEN: RULERS, REBELS (AND WHAT THE NEIGHBORS THOUGHT), written by Kathleen Krull and illustrated by Kathryn Hewitt (Harcourt); a title in the delightful, informative series; 20 brief, humorous bios include Joan of Arc, Elizabeth I, Eva Peron, and Indira Gandhi.

- BULLY FOR YOU, TEDDY ROOSEVELT, by Jean Fritz (Penguin). Filled with interesting details, this biography is an absorbing read about a well-loved, boyish American hero.

- HARVESTING HOPE: THE STORY OF CESAR CHAVEZ, written by Kathleen Krull and illustrated by Yuyi Morales (Harcourt); see the read-aloud plan elsewhere in this resource.

• CARVER: A LIFE IN POEMS, by Marilyn Nelson (Front Street); biography in poems that garnered the author the Newbery Honor Award, the Coretta Scott King Honor Award, a National Book Award Finalist distinction, and the Boston Globe-Horn Book Award.

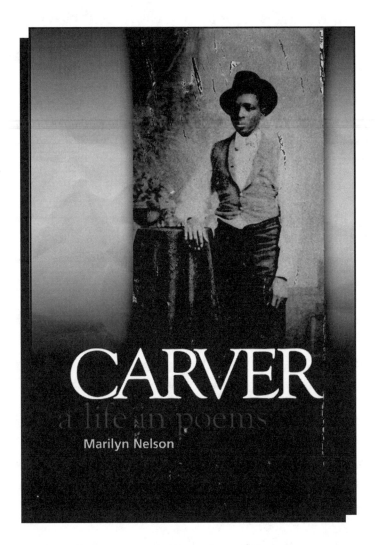

CARVER: A LIFE IN POEMS, by Marilyn Nelson. Copyright © 2001. Published by Front Street, an imprint of Boyds Mills Press. Reprinted by permission.

• THE BOY ON FAIRFIELD STREET: HOW TED GEISEL GREW UP TO BECOME DR. SEUSS, written by Kathleen Krull and illustrated by Steve Johnson and Lou Fancher (Random House); details the childhood of this legendary children's author and illustrator; see the read-aloud plan in *Children's Book Corner, Grades 3–4.*

- ALBERT EINSTEIN: A LIFE OF GENIUS, written by Elizabeth MacLeod (Kids Can Press); straightforward picture book biography accompanied by appealing illustrations, photographs, and quotations from Einstein and those who knew him; backmatter includes a time line of Einstein's life and an index.

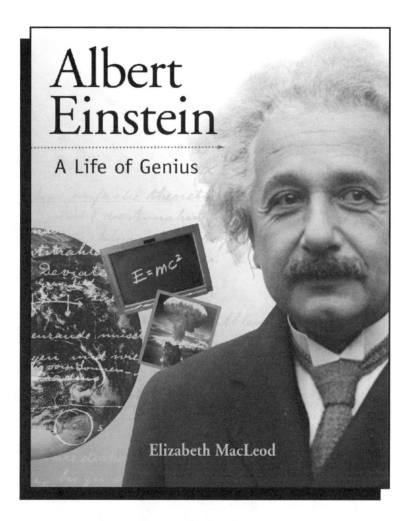

ALBERT EINSTEIN: A LIFE OF GENIUS by Elizabeth MacLeod. Published by Kids Can Press. Reprinted by permission.

- ROSA PARKS: MY STORY, by Rosa Parks with Jim Haskins (Penguin); the autobiography of the woman who refused to give up her seat on a bus to a white man, an act that led to the end of segregation on buses.

- LIVES OF THE PRESIDENTS: FAME, SHAME (AND WHAT THE NEIGHBORS THOUGHT), written by Kathleen Krull and illustrated by Kathryn Hewitt (Harcourt); brief, factual, yet humorous sketches giving insight into the human side of these historical figures. Learn who had "feet bigger than his ego", who barked like a seal, and who had a messy closet.

- LIVES OF THE WRITERS: COMEDIES, TRAGEDIES (AND WHAT THE NEIGHBORS THOUGHT), written by Kathleen Krull and illustrated by Kathryn Hewitt (Harcourt); brief, informative yet humorous sketches offering the "inside scoop" on historical figures in the field, from William Shakespeare and Miguel De Cervantes to Emily Dickinson and Langston Hughes. Did you know that Robert Louis Stevenson agreed with his wife's opinion that he was beautiful, and that he never passed a mirror without checking himself out; that E. B. White once sold roach powder; or that Carl Sandburg was jailed at fourteen for swimming in the nude?

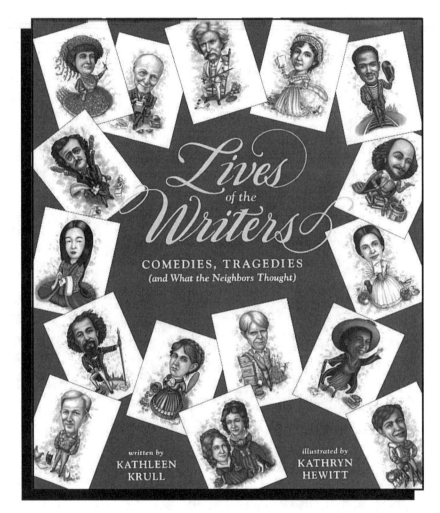

Courtesy Harcourt, Inc.

- LIVES OF THE MUSICIANS: GOOD TIMES, BAD TIMES (AND WHAT THE NEIGHBORS THOUGHT), written by Kathleen Krull and illustrated by Kathryn Hewitt (Harcourt); brief, informative yet humorous sketches offering the "inside scoop" on what these notable (ha ha) figures in the field were *really* like; includes bios on 19 musicians from different countries, eras, and musical styles, from Vivaldi and Beethoven to Stravinsky and Guthrie.

- LIVES OF THE ARTISTS: MASTERPIECES, MESSES (AND WHAT THE NEIGHBORS THOUGHT), written by Kathleen Krull and illustrated by Kathryn Hewitt (Harcourt); brief, informative yet humorous sketches offering the "inside scoop" on artsy folk, from Michelangelo and Rembrandt to Dali and Warhol.

- STEALING HOME: THE STORY OF JACKIE ROBINSON, by Barry Denenberg (Scholastic); biography of the first black man to play in the major leagues.

- LIVES OF THE ATHLETES: THRILLS, SPILLS (AND WHAT THE NEIGHBORS THOUGHT), written by Kathleen Krull and illustrated by Kathryn Hewitt (Harcourt); 20 true stories of athletes who broke records, barriers, hearts, and bones in their quest for excellence in the world of sports; includes bios of Jim Thorpe, Babe Ruth, Jesse Owens, Jackie Robinson, Wilma Rudolph, Arthur Ashe, and Bruce Lee.

- STEVEN SPIELBERG: CRAZY FOR MOVIES, by Susan Goldman Rubin (Abrams); includes photos and family interviews that recall Spielberg's boyhood as well as his accomplishments as an adult.

- TALLCHIEF: AMERICA'S PRIMA BALLERINA, written by Maria Tallchief with Rosemary Wells and illustrated by Gary Kelley (Penguin); picture book autobiography for older children.

- Who Was? series (Grosset & Dunlap); accessible biographies illustrated with black-and-white drawings; titles by various authors include WHO WAS HARRY HOUDINI?, WHO WAS MARK TWAIN?, WHO WAS SACAGAWEA?, WHO WAS THOMAS JEFFERSON?, WHO WAS ALBERT EINSTEIN?, WHO WAS ELEANOR ROOSEVELT?, WHO WAS HARRIET TUBMAN?, WHO WAS ANNIE OAKLEY?, and WHO WAS BEN FRANKLIN?

- Smart About Art series (Grosset & Dunlap); scrapbook format, with simple language; written in the style of elementary school reports; titles by various authors include VINCENT VAN GOGH: SUNFLOWERS AND SWIRLY STARS; PABLO PICASSO: BREAKING ALL THE RULES; CLAUDE MONET: SUNSHINE AND WATERLILIES; EDGAR DEGAS: PAINTINGS THAT DANCE; FRIDA KAHLO: THE ARTIST WHO PAINTED HERSELF; and HENRI MATISSE: DRAWING WITH SCISSORS.

MEMOIR

- BOY: TALES OF CHILDHOOD, by Roald Dahl (Farrar Straus Giroux). Stories from this colorful author's unconventional childhood give insight into where some of his story ideas came from. See also the sequel, GOING SOLO, which tells of his exciting adventures during World War II, his fist job, his African safaris, and more escapades in his adult life.

BOY: TALES OF CHILDHOOD © 1984 by Roald Dahl; Cover Art © 1985 by Quentin Blake. Used with the permission of Farrar Straus Giroux.

- THE MAKING OF A WRITER, by Joan Lowery Nixon (Random House). This memoir by one of the most beloved mystery writers for preteens and teens includes sage advice for young writers along with anecdotes about events in Nixon's life that shaped her as a writer.

- SMALL STEPS: THE YEAR I GOT POLIO, by Peg Kehret (Whitman); award-winning account of the author's twelfth year, when she contracted polio.

SMALL STEPS: THE YEAR I GOT POLIO by Peg Kehret. Copyright © 1996 by Peg Kehret. Cover reprinted by permission of Albert Whitman & Company.

- DON'T TELL THE GIRLS: A FAMILY MEMOIR, by Patricia Reilly Giff (Holiday House); vignettes of Giff's family history; see the read-aloud plan elsewhere in this resource.

- THE ABRACADABRA KID: A WRITER'S LIFE, by Sid Fleischman (Greenwillow); events in the life of this reluctant reader who turned out to be a magician, as well as a successful screenwriter and award-winning children's author.

- WOODSONG, by Gary Paulsen (Simon & Schuster); autobiographical account of Paulsen's experiences dog sledding and his first Iditarod, a race across Alaska's frozen wilderness.

- HEADING OUT: THE START OF SOME SPLENDID CAREERS, edited by Gloria Kamen (Bloomsbury); excerpts from autobiographies and reflections written by those with careers in writing, the arts, business, politics, science, and medicine, who overcame obstacles to reach their dreams; contributors include Dan Rather, Sidney Poitier, Pablo Casals, Nelson Mandela, Lance Armstrong, Isaac Asimov, and Katherine Paterson.

- I WAS A TEENAGE PROFESSIONAL WRESTLER, written and illustrated by Ted Lewin (Hyperion); autobiography of Lewin's teen years, when he went to school by day and wrestled professionally at night.

VALUES/CHARACTER EDUCATION

- THE LIBRARIAN OF BASRA: A TRUE STORY FROM IRAQ, by Jeanette Winter (Harcourt); see the read-aloud plan elsewhere in this resource.

- THE SECRET OF SAYING THANKS, written by Douglas Wood and illustrated by Greg Shed (Simon & Schuster); explores the wisdom of appreciating what we have and living in a spirit of gratitude for the beauty of the world around us rather than focusing on what we lack.

THE SECRET OF SAYING THANKS by Douglas Wood, illustrated by Greg Shed. Copyright © 2005. Used with permission of Simon & Schuster Books for Young Readers, an imprint of Simon & Schuster Children's Publishing.

- A DAY, A DOG, by Gabrielle Vincent (Front Street); wordless wonder about a day in the life of an abandoned dog ends with hope—and opens the door to a number of discussions.

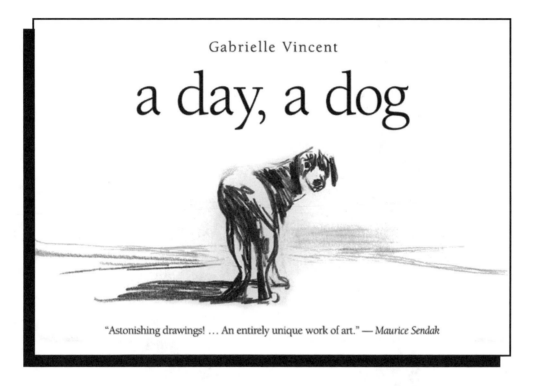

A DAY, A DOG, by Gabrielle Vincent. Copyright © 1982. Published by Front Street, an imprint of Boyds Mills Press. Reprinted by permission.

• GRANDPA'S ANGEL, by Jutta Bauer (Candlewick); a lovely perspective, an elegant story first published in Germany about the wisdom a grandpa imparts to his grandson about life's blessings.

GRANDPA'S ANGEL. Copyright © 2001 Carlsen Verlag Gmbh. English Translation Copyright © 2005 Walker Books Ltd., London. First published in Germany as Opas Engel. Candlewick Press, Inc. on behalf of Walker Books Ltd.

• HACHIKO: THE TRUE STORY OF A LOYAL DOG, written by Pamela S. Turner and illustrated by Yan Nascimbene (Houghton Mifflin); the story of a real dog in whose honor a statue stands in Shibuya Station in Tokyo, commemorating his devotion to his master.

Cover from HACHIKO: The True Story of a Loyal Dog by Pamela S. Turner, illustrated by Yan Nascimbene. Jacket art copyright © 2004 by Yan Nascimbene. Reprinted by permission of Houghton Mifflin Company. All rights reserved.

• THE HERO'S TRAIL: A GUIDE FOR A HEROIC LIFE, by T. A. Barron (Philomel); short profiles of heroic young people in themed chapters; quotations; reflections of the author.

• LET THERE BE LIGHT: POEMS AND PRAYERS FOR REPAIRING THE WORLD, compiled and illustrated by Jane Breskin Zalben (Dutton). Reflecting a cross-section of faiths, these timely poems, illustrated with collages, offer comfort and hope.

- SEQUOYAH: THE CHEROKEE MAN WHO GAVE HIS PEOPLE WRITING, by James Rumford (Houghton Mifflin); a Sibert Honor Book written in verse about the man who brought reading and writing to his people in the early 1800s by creating a writing system.

- IN A SACRED MANNER I LIVE: NATIVE AMERICAN WISDOM, edited by Neil Philip (Clarion); an anthology of speeches, poems, songs, stories, and photographs that reflect the beliefs, values, and struggles of Native Americans throughout history.

- THANK YOU, SARAH! THE WOMAN WHO SAVED THANKSGIVING, written by Laurie Halse Anderson and illustrated by Matt Faulkner (Simon & Schuster); a most incredible picture book written by an inspired, award-winning author, with art by an illustrator who knows what makes a picture book stand out; biography, history, power-of-the-pen message.

- TAKE THE LEAD, GEORGE WASHINGTON, written by Judith St. George and illustrated by Daniel Powers (Philomel); the second in a series of picture storybooks, written by the author of SO YOU WANT TO BE PRESIDENT? and SO YOU WANT TO BE AN INVENTOR? (see *Children's Book Corner, Grades 1–2*), that describe momentous events in the young lives of American presidents that led them to become the men they were.

- HARVESTING HOPE: THE STORY OF CESAR CHAVEZ, written by Kathleen Krull and illustrated by Yuyi Morales (Harcourt); see the read-aloud plan elsewhere in this resource.

- THE FLAG WITH FIFTY-SIX STARS: A GIFT FROM THE SURVIVORS OF MAUTHAUSEN, written by Susan Goldman Rubin and illustrated by Bill Farnsworth (Holiday House); true account of a heartrending episode during World War II; see the read-aloud plan elsewhere in this resource.

- FLY HIGH! THE STORY OF BESSIE COLEMAN, written by Louise Borden and Mary Kay Kroeger and illustrated by Teresa Flavin (McElderry); IRA Teachers' Choice Book about the African American pilot and role model, for whom the sky was the limit.

- HEADING OUT: THE START OF SOME SPLENDID CAREERS, edited by Gloria Kamen (Bloomsbury); excerpts from autobiographies and reflections written by those with careers in writing, the arts, business, politics, science, and medicine, who overcame obstacles to reach their dreams; contributors include Dan Rather, Sidney Poitier, Pablo Casals, Nelson Mandela, Lance Armstrong, Isaac Asimov, and Katherine Paterson.

- THE SEVEN WONDERS OF SASSAFRAS SPRINGS, written by Betty G. Birney and illustrated by Matt Phelan (Atheneum). A boy finds wonders equal to the Seven Wonders of the World in his own small town; see the read-aloud plan elsewhere in this resource.

- ELLA ENCHANTED, by Gail Carson Levine (HarperCollins); Newbery Honor Award. What was the fairy thinking, giving a gift of obedience? Ella's determination to break the curse is a memorable story indeed.

- JUST ELLA, by Margaret Peterson Haddix (Simon & Schuster); a Cinderella story with a twist; the heroine is strong and wise in this version of the fairy tale.

- KNEE-KNOCK RISE, by Natalie Babbitt (Farrar Straus Giroux); a fable about Egan, who dares to think outside the box to solve a mystery that has been tradition in mythic Instep.

- THE GOLDEN FLEECE AND THE HEROES WHO LIVED BEFORE ACHILLES, by Padriac Colum (Macmillan). This telling of the story of Jason and the Argonauts won a Newbery Honor.

COUNSELING/ADVICE/SELF-HELP

- MY PARENTS ARE GETTING DIVORCED: HOW TO KEEP IT TOGETHER WHEN YOUR MOM AND DAD ARE SPLITTING UP, written by Florence Cadier with Melissa Daly and illustrated by Claire Gandini (Abrams); useful advice for coping with a trying situation.

MY PARENTS ARE GETTING DIVORCED: HOW TO KEEP IT TOGETHER WHEN YOUR MOM AND DAD ARE SPLITTING UP by Florence Cadier with Melissa Daly, illustrated by Claire Gandini. Reprinted with permission of Abrams Books for Young Readers and Amulet Books (www.abramsyoungreaders.com).

- HELP! A GIRL'S GUIDE TO DIVORCE AND STEPFAMILIES, written by Nancy Holyoke and illustrated by Scott Nash (American Girl); straightforward, accessible information and tips for coping with parents' divorce and blended families.

- DIVORCE IS NOT THE END OF THE WORLD: ZOE AND EVAN'S COPING GUIDE FOR KIDS, by Evan Stern, Zoe Stern, and Ellen Sue Stern (Tricycle Press). Written by siblings (15 and 13 years old), this helpful guide offers advice to kids adjusting to their parents' split.

- A SMART GIRL'S GUIDE TO STICKY SITUATIONS: HOW TO TACKLE TRICKY, ICKY PROBLEMS AND TOUGH TIMES (American Girl); simple, straightforward advice on topics from boys to tough days at school.

- 100 THINGS GUYS NEED TO KNOW, by Bill Zimmerman (Free Spirit); advice, stories, quotes, facts, and survey results in an appealing package with graphic novel–style illustrations.

- REAL SPIRIT: FUN IDEAS FOR REFRESHING, RELAXING, AND STAYING STRONG, written by Elizabeth Chobanian and illustrated by Carol Yoshizumi (American Girl); advice on how to manage stress, yoga poses, and simple suggestions for dealing positively with life's busy-ness and unexpected challenges.

Reprinted with permission of Pleasant Company Publications from REAL SPIRIT © copyright 2005 American Girl, LLC.

- THE FEELINGS JOURNAL, written by Dr. Lynda Madison and illustrated by Norm Bendell (American Girl); specific how-to suggestions for getting in touch with and managing a variety of feelings; includes checklists, fill-in-the blank exercises, and quizzes.

- A SMART GIRL'S GUIDE TO STARTING MIDDLE SCHOOL, written by Julie A. Williams and illustrated by Angela Martini (American Girl); confidence-building advice and activities helpful in preparing for the transition to middle school; upbeat and positive approach.

Reprinted with permission of Pleasant Company Publications from A SMART GIRL'S GUIDE TO STARTING MIDDLE SCHOOL copyright © 2004 American Girl, LLC.

- SCHOOL SMARTS PLANNER (American Girl). Getting organized in school is made fun with stickers, tear-out notes, and simple suggestions.

- MICHAEL ROSEN'S SAD BOOK, written by Michael Rosen and illustrated by Quentin Blake (Candlewick); explores sadness in simple, spare language and signature art.

- GOOD SPORTS: WINNING, LOSING, AND EVERYTHING IN BETWEEN, by Therese Kauchak (American Girl); advice on being sportsmanlike.

- THE BEHAVIOR SURVIVAL GUIDE FOR KIDS: HOW TO MAKE GOOD CHOICES AND STAY OUT OF TROUBLE, by Thomas McIntyre, Ph.D. (Free Spirit); explanations of behavior problems, advice, tips, and strategies children with learning problems can use; includes anecdotes from real kids.

- A SMART GIRL'S GUIDE TO MANNERS, by Nancy Holyoke (American Girl); practical advice for common situations.

- DRUGS EXPLAINED: THE REAL DEAL ON ALCOHOL, POT, ECSTASY, AND MORE, written by Pierre Mezinski with Melissa Daly and Francoise Jaud and illustrated by Redge (Abrams); straightforward and factual.

DRUGS EXPLAINED by Pierre Mezinski with Melissa Daly and Francoise Jaud, illustrated by Redge. Reprinted with permission of Abrams Books for Young Readers and Amulet Books (www.abramsyoungreaders.com)

FAIRY TALES, FOLK TALES, FABLES, TALL TALES, LEGENDS, AND MYTHS

• THE POND GOD AND OTHER STORIES, written by Samuel Jay Keyser and illustrated by Robert Shetterly (Front Street); one-page fables in verse about gods with some very human qualities.

• MIKHAIL BARYSHNIKOV'S STORIES FROM MY CHILDHOOD, edited and compiled by Joan Borsten and Oleg Vidov (Abrams); fairy tales, including "The Snow Queen", "Cinderella", and "Pinocchio and the Golden Key."

• JACK AND THE BEANSTALK: HOW A TALL FELLOW SOLVED A BIG PROBLEM, retold and illustrated by Albert Lorenz with Joy Schleh (Abrams); lushly illustrated. Can you find Jack?

JACK AND THE BEANSTALK: HOW A TALL FELLOW SOLVED A BIG PROBLEM by Albert Lorenz with Joy Schleh. Reprinted with permission of Abrams Books for Young Readers (www.abramsyoungreaders.com).

- RUMPELSTILTSKIN'S DAUGHTER by Diane Stanley (Morrow); no weepy maiden in a tower here! See the read-aloud plan in *Children's Book Corner, Grades 3–4.*

- THE TRUE STORY OF THE 3 LITTLE PIGS! BY A. WOLF, written by Jon Scieszka and illustrated by Lane Smith (Viking); told from the point of view of the much-maligned wolf; hilarious.

- THE STINKY CHEESE MAN AND OTHER FAIRLY STUPID TALES, written by Jon Scieszka and illustrated by Lane Smith (Penguin); zany fun that is par for the course for this dynamic duo.

- AN UNDONE FAIRY TALE, written by Ian Lendler and illustrated by Whitney Martin (Simon & Schuster); hilariously clever tale about a pie-making princess trapped in a tower, and Ned, the painter and costume-maker, who can't keep up with you, the speedy reader who keeps turning the page!

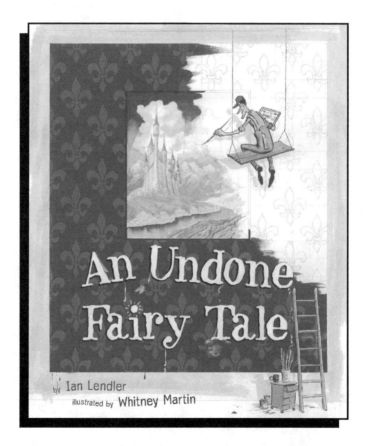

AN UNDONE FAIRY TALE by Ian Lendler, illustrated by Whitney Martin. Copyright © 2005. Used with permission of Simon & Schuster Books for Young Readers, an imprint of Simon & Schuster Children's Publishing.

- ELLA ENCHANTED, by Gail Carson Levine (HarperCollins); Newbery Honor Award. What was the fairy thinking, giving a gift of obedience? Ella's determination to break the curse is a memorable story indeed.

- JUST ELLA, by Margaret Peterson Haddix (Simon & Schuster); a Cinderella story with a twist; the heroine is strong and wise in this version of the fairy tale.

- NEWFANGLED FAIRY TALES: CLASSIC STORIES WITH A TWIST, edited by Bruce Lansky (Meadowbrook); a collection of original fairy tales written by well-known and well-loved authors.

- THE RUMPELSTILTSKIN PROBLEM, by Vivian Vande Velde (Scholastic); twists on the tale; see the read-aloud plan elsewhere in this resource.

- THE PEOPLE COULD FLY: THE PICTURE BOOK, written by Virginia Hamilton and illustrated by Leo and Diane Dillon (Knopf); winner of Coretta Scott King Honor Award and New York Times Book Review Award for Best Illustrated Children's Book. This is the picture book version of the title story in Hamilton's American black folk tale collection, published in 1985.

- APPLES TO OREGON, BEING THE (SLIGHTLY) TRUE NARRATIVE OF HOW A BRAVE PIONEER FATHER BROUGHT APPLES, PEACHES, PEARS, PLUMS, GRAPES, AND CHERRIES (AND CHILDREN) ACROSS THE PLAINS, written by Deborah Hopkinson and illustrated by Nancy Carpenter (Atheneum); tall tale "loosely based on the life of a real fruiting pioneer."

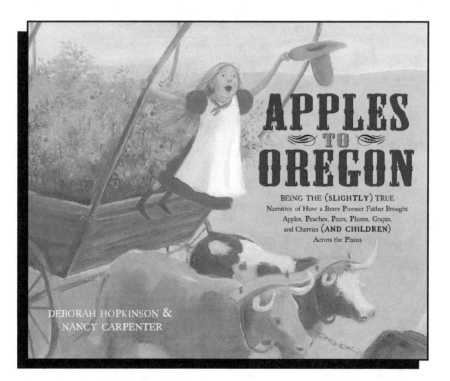

APPLES TO OREGON: BEING THE (SLIGHTLY) TRUE NARRATIVE OF HOW A BRAVE PIONEER FATHER BROUGHT APPLES, PEACHES, PEARS, PLUMS, GRAPES, AND CHERRIES (AND CHILDREN) ACROSS THE PLAINS by Deborah Hopkinson, illustrated by Nancy Carpenter. Copyright © 2004. Used with permission of Atheneum Books for Young Readers, an imprint of Simon & Schuster Children's Publishing.

- AMERICAN TALL TALES, written by Mary Pope Osborne and illustrated by Michael McCurdy (Knopf); attractive volume for middle graders of a handful of well-known tales; illustrated with wood engravings.

- KNEE-KNOCK RISE, by Natalie Babbitt (Farrar Straus Giroux); a fable about Egan, who dares to think outside the box to solve a mystery that has been tradition in mythic Instep.

- THE GOLDEN FLEECE AND THE HEROES WHO LIVED BEFORE ACHILLES, by Padriac Colum (Macmillan). This telling of the story of Jason and the Argonauts won a Newbery Honor.

- HOLES, by Louis Sachar (Farrar Straus Giroux); popular Newbery Medal book about Stanley Yelnats, who digs holes at Camp Green Lake detention center to serve out a sentence he didn't deserve, and what he unearths about the warden, and ultimately, himself.

- MANIAC MAGEE, by Jerry Spinelli (Little, Brown). A modern folk tale/tall tale explores the search for home, racism, heroism, and strength of spirit, while also managing to be funny; Newbery Medal.

SEASONAL/HOLIDAY

- FESTIVALS, poems by Myra Cohn Livingston and illustrated by Leonard Everett Fisher (Holiday House); a collection of poems about festivals celebrated by people of different faiths and cultures.

- A CIRCLE OF SEASONS, written by Myra Cohn Livingston and illustrated by Leonard Everett Fisher (Holiday). See also SKY SONGS, EARTH SONGS, SEA SONGS, and SPACE SONGS by this incredible team (Holiday).

- WINTER LIGHTS: A SEASON IN POEMS & QUILTS, by Anna Grossnickle Hines (Greenwillow). Poems illustrated with quilts celebrate the winter holidays. Backmatter offers information on how the quilts were made and photographs of the process. See also PIECES: A YEAR IN POEMS & QUILTS, winner of the 2002 Lee Bennett Hopkins Award for Children's Poetry.

- STOPPING BY WOODS ON A SNOWY EVENING, written by Robert Frost and illustrated by Susan Jeffers (Dutton); lovely picture book presentation of the well-loved poem.

- WINTER EYES, by Douglas Florian (Greenwillow); seasonal collection of delightful poems.

- WINTER POEMS, selected by Barbara Rogasky and illustrated by Trina Schart Hyman (Scholastic); 25 poems from Shakespeare to Sandburg to haiku celebrating the season.

- AUTUMNBLINGS, by Douglas Florian (Greenwillow). Wonderful word play celebrates the season.

- HIST WHIST, written by e. e. cummings and illustrated by Deborah Kogan Ray (Crown); Halloween poem; exquisitely illustrated.

- SUMMERSAULTS, by Douglas Florian (Greenwillow); see description of AUTUMNBLINGS, above.

Christmas

- A NEWBERY CHRISTMAS, selected by Martin H. Greenberg and Charles G. Waugh (Delacorte); 14 holiday stories written by Newbery Award–winning authors, including Beverly Cleary, Madeleine L'Engle, Nancy Willard, and Katherine Paterson.

- NO ROOM IN THE INN AND OTHER STORIES FROM A MIDNIGHT CLEAR, by Katherine Paterson (Penguin); four stories by the well-known and well-loved Newbery author.

- JOSIE'S GIFT, written by Kathleen Long Bostrom and illustrated by Frank Ordaz (Broadman & Holman). The message of this Christmas story, set in the 1940s, is that contentment is not about what we want, but rather about what we have, a piece of wisdom Josie's Papa, who died in the past year, imparted to her. How Josie finds joy in a gift she gets and then gives is an affirming story.

Hanukkah

- HANUKKAH, SHMANUKKAH!, written by Esmé Raji Codell and illustrated by LeUyen Pham (Hyperion). In true Codell style, this witty Jewish remake of Dickens's classic Christmas tale teaches while it entertains. Follow along as Scroogemacher learns the errors of his ways and comes to terms with his past at the hand of the Rabbi of Hanukkah Future, a woman with an attitude. Don't miss the Author's Note and the glossary of Yiddish words at the back of the book.

Hyperion Books for Children.

• JEWISH HOLIDAYS ALL YEAR ROUND: A FAMILY TREASURY, written by Ilene Cooper and illustrated by Elivia Savadier in association with The Jewish Museum, New York (Abrams), From an explanation of the Sabbath to Tisha B'Av, this book of facts, stories, crafts, and recipes introduces children to the Jewish holidays.

JEWISH HOLIDAYS ALL YEAR ROUND: A FAMILY TREASURY by Ilene Cooper, illustrated by Elivia Savadier. Reprinted with permission of Abrams Books for Young Readers (www.abramsyoungreaders.com).

• THE STONE LAMP: EIGHT STORIES OF HANUKKAH THROUGH HISTORY, written by Karen Hesse and illustrated by Brian Pinkney (Hyperion); free verse, first-person accounts of key events in Jewish history as seen through the eyes of a child; written by a Newbery Award winner and illustrated by a Caldecott Honor Award winner.

WORDLESS BOOKS

- A DAY, A DOG, by Gabrielle Vincent (Front Street); wordless wonder about a day in the life of a dog that begins with harsh treatment of an animal and ends with hope in the form of a child.

- THE MYSTERIES OF HARRIS BURDICK, by Chris Van Allsburg (Houghton Mifflin); story-starters galore in the form of illustrations that were left mysteriously at a publisher's office.

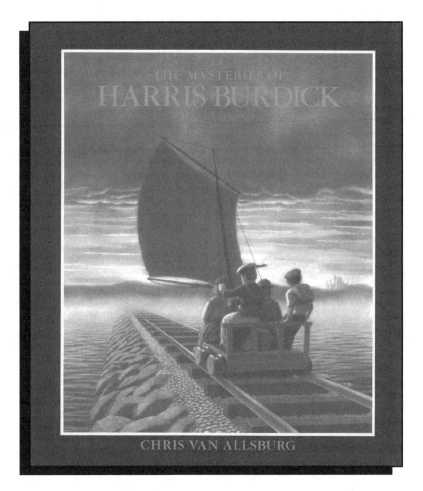

Cover from THE MYSTERIES OF HARRIS BURDICK by Chris Van Allsburg. Copyright © 1984 by Chris Van Allsburg. Reprinted by permission of Houghton Mifflin Company. All rights reserved.

- SIDEWALK CIRCUS, presented by Paul Fleischman and illustrated by Kevin Hawkes (Candlewick); a wordless book about imagination and observation.

- TIME FLIES, by Eric Rohmann (Crown); Caldecott Honor; great to jump-start a writing activity.

- TUESDAY, by David Wiesner (Clarion); Caldecott Medal; another wordless wonder great for imagination start-up.

POETRY

See the Tips and Techniques for Teachers and Librarians section of this book for recommended poetry anthologies and collections.

For recommended books listed by genre, refer to the Parent Pull-Out Pages.

Subject Index

Title Index

Titles of books that have read-aloud plans are boldface.

Author Index

Illustrator Index

Index of Resource
Books and Authors

About the Author

JUDY BRADBURY is the author of the Christopher Counts! children's picture book math series published by McGraw-Hill/Learning Triangle Press. She is also a frequent workshop presenter.

Judy has over 20 years of teaching experience. A lifelong advocate of promoting reading, Judy pioneered a New York State–funded summer community remedial reading program for children in grades 1–6 and has developed remedial as well as enrichment reading and writing programs for high school students. She is an active member in organizations such as the International Reading Association, the Niagara Frontier Reading Council, the Society of Children's Writers and Illustrators, and the Association of Professional Women Writers. She lives in western New York with her husband, her daughter, one big dog, and one tiny cat that came for Christmas and stayed.